People Who Care

[redacted]

People Who Care

An Illustrated History of Human Compassion

by HEINZ VONHOFF

[redacted]

FORTRESS PRESS

Philadelphia

[redacted]

This book is a translation of *Herzen gegen die Not,* copyright © 1960 by J. G. Oncken Verlag in Kassel, Germany.

Library of Congress Catalog Card Number 76-137752

ISBN 0-8006-0052-5

1391G70 Printed in U.S.A. 1-52

Contents

Foreword

I would hope that many people would have the opportunity of reading *People Who Care*. In an age when Christian people everywhere are being beset by materialistic values and not very inspiring personal examples, here is a book which reaches far into the past to Egypt and Greece and ancient Israel, and on through the Christian era into the present to give us the inspiring history of "people who care" in a variety of philosophical and religious traditions.

I have long believed that people learn more by example than they do by words. It is for this reason that this book is so different and so helpful, that it is based entirely upon the personal examples of those who took seriously the words of Our Lord: "I was hungry and you gave Me to eat, thirsty and you gave Me to drink, naked and you clothed Me, in prison and you visited Me . . . whatsoever you did for one of these, My least brethren, you did it for Me." This, of course, was Our Lord's personalization of the ancient Hebrew injunction, "Treat your neighbor as you would like to be treated." The lasting Christian inspiration behind all of these Christians who cared was the thought that in serving the poor, the hungry, the weak, the sick, the suffering, they were serving Christ, Our Lord, Himself.

One should be grateful to Heinz Vonhoff for the time and effort and research that has gone into the writing of this book which provides us with innumerable examples through the ages of what each of us should be attempting to do today to prove that we, too, are "people who care."

REV. THEODORE M. HESBURGH, C.S.C.

Preface

Since the dawn of human history, man's existence has been threatened by famine, disease, privation, affliction, disaster, and the forces of terror. Man has tried to secure himself against these perils in many ways, but in the end only one thing has made it possible for him to survive—the power of love, that love of neighbor, of fellowman and brother, which found its pure and perfect expression in the life of Jesus of Nazareth, the Son of God. Wherever man has been touched by this love, he has been enabled to become the helper, benefactor, and deliverer of his fellowman.

If we follow the destinies of nations through the centuries and look at the endless succession of calamities that has been visited upon whole peoples, it appears little short of miraculous that mankind has survived at all. In our time the mortal peril has become so great as to be altogether terrifying. Never was the threat of human extinction so great, and never did all man's efforts to defend against it appear so futile.

But history speaks not only of the perils, of war and disaster. It also bears record of the heroic efforts made by men and women whose motive force was the love of God and whose guide was selfless compassion. In their lives we see the sustaining power of love.

People Who Care is the story of this power. Its purpose is threefold: to show the imprint that mercy and love of neighbor have left upon history; to describe how men, singly and together, have set about doing good in a world of anguish and turmoil; and to recall those events upon which are based the consolation and hope of this and every age.

The earliest beginnings of charity are to be found in ancient Egypt, where we find the canon of the seven works of mercy.

The philosophers of classical Greece and Rome taught the principles of humanity and kindness, laying the foundations of that *humanitas* toward which mankind is still striving.

Tiny Israel, God's Chosen People, preserved through centuries of tribulation and adversity, of flagrant disobedience and earnest repentance, the divine command which had been given it: "Thou shalt love thy neighbor as thyself."

Then in the midst of this particular people there came to live the one who not only practiced love but was and is love incarnate: Jesus Christ, God's Son. From that moment on, mercy and love of neighbor have been clearly woven into the fabric of human history, and love-in-action has inspired deeds of charity among both Christian and non-Christian men and nations. The heroism of individuals has provided the impetus for large-scale relief efforts in time of disaster and plague, war and tyranny. The public and private relief and welfare programs of modern times are inconceivable apart from the example and zeal of those great pioneers who followed the obstacle course of well-doing, often alone, misunderstood, ridiculed, and persecuted.

The many well-known and lesser-known figures whose life and work are here presented may stand as representative of all those who likewise sought to follow the example of the Good Samaritan, and who in loving their neighbor with a love that transcended all barriers and prejudices came to discover that which alone gives dignity and worth to human existence. The picture of suffering and want in every age is brighter for their having lived. They introduced into the history of mankind the one thing which could save it from extinction.

It is our hope that this book may contribute modestly to a more comprehensive understanding of human history, one that is not narrowly circumscribed by political, economic, or cultural bounds. We would also hope that it might inspire the reader, in his own way and in his own situation, to do what he can to augment this sustaining power of love in our foreboding times. It is not enough just to preach Christ's command to love our neighbor. Nor is it enough just to keep fresh the memory of all those who have lived his command. We ourselves must live it; for the salvation and peace of the world are wholly dependent upon whether we human beings will love one another as God loves us.

The numerous drawings and etchings included in the book come chiefly from ancient sources. Together with the more contemporary photographs they serve not only to illustrate but also to supplement and document the text. I would express here a word of thanks to my publishers for their extensive efforts in procuring the pictures and plates, and for their cooperation throughout. My warm appreciation goes also to all the church-related and independent charitable institutions that willingly provided me with material. Finally, special thanks are due to Günther S. Wegener for his untiring assistance and counsel during the editing of both text and pictures.

HEINZ VONHOFF

1. Mercy in Ancient Times

Egypt and the Seven Works of Physical Mercy

Egypt. Land of the pyramids. Here emerges, some five thousand years ago, one of the earliest civilizations known to man. Here too we discover the first evidences of the works of charity. We find them on inscriptions in pyramids, in tombs, and on obelisks, and we also learn of them from the wisdom and didactic literature of the time, written on yards of papyrus scrolls. We are thus introduced to a people ruled by a divine king, who is also known as the "helper of the poor" and who enjoins his officials to exercise social concern wherever need exists.

The fortunes of the Egyptian people rise and fall with the Nile, the great river which gives the land its wealth. Harvest and sustenance depend on it. It can also bring famine and privation. The Egyptians learn early to distribute the increase of the land wisely and to store the remainder. Granaries are filled in times of plenty and opened in times of want. Early biblical records tell us of Joseph, the prudent manager of these provisions; but centuries after Joseph high officials are still put in charge of the granaries and are accountable to pharaoh for an equitable distribution.

One of these officials is named Amenemope. Had he been merely an administrator, like all the others before and after him, we would never have heard of him. But Amenemope aspires to something more. He lives in an age of political ebb tide, and he does some thinking about this. He studies the old wisdom books, searching through the ephemeral for traces of the enduring. When his son becomes a priest, the father decides to collect in book form the imperishable values he has found in the wisdom of the past. In thirty chapters Amenemope sets forth the conclusions of his inquiries, admonishing his son to heed them, preserve them, and pass them on.

In his writing, this loyal and honest official does not bewail the dwindling might of Egypt. He does not despair at the dissolution of a political and social order that had been carefully preserved for centuries. Instead he sees, over against the ephemeral, the one thing that endures—the Good. And good comes from God, so Amenemope admonishes his son to do good for God's sake.

Justice, helpfulness, and a friendly and accommodating spirit are the three precepts of this Egyptian teacher. "God loveth him who cheereth the lowly more than him who honoreth the exalted," says Amenemope. "Be unfair to no man in court, take not the gifts of the strong, and oppress not the weak for his sake. The law is a great gift of God."

Amenemope sees selfishness and greed multiplying in this period of decay, leading even the officials to become unjust; and so he repeatedly admonishes: "Be not greedy when thou findest abundance, covet not the possessions of the lowly, have respect unto the boundaries of a widow, alter not thy balances, and falsify not their weights." Nor does he forget the humblest of all: "Mock no dwarf and scorn not the limbs of the deformed."

A dominant theme runs through every chapter of *The Instruction of Amenemope,* and that theme is God. It is God who fills all Amenemope's pondering and searching. He will trust this God, however inscrutable His purposes. And it is God's will that men do good. Thus does this manager of the king's storehouses gather together the wisdom of his people as the grain is gathered; along with the fruits of the field is harvested the vintage of a two-thousand-year-old culture.

Such precepts are not only written down—by Amenemope and others—they are also followed. Particularly noteworthy is the concern for man's soul and spirit as well as his body. "It is more important to the troubled one that his heart be lifted up than that his petition be granted," says Ptahhotep twenty-five hundred years before Christ. A thousand years later another writer exhorts his son: "Double the bread thou givest to thy mother, and bear her as she bore (thee). Thou wast a great burden to her. . . ." In state-

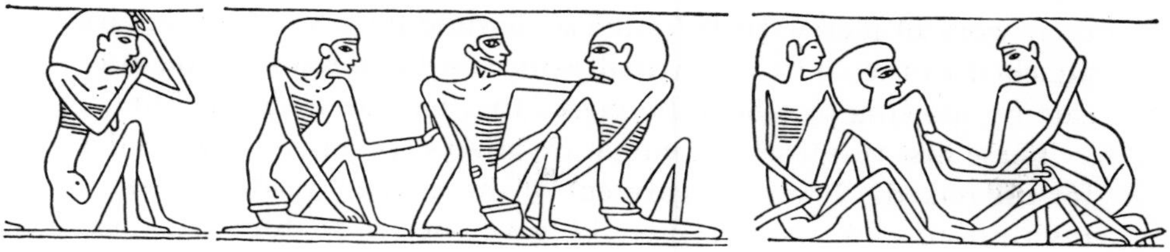

The drastic effects of a drought in Egypt are shown by this relief-drawing of a starving people. Found in the Pyramid of Unas, the picture is both a commemoration and an exhortation to active concern.

Sigbert Mohn Verlag, Gütersloh

ments like these we can see the beginnings of a true ministry to the human spirit, what we today would call psychotherapy.

The Egyptians' primary concern, however, is with taking care of the needs of the body. Thus we find at a very early stage the canon of the "seven works of physical mercy": feeding the hungry, giving drink to the thirsty, clothing the naked, sheltering the stranger, setting the prisoner free, caring for the sick, and burying the dead. The history of Egypt provides abundant evidence that these seven precepts were practiced.

At the head of the list is relief for the hungry. The economic planning of the pharaohs clearly shows the stress laid on this precept. In times of famine, pharaoh, acting through his ministers, becomes family provider for the whole people. He distributes, rations, and if necessary grants tax exemptions to the needy. Beyond these state relief measures there remains plenty for the individual to do. Numerous tomb inscriptions bear witness to this: "I gave bread to the starving." "I filled him who had nothing."

The second work of mercy, relief for the thirsty, is regarded in the same spirit: "Pass not over the stranger with thy jug," we read in as early a source as Amenemope. And Sinuhe, an Egyptian official who is forced to flee when his king dies and who in exile writes down the story of his life, gratefully tells how he was saved from dying of thirst in the desert. Bedouins found him and took him with them. The bedouin sheik himself served him water and boiled milk for him. "It was good what they did unto me," writes Sinuhe, who never forgot the sons of the wilderness and their work of mercy. In Palestine some time later Sinuhe becomes attached to the court of a tribal prince and endeavors to reciprocate by showing to others the mercy that had been shown him.

These first two works of mercy are always accompanied by relief for the naked. "I was the garment of the naked," reads one tomb inscription, and another says: "I gave shelter to him who was naked." When Ramses IV ascends the throne, the people join in jubilant song: "Those who were naked are clothed in fine linen, and those who were in filth wear white raiment." Thus clothing the poor appears here as one of the noblest works of the king.

The fourth work of mercy is directed toward the stranger. Throughout Egypt it is customary to accommodate the stranger, whether friend or enemy, in one's own dwelling. This rule—and the safety of the guest—is inviolable. "One should share his meal even with the enemy, and feed the uninvited guest," writes Ani in the second millennium before Christ. Hospitality also includes giving the departing guest directions, accompanying him part of the way, or leading him to the next source of water. Those who live by the Nile see to transportation for the stranger. In many ancient documents the writers speak of having ferried across the river people who had no boat. Ferrymen who take only paying passengers are sternly reproved: "Keep no man from crossing the river when thou hast room in thy boat."

We hear somewhat less often about relief for prisoners. The reason may be that the Egyptian penal system was so scrupulously regulated that prisoners rarely suffered any serious hardship. Even so, petitions to the God Amun (Amon) ask that he hear "the prayer of the prisoners" and that he be "a pleasant wind for them." In the hymn of praise to Ramses IV mentioned above we read, "Those in prison are set free, and he who was bound is full of joy." The reference here is perhaps to an amnesty. There is also this advice, found in a book of wisdom: "If thou art rich, redeem him whom thou findest in bonds. Be thou a shield to the unfortunate."

In the late period of ancient Egypt the state grants a singular privilege to the oppressed. Farmers and peasants, hired laborers and slaves who incur debts and are hard-pressed by their creditors may flee for refuge to the temple altars. Reverence for deity keeps them and their possessions free from harm. This privilege of asylum in the temple is mentioned as early as the time of Ramses III, who reigned after the exodus of the children of Israel. But it does not acquire its full importance until later, when Egypt is suffering under a burden of Roman taxation so great that it threatens to crush the farmers and laborers.

Care for the sick is provided or supervised by doctors, who are officials of the state. To a remarkable degree, most of their methods are medically sound and are based on careful observation. Not until the eclipse of the political order do the doctors revert in part to magic and alchemy, and in the meantime Egyptian medical arts flourish for two thousand years. As there are no hospitals, however, the sick have to be cared for by their families. It is noteworthy that any Egyptian traveling within the borders of the land is entitled to free medical care. Egyptian doctors, incidentally, are all specialists in some branch of medicine, be it surgery or whatever. In addition there are skilled lay assistants, nurses, and "bandagers." Understandably, with medical care organized to such a degree, little remains for the individual to do in fulfilling this work of mercy. But even so, we read again and again that all possible care should be given the sick, the crippled, and the mentally ill.

The last of the seven works of physical mercy has to do with the dead. The Egyptian believes in an afterlife, which explains his veneration of the dead and his funerary cults. As the dead are buried, so shall they live in the hereafter. Thus care is taken to preserve the body as long as possible and to provide it with all the common things of everyday life. The families of the deceased must be concerned at all times about the protection, care, and provision for their dead, so that it will be well with them. It follows, then, that great importance attaches to the funeral rites themselves. No one neglects his duty to render to the departed every possible service, and those who cannot afford the expense involved are given assistance as a matter of course. If someone dies and leaves no survivors, it is a certainty that others will step in to take care of the arrangements: the tomb, the cerements, and if at all possible, the embalming as well.

To be sure, the funerary cults are often carried to extremes; and in the case of the other works of mercy as well, light is often mixed with darkness. The land of the Nile is repeatedly shaken by social upheaval, her people groan under their pharaoh's yoke, and hardship and misery are rife. Yet the fact remains that here in Egypt, for the first time on such a comprehensive scale, man preaches and practices the works of mercy. It is not the "war god" but the "corn god" who gives Egyptian history its distinguishing features: social order, mature practical wisdom, and active love for one's neighbor. No other ancient civilization begins to approach Egypt in this regard. The history of mercy truly begins in the land of the Nile.

Aristotle and Almsgiving

We encounter a totally different idea of mercy in classical Greece. Here in the sixth and fifth centuries before Christ live the great philosophers whose thought has such an impact that it becomes virtually the foundation of Western culture. Modern philosophy is still heavily influenced by the writings of Plato and Aristotle, as is science by the research of Democritus, Heraclitus, and Xenophanes. From these philosophers come the concepts of *humanitas* and *bonitas*—humaneness and goodness or kindness. These are fundamentally different from the concepts of mercy and love of neighbor.

The reason for the difference lies in the ancient Greeks' peculiar notion of divinity. A god is not a lawgiver who proclaims his will to men and sees to it that they obey it. A god is an example, an ideal. Beyond man's reach and unmoved by man's fortunes or misfortunes, he lives in a lofty sphere in eternal beauty, eternal serenity, and eternal tranquillity. The Greek gods are not merciful and the Greek man expects no mercy from them. His consolation is that they are there, and accordingly his own aspiration is to find harmony, serenity, and beauty here on earth. This world view leaves no room for pity. Indeed, pity is considered weakness, unworthy of a man. If the gods mete out hardship and suffering, mortals must bear it philosophically and with dignity.

Aristotle is known to have given alms one day to an indigent. The philosopher's friends promptly engage him in argument, criticizing his gesture. Everyone knows the recipient to be a sluggard, they say; he was not worthy of your gift; giving help to the undeserving is not a good deed. But Aristotle defends himself: "I had mercy on the man, not on his bad morals." To give to one's fellowman, he contends, is indeed good; it is an act worthy of an excellent and honorable man. Thus in the last analysis Aristotle gave alms for his own sake, not for the sake of the recipient. Good deeds abide, then, but they are more narrowly defined. Aristotle praises generosity as the golden mean between extravagance and parsimony; the concept of charity is not to be found in him. Friends should practice kindness toward each other, and he who knows his friend to be in trouble should hasten to his aid unasked. But here again there are limits. For example, Aristotle holds that friendship with a slave is impossible, because a slave is not a human being in the proper sense of the word but at best only an animated tool. For two millenniums this notion will emerge and reemerge, preventing man from becoming truly merciful.

The Greek ideal of a well-ordered and wisely administered state that provides for its citizens a life of peace and calm and unclouded serenity does not include any comprehensive provision for the poor. The pauper and the beggar actually disturb that peace. The best way to deal with disturbance is to get rid of the disturbers.

This harsh logic is carried still further: abortion, for example, is countenanced, and weak or deformed children may be put to death after birth. This calculated, pragmatic thinking of the Greeks, coupled with their eternal longing for harmony and beauty, leaves no room for compassion.

To be sure, even in the history of Greece we meet individuals who show mercy—as individuals. There is, for example, Cimon of Athens, who in the fifth century before Christ has the fences around his land torn down so that the needy can pick the fruit in his orchards without hindrance. In his house each day a table for the poor is spread, to which everyone is invited. Of course it is possible, especially in Cimon's case, that some elements of an early communism are involved: as a full-fledged citizen of the state, he believes that collective ownership is a sign of the commonweal.

In the golden age of Athens, we are told, impoverished citizens are cared for by state agencies, and the unemployed receive temporary public assistance. Disabled veterans also get a kind of pension for a time. But all these provisions are solely for the benefit of the citizen. The poor, the beggars, the unfortunate, since they do not enjoy the rights of citizenship, are excluded from such beneficence. Often they have no more than a tub to live in. Indeed, the curious one-man protest movement of Diogenes, who lives in a beggar's tub and goes about with a lantern in broad daylight "in search for an honest man," may include an element of social protest.

Public Assistance in Ancient Rome

The situation in ancient Rome develops differently. In the early days, when even Rome's population is predominantly rural, poverty can hardly have been a problem, as the people would have still lived off the land; but later, when the city grows to a metropolis of millions, there emerges a proletariat that is cut off from all of the natural, primary means of earning a living and is dependent on state support.

This support is organized, and on a large scale. During the imperial age of Rome, between 100,000 and 150,000 families live wholly on public assistance. There is first of all the *annona,* the distribution of the grain, which is operated on a permanent basis. In addition, every ranking state official, every dictator, and every emperor counts it a matter of personal prestige to lavish grain and wine in abundance on the common people. Unquestionably this is done largely for the sake of popular support, but it is nonetheless an effective form of relief.

The Roman citizen is also responsive in cases of disaster. After the great fire in A.D. 64 during the reign of Nero, the emperor himself has quantities of food distributed and opens his gardens to the public. Fifteen years later, when erupting Vesuvius buries the cities of Pompeii and Herculaneum under a rain of cinder and ash, a spontaneous relief operation springs up. And when an amphitheater collapses in the provinces, the Romans dispatch doctors and medical supplies to the scene, and the houses of the upper classes are opened to the victims.

But in Rome too it is clear that not all of these actions are motivated by compassion. Lucius Annaeus Seneca, the philosopher who commits suicide on Nero's orders, leaves numerous writings

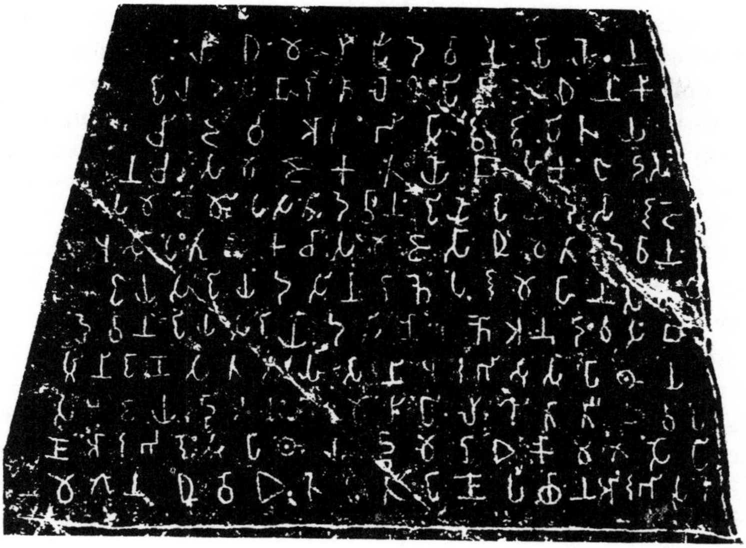

"No living thing may be killed." This edict, issued by Emperor Asoka of India, was found in Gujarat and dates from about 240 B.C.

in which he states his views on the question of mercy. In his seven treatises on good deeds, he discusses in detail man's obligation to do good to everyone. But pity he holds in execration. Only old wives have pity, says Seneca. He will help those that weep, but he will not weep with them. What he does is rationally motivated, and good deeds make for a good conscience. Still, in his doctrine of charity to all, he goes a step beyond the Greeks; for, he says, all men are by nature brothers. But it must not be overlooked that his is not the kind of spirit that produces a genuine and broadly conceived kind of mercy.

Israel and the Commandments of Mercy

A totally different motivation for good deeds is to be found in ancient Israel. On Mount Sinai God gives his Chosen People his commandments. The first and great commandment is to fear and love God. But the very next commandment is to love one's neighbor. No state socialism, no philosophically based *humanitas* is needed as incentive to keep this commandment. The laws of true philanthropy as they ring out in the Torah have a different and profoundly significant basis: Your neighbor is God's creation; therefore you, who are also God's creation, are to love him as yourself. You are to do so because God loves you, and you *will* do so if you are obedient to God. Love of neighbor is thus an expression of thanks and obedience to God.

Whenever the children of Israel forget God's kindness toward them, they also forget the commandment to love their neighbor. When they are disobedient (and they often are) this commandment is vitiated. But when they keep God's commandments in grateful obedience, they are blessed. And the blessing is contagious, spreading to neighboring peoples and to aliens and strangers.

An illustration of this is the story of Ruth. Ruth is a foreigner in Israel. She enters the land as the daughter-in-law of Naomi, after Naomi has lost husband and children in a strange land. Your people shall be my people, Ruth says to Naomi; nothing but death can part us.

So Ruth the Moabitess now lives in Bethlehem. As Naomi is without means, Ruth makes herself useful by going to the fields and gleaning the ears of grain. The servants, who in accordance with the customs of the day leave her to her gleaning, are astonished at the industry of this foreigner. The field belongs to a man named Boaz, a kinsman of Naomi; and Boaz honors the Mosaic statute that says, "When ye reap the harvest of your land, thou shalt not wholly reap the corners of thy field, neither shalt thou gather the gleanings of thy harvest. And thou shalt not glean thy vineyard, neither shalt thou gather every grape of thy vineyard; thou shalt leave them for the poor and stranger."

But Boaz does more than he has to. He instructs his reapers to pull ears of grain out of the sheaves and leave them for Ruth to glean. Thus Ruth and Naomi experience the mercy that the Israelites are to show especially to strangers, widows, and orphans. Boaz is mindful that he has received his possessions in trust from God, and that the fruit of his fields does not belong to him alone. What he manages is God's, and he is accountable to God for the way he manages it.

Two things become clear in this story: First, when Naomi returns destitute to her homeland, there is no state or public assistance for her. Israel is different in this respect from Egypt and Rome. All works of mercy are performed by individuals; and in this personal, neighbor-to-neighbor ministry we can see the outlines of the neighbor-loving-neighbor principle that will appear in the Christian era. Second, the story of Ruth is evidence that in Israel concern is not bounded by nationality. Although the Chosen People are careful to avoid foreign influences, they are just as careful to be generous when it comes to helping others, including foreigners.

To be sure, Israel goes through the same phases as other nations. There are times when its norms are abandoned, the commandments flouted, and selfishness and greed proliferate. But in Israel there are always men who rise up to rally the people, rouse them from their torpor, and lead them back to the right way. The mighty figures of the prophets are a case in point. During the reign of Jeroboam II, which was one of Israel's flourishing periods, material prosperity is accompanied by a turning away from the divine precepts. Thereupon the shepherd Amos rises up and preaches judgment upon the usurious Israelites who "trample upon the needy, and bring the poor of the land to an end," who "afflict the righteous," "take a bribe," "make the ephah small and the shekel great" (shrink the measure and raise the price), and "deal deceitfully with false balances." Not many years later Isaiah hurls his sixfold indictment at the Jews in Jerusalem who do evil and pervert what is right.

From the period of the Assyrian captivity comes the story of Tobit, who goes about daily with his entire family, distributing his possessions and comforting the afflicted. He feeds the hungry, clothes the naked, and buries the dead. This story from the Old Testament Apocrypha gives an uncommonly vivid picture of the religiously motivated mercy which is characteristic of the people of Israel.

Upon their return from exile the Jews are forced to maintain strict precautions against foreign influences; the religions and cults of the procession of nations that oppress or occupy Israel threaten to make inroads into the monotheism of the Jews. Unfortunately this narrowing and sealing-off process gradually produces the legalism that typifies the Jewish mind-set in Jesus' day. At the same time, a number of old statutes are falling into oblivion, for example the sabbatical year. The sabbatical, observed every seven years, is a hallowed year during which the fields may not be planted or harvested. The harvest of the previous year must be made to last two years. Whatever comes up by itself is God's gift to the poor. Another forgotten statute concerns the Year of Jubilee, when all slaves are to be freed and all expropiated land restored to the dispossessed. Celebrated every forty-nine years, the Year of Jubilee appears to be an early and daring experiment in a kind of reparations policy aimed at social equity. The ban on interest is also increasingly ignored. As a people, the Jews are no longer tillers of the soil; they are becoming a nation of traders. Usury and profiteering grow apace, augmented by the peculiar tribute laws imposed by Rome. When one adds to this the hordes of beggars, and of lame persons, most of whom are the casualties of an uprooted rural population, the picture of human misery is complete. Thus by the time of the Gospels the picture is largely one of a fragmented and, in many ways, impoverished people.

The commandment to love one's neighbor also seems in virtual limbo. The Proverbs had exhorted, "If your enemy is hungry, give him bread to eat; and if he is thirsty, give him water to drink." Now, although one is still enjoined to love his friends, the commandment continues in shameful fashion, "and hate your enemy." The orthodox Jew now confines himself strictly to the letter of the law. When he does mercy, he goes only as far as the law goes. His motivation to do good is now a concern for his own standing in God's sight and for blotting out his own sin. Benevolences now exalt their dispenser—and frequently debase their object.

Notwithstanding, here and there within the Jewish nation are devout communities that preserve and faithfully proclaim the meaning of true mercy. And it must never be forgotten that here for the first time the principles of mercy and of love for one's neighbor are understood and applied in their only proper frame of reference: that of man's duty to obey God.

2. Love of Neighbor in the Early Christian Era

Jesus and the New Commandment

Jesus Christ brings a new Way into the world. A new chapter in the history of mankind begins with the life and death of the Redeemer. If we wanted to sum up that life and death in a word, we would have to say that what he brought to men was love. It is not enough to say that love and mercy is something Jesus *practiced*; we must see that love and mercy is something Jesus *was*. His words and acts have become the criterion, the definition, of love and mercy.

The new Way is heralded by a voice crying in the wilderness. John the Baptist prophesies at a time when the land is occupied by Roman soldiers, and when the Torah-minded Pharisee is isolating himself more and more, both from his and Israel's despised enemies and from his less devout countrymen. The Baptizer calls the people to turn and repent. At the same time he proclaims the coming of the Messiah, the hope of the Jews since the days of the prophets. "Repent," he cries, "the kingdom of heaven is at hand!" God's anointed, the Christ, is coming.

John, who stands at the threshold of the new era, explains the commandment to "love thy neighbor" in the simplest possible terms. When the listening multitudes are troubled by his message and ask what they should do, he answers, "He who has two coats, let him share with him who has none; and he who has food, let him do likewise." John exhorts the tax collectors not to demand more than is due, and he cautions the soldiers who, like the tax collectors, have long been ostracized by the Jewish community,

"Rob no one by violence or by false accusation, and be content with your wages." The message is clear: Let him who would please God not forget his neighbor. Even before Jesus begins his own ministry, John fuses into an indivisible whole the old Mosaic laws enjoining love of God and neighbor. At the same time he begins to tear down the legalistic hedges and barriers erected by the Pharisees in their anxious concern for the Law. John identifies the notorious tax collector and the equally despised soldier as neighbors.

People helping people, ignoring all barriers and all questions about the worthiness of those being helped—that is the principle ancient Israel had learned and then forgotten. John revives the original commandment, and the One whom he heralds comes and fulfills it with his life and with his death.

Jesus takes up the call to repentance, but instead of remaining in the desert he goes to where the people are, preaching in Judea and in Galilee, in Jerusalem and by the Lake of Gennesaret, testifying to the mercy of God. God wants to help, heal, save; he wants men to find their way back to him, and so he has sent Christ into the world. That is Jesus' message. The Master becomes a servant, the king a minister. In both his preaching and his deeds Jesus himself undergoes this transformation from master to servant in obedience to God. For him words and works belong together. The love of the man of Nazareth for his neighbor is perfect, like the love of God.

The life of Jesus is permeated by his concern for the whole man; meeting physical needs is not enough. However, Jesus takes the physical needs of his fellowman seriously. He is moved with compassion by the misery he sees. He identifies with the sufferers and takes their burdens upon himself. He puts out his hand and touches the leper by the wayside; he heals the servant of the Roman centurion; he raises Jairus's daughter; he lays his hand on the blind man and restores his sight. Wherever someone is in trouble, wherever there is disease or misery, Jesus is there to help. He is there in the moment of need. But his primary concern is not to make the world a better place, not to eliminate poverty. As he himself says to his disciples, "The poor you have always with you." He does not stir up the poor against the Pharisees; he mobilizes no armies of the unfortunate against the rich and the well-fed. He proclaims no social reform program. He helps.

It is remarkable to observe how his spontaneous action moves others. Suddenly people are willing to help their neighbors get to where Jesus is. The feeble are escorted, the lame are carried. Four men, bearing the bed of a paralytic, work their way through to Jesus, allowing nothing to obstruct them. Another man takes the hand of a blind man and leads him to the Savior. They bring the sick from far and near, and they cry to him, "Come and help!" A Canaanite woman pleads for her daughter, a Roman centurion for his servant, a father for his epileptic son. Mary and her sister Martha send a message to him saying that Lazarus, their brother, is fatally ill. The disciples go out on mission in the same spirit: to do the works their master has done.

The ministry of Jesus is an example of perfect love, enabling men to see what is demanded of them in turn. They begin to see what they can do to deal with human need and misery.

They fail repeatedly, of course. The disciples want to send the children away, and their parents with them, so that Jesus will not be bothered. Or they suggest that the thousands listening to Jesus can find their own food. Peter denies his Master in the hour of crisis. But the love of the Redeemer covers all human failure. He does not reject Peter after being denied by him; he heals the ear of Malchus, who has come to take him prisoner; and he prays for those who have nailed him to the cross. For Jesus, human barriers do not exist. He eats with publicans and sinners, he extends his hand on behalf of the woman taken in adultery, he is gentle with the harlot, and he washes the feet of his own disciples, thus performing the humble function of a slave.

The Good Samaritan

What love of neighbor meant to Jesus is nowhere clearer than in the parable of the Good Samaritan:

> And behold, a lawyer stood up to put him to the test, saying, "Teacher, what shall I do to inherit eternal life?" He said to him, "What is written in the law? How do you read?" And he answered, "You shall love the Lord your God with all your heart,

> and with all your soul, and with all your strength, and with all your mind; and your neighbor as yourself." And he said to him, "You have answered right; do this, and you will live." But he, desiring to justify himself, said to Jesus, "And who is my neighbor?" Jesus replied, "A man was going down from Jerusalem to Jericho, and he fell among robbers, who stripped him and beat him, and departed, leaving him half dead. Now by chance a priest was going down that road; and when he saw him he passed by on the other side. So likewise a Levite, when he came to the place and saw him, passed by on the other side. But a Samaritan, as he journeyed, came to where he was; and when he saw him, he had compassion, and went to him and bound up his wounds, pouring on oil and wine; then he set him on his own beast and brought him to an inn, and took care of him. And the next day he took out two denarii and gave them to the innkeeper, saying, 'Take care of him; and whatever more you spend, I will repay you when I come back.' Which of these three, do you think, proved neighbor to the man who fell among the robbers?" He said, "The one who showed mercy on him." And Jesus said to him, "Go and do likewise."*

The lawyer's question has been turned around. It is no longer, "Who is my neighbor?" but "To whom am I a neighbor?" And Jesus adds pointedly, "Go and do likewise." Merely knowing the commandment to love our neighbor is not enough. Talking about it is not enough either, no matter how eloquent we are. Nor is it enough to wait until a "worthy" neighbor turns up, someone on whom we can have compassion without losing our dignity or getting our hands dirty. The commandment to love our neighbor is in effect *now,* regardless of time, place, or circumstance. "To whom am I a neighbor?" means "Where is someone who needs my help?"

Jesus' interpretation of the commandment of love is radical and unconditional. Not even a collision with the law deters him. He heals on the Sabbath as well as on other days, though legally forbidden to do so according to the interpretations of the day. He demands what no man has ever demanded. When Peter asks him whether forgiving seven times is enough, Jesus answers: not seven times but seventy times seven. In other words, forever.

Before Jesus leaves his disciples, before he goes the way of

* Sources of the indented quotations are listed on pp. 289-292.

obedience that leads to the cross, he gives them one more object-lesson, in order to teach them to do as he has done.

> Now before the feast of the Passover, when Jesus knew that his hour had come to depart out of this world to the Father, having loved his own who were in the world, he loved them to the end. And during supper, when the devil had already put it into the heart of Judas Iscariot, Simon's son, to betray him, Jesus, knowing that the Father had given all things into his hands, and that he had come from God and was going to God, rose from supper, laid aside his garments, and girded himself with a towel. Then he poured water into a basin, and began to wash the disciples' feet, and to wipe them with the towel with which he was girded. He came to Simon Peter; and Peter said to him, "Lord, do you wash my feet?" Jesus answered him, "What I am doing you do not know now, but afterward you will understand." Peter said to him, "You shall never wash my feet." Jesus answered him, "If I do not wash you, you have no part in me." Simon Peter said to him, "Lord, not my feet only but also my hands and my head!" Jesus said to him, "He who has bathed does not need to wash, except for his feet, but he is clean all over; and you are clean, but not all of you." For he knew who was to betray him; that was why he said, "You are not all clean." When he had washed their feet, and taken his garments, and resumed his place, he said to them, "Do you know what I have done to you? You call me Teacher and Lord; and you are right, for so I am. If I then, your Lord and Teacher, have washed your feet, you also ought to wash one another's feet. For I have given you an example, that you also should do as I have done to you. Truly, truly, I say to you, a servant is not greater than his master; nor is he who is sent greater than he who sent him. If you know these things, blessed are you if you do them."

In the Footsteps of the Master

Jesus sends his disciples forth, and these sent-ones or "apostles" follow the example he has given them. They preach the good tidings of Jesus the Christ, and they do good for God's sake. The Acts of the Apostles in the New Testament is full of such reports. From the beginning the faithful are together with one accord, and they help all the poor and needy in their midst. We hear of members of that first Christian community who sell all their possessions and give the proceeds to the poor. We hear that certain men

Sheltering the homeless has always been one of the supreme commands of mercy. This old woodcut shows the sleeping quarters of a hostel.

are set apart to serve the poor. These deacons, as they are called, assist the apostles and divide the gifts among the needy, particularly the widows and orphans. When the church in Jerusalem runs out of funds (perhaps because of its own generosity) the churches in Asia Minor and Greece take up a collection for their brothers. The collection is delivered by Paul.

In such examples of the early Christians' love the "neighbors" are chiefly other Christians; but mercy and charity in this period are by no means limited to fellow believers. The pattern here is no different from the one Jesus followed. No banners proclaim social reform programs, no one proposes to usher in the Millennium single-handed. The early Christians help their fellowman because they have experienced the love of God and desire to live in obedience to him. They are servants of their Master and do his bidding.

The first three centuries after Christ bring severe persecution and suffering upon the young churches. From the bloodbath under Nero and the systematic campaign of arrests and trials under Decius to Diocletian's reign of terror, Christians are blamed, hounded, and persecuted on all sides. Even so, the commandment to love one's neighbor and show mercy to him is not forgotten. Thousands of Christians, though persecuted themselves, help their neighbors whenever they can, even if the neighbor is actually the enemy.

In the middle of the third century, Ethiopia is hit by one of mankind's most fearful scourges: the bubonic plague. Soon the "black death" is raging throughout North Africa, and people are seized with panic. Daily the epidemic sweeps away countless numbers of lives, while those it does not touch take desperate flight. Family members who have become infected are abandoned, and children are turned out of their homes. A fierce greed fastens upon men's minds. The diseased are shunned, but their possessions are seized. In the cities, as the bodies of the victims are heaped up, their houses are invaded and looted. Men succumb to both fear and greed, and often it is greed that predominates.

Cyprian and Identification with the Victim

Carthage, A.D. 253. The plague is raging unabated. Again the people are saying that the Christians must be to blame, that the plague is the visible judgment of the gods upon those who have turned to this new superstition. One wave of bitter persecution barely over, the wrath of the people is again stirred up against the Christians. Especially vocal among the accusers is a man named Demetrius. In the midst of all the fear and misery Demetrius can find nothing better to do than inflame the hatred of the masses toward the Christians. Whereupon Bishop Cyprian confronts him with the words: "The sick are shown no mercy by you; greed and rapacity gape upon the dead. Those who lack the courage to do the works of mercy instead plunge into the pursuit of iniquitous gain. Those who shrink from burying the dead instead covet their possessions!"

Cyprian sees that universal disaster leads the unbelievers not to relief action but to crime; everywhere they are burning, robbing, and looting. Cyprian then does what he has been unable to challenge them to do. He gathers his people and calls upon them for the sake of Christ to include the unbelievers in their aid, the very unbelievers who so severely persecuted him. He himself leads his people into the houses of the diseased. He ministers to those in agony and comforts those who are dying. He does not ask whether the home is Christian or heathen. He asks only where the plague victims are, where to find those who are dying alone and forsaken. There he is needed, and there he goes.

Before long he abandons this largely hit-or-miss approach and organizes a relief program in his parish. Everyone is put to work at a specific task where his talents will do the most good. Numbers of these volunteers succumb to the plague themselves; they end their service with the sacrifice of their own lives.

One of the primary tasks of Cyprian's program is the burial of the dead. In the plague year of 253 cadavers lie in heaps everywhere. The heathen let them lie there, prey for the buzzards. But the Christians revive the Egyptians' seventh work of mercy. Christians believe that it is man's duty to bury his dead, and for them this means not only those of the family circle but all whom they find. By systematically carrying out this principle the Christians accomplish something they cannot have been aware of: they check the spread of the plague. Proper burial is itself a hygienic measure of vital importance.

During the same year that the plague spreads through North Africa, hordes of bandits appear along the borders of ancient Numidia and raid the nearby towns and villages. They scatter over the countryside, looting and robbing and cutting down everything that opposes them. Those who are not killed are driven into captivity and slavery. Among the captives are many Christians—men, women, and children. A dreadful future awaits them; the men are sold as chattel, the women and girls are raped. The Numidian bishops find out about this and send an urgent appeal to Cyprian in Carthage.

Cyprian has his hands full with his own plague relief program, but he does not hesitate to launch another campaign. He knows that if there is any rescuing to be done in this case, it will have to be done with money; he must try to ransom the captives. Cyprian therefore issues a call for funds, and the result is almost unbelievable. The church of Carthage, already bled white, decimated by the plague, laboring under the almost insupportable weight of misfortune in its own country, musters its reserves and collects a total of 100,000 sesterces (about 5,000 dollars).

Cyprian immediately sends the money to Numidia, along with a letter in which he writes, "So we must now consider the captivity of our brothers as our own captivity, and the pain of our companions as our own pain." The identification of the deliverer with the victim is here unmistakable, and it is this alone which makes compassion possible, indeed translates compassion into action.

Cyprian's letter also makes clear mention of the dynamic for such action, the true source of the Christian's love of neighbor: "Thus we must see Christ in our captive brethren and rescue him from the perils of captivity; for he rescued us from the perils of death." But Cyprian is not minded to help once and let it go at that, and so he adds, "Should, however . . . something similar recur, do not hesitate to communicate it to us in writing."

As Cyprian's plague relief program becomes a model for similar programs in other localities, so too his efforts in ransoming captives also have a widespread impact. His name and his deeds may stand as representative of many similar deeds by many other willing workers. There are even some Christians who sell their own freedom, submitting to bondage in order that others may go free.

The moral and spiritual support of Christian brothers, especially on behalf of those who have been put in prison for their faith, remains of vital importance. The deacons in Carthage voluntarily assume the responsibility for a regular prison ministry. We know from the prison writings of the martyred St. Perpetua that these deacons secure jobs as guards in order to minister to the prisoners' physical and spiritual needs, even though anyone who does so is in constant danger of being arrested and thrown into prison himself. "And so we were put in jail," writes Perpetua, "and I was horrified, as I had never before experienced such darkness. O dreadful day! Tremendous heat! for the soldiers were throwing in whole heaps of people at a time; and besides all this I was torn by anxiety for my child. Then the good deacons Tertius and Pomponius, who minister unto us, arranged to buy us a few hours in a better part of the jail, where we could refresh ourselves."

Anthony and the Bonds of Love

One of the finest examples of prison ministry is the work of St. Anthony, the Hermit of Coma. At the age of sixty he leaves his desert hermitage in order to accompany a group of Christian captives to Alexandria where they are to be tried and sentenced. For months the hermit stays with them during their trial. He comforts those who are sentenced, cares for the sick, and rallies those in despair. Again and again he goes to the place of execution and stands watch with the prisoner until the moment of execution.

Anthony soon begins to attract attention. The complaints which would inevitably have brought him to trial, however, are never filed. Even the vigilant enforcers of the law seem to respect the selfless efforts of this old man. He gains access to all the jails and goes from cell to cell, distributing bread and comforting the prisoners with prayer and words of cheer. He attends the sick and the crippled and the wounded. No effort seems too great to make. He goes down into the mines to visit those who have been sentenced to hard labor. He even steps in to work in the place of some exhausted prisoner until the overseers drive him away. Only when the persecution abates and conditions in the land return to normal does he go back to his hermitage on Mount Colzim, site of the present Monastery of St. Anthony. And even here he remains active, giving spiritual counsel to all who come to him in need. Is it any wonder that the word of such a man is believed? Even the emperor has occasion to send to him for advice. Anthony is sometimes referred to—justifiably—as the secret conscience of the Roman Empire.

St. Anthony is over a hundred years old when he dies in about the year 356. By this time the persecution of Christians has long passed. Constantine the Great has given Christianity the official recognition of the state. Many activities of the Christian churches are now taken over by state and public agencies and authorities. But as always, the real ministry of love from neighbor to neighbor devolves upon the individual. And the call for such ministry is great, for although the era of Christian persecution has ended, want and misery has not ended.

Basil and the City of Mercy

The church, however, has now been given other means of combatting want. It is not unheard of now for a single bishop to build a whole city for the poor and the sick. One such bishop is Basil, whose field of ministry is Caesarea of Cappadocia.

Basil's childhood years are not easy ones. He is brought up as an orphan by his grandmother Macrina, who hides him in the dense forests by the Black Sea for seven years during the persecution of Christians under Diocletian. Basil later attends the university in Athens together with his friend Gregory Nazianzen. Even in his youth Basil's purity and asceticism are widely known, and like Anthony before him Basil first seeks his salvation in solitude. He visits the anchorites in Egypt, and he gives away all that he owns. Subsequently he comes to see, however, that his real vocation lies in the world.

In 364 Basil goes to Caesarea to become an assistant and advisor to the bishop there. When a severe drought results in widespread famine and want, Basil calls upon the rich for aid. It is reported that his appeal opened the storehouses of the prosperous citizens, and that he distributed food to the poor in the manner of a "second Joseph." He gathers the hungry together and feeds them community-style. Vegetables and salted meat are cooked in large pots, and then doled out. While the hungry are eating, Basil stands nearby, preaching to them the word of God. He is able to provide for the people in this way for the better part of a year, thus averting a crisis.

Six years later, when the bishop of Caesarea dies, Basil is unanimously chosen to take his place. He is now able to take up the work he has begun and to carry it on with purpose and vigor.

On the outskirts of the city, Basil builds a xenodochium—a hospital and hospice that becomes one of the best-known institutions of mercy of the entire early-church period. Situated around the main building is a colony of separate units for strangers, the sick, and the poor. Even lepers, traditionally the outcasts in every age, have a house of their own here. Basil secures doctors, nurses, and orderlies. He personally hires the janitors and maintenance men.

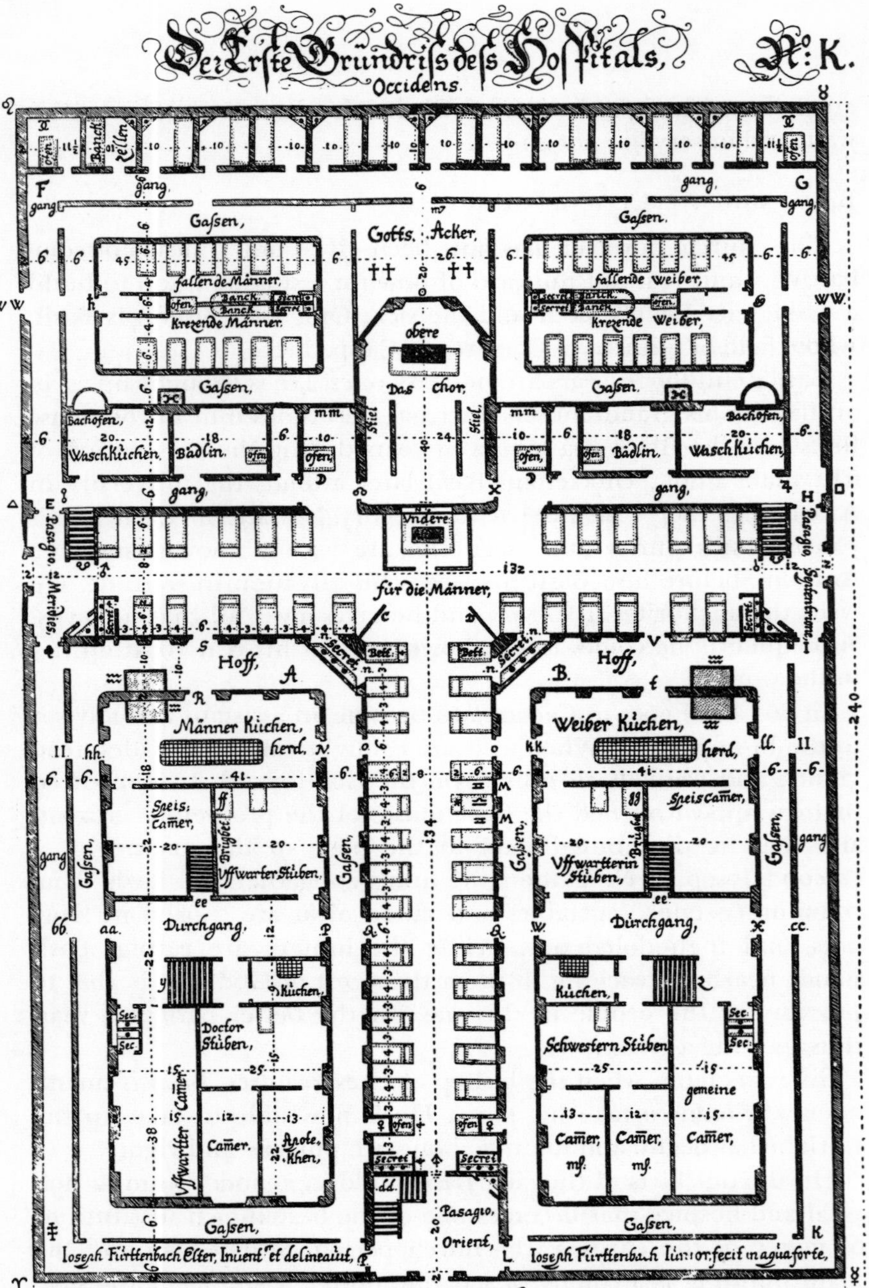

The movement that began in Basil's time with the xenodochium—the hostel and early "hospital"—advanced significantly during the time of the Crusades under the leadership of the Knights of St. John, culminating in the progressive hospital care of the Middle Ages. Above, the floor plan of a hospital built to accommodate 200 needy people: aged, sick, lepers, epileptics, and the feebleminded. From a treatise on hospital construction by Joseph Furttenbach (Ulm, 1655).

Thus a whole city comes into being, a city of mercy, which later comes to be called the Basileiad after its founder.

Basil himself stays on the front lines. He helps to care for the sick, he plans and advises, he is on hand wherever needed, and he is always concerned for the spiritual care of those entrusted to his charge.

Not being able, of course, to finance the work out of his own pocket, Basil issues an appeal for support. The gifts pour in; for Basil manages, through the use of flaming exhortations, to stir up a diocesan-wide competition in the cause of mercy. All the more deplorable, then, is the malicious gossip that circulates about him and his money. The emperor Valens, who finds the bishop a nuisance anyway (because of doctrinal disagreements), is only too glad to pounce on such gossip; and one day he threatens to strip Basil of his fortune. Basil answers merely, "My fortune? Take this worn-out robe and my books. More I do not own!" The fact is that Basil has never used even the smallest part of the money entrusted to him for anything but his hospital. Every single donation was meant for the needy who depended upon his protection, and they alone would have it. And the people know this very well; there is none among them who does not honor this man of mercy. An angry crowd gathers outside the emperor's palace, demanding that their benefactor be released. Valens has to yield to the will of the people. The poor have not forgotten their champion.

Basil's brothers and sisters follow similar paths. His sister Macrina founds a monastic community that serves as a haven for needy persons of every kind; his brother Naucratius takes care of helpless old folk in a villa on the river Iris, going on mountain hunting expeditions to provide the necessary food. Gregory, Basil's second brother, also rises to prominence, becoming the bishop of Nyssa.

Basil dies on January 1, 379, and the renowned Gregory Nazianzen delivers the eulogy: "Go to the gates of the city and see the city of mercy, the storerooms of godliness, the treasurehouse of love, where the abundance of the rich and the pennies of the poor are gathered, where love is practiced, compassion demonstrated, and suffering exalted. What is Thebes with its seven gates, what are the pyramids of the pharaohs compared with this work of love? Basil taught us to lend our mercy to God, just as we ourselves are in need of God's mercy."

The influence of Basil and men of his stature spreads to the non-Christian world. When Julian attempts, in his three-year reign as emperor, to restore the polytheism of bygone days and to undermine the position of Christianity, he is unable to ignore the Christians' works of love. If his pagan restoration is to succeed, he must at least carry on their charitable institutions. Accordingly he orders Arsacius, the chief priest of Galatia, to "build many hostels in each city. Travelers should enjoy the benefits of our care, not only those who belong to us but also those of the other side, and indeed anyone without money." Above all, the chief priest is to urge humanitarian goals upon the Gentiles; for, as the emperor writes, "We ought to be ashamed. Not a beggar is to be found among the Jews, and those godless Galileans (the Christians) feed not only their own people but ours as well, whereas our people receive no assistance whatever from us."

Julian's design fails. His attempts at restoration are foredoomed, for the wheel of history cannot be reversed. Christianity has conquered the ancient world. But the growing power of the church has its ominous side: the church now assumes the role of persecutor. Pagan temples are destroyed, unbelievers forcibly proselyted, and apostates severely punished. Nonetheless, these political measures do not disrupt the works of mercy. The churches continue to love and serve. Doing mercy also remains the noblest office of the bishops and their deacons. New hospitals and hostels spring up everywhere, and reports of emergency relief efforts, especially for the ransoming of prisoners, continue to abound.

Around the year 375, the Syrian city of Edessa is hit by a severe famine. The victims get neither food nor medical treatment. But there are Christians living in the city, among them the old church father Ephraem Syrus, a religious teacher and hymnwriter who confronts his fellow believers with the need and reproaches them for their hardness of heart. It is up to the Christians, he cries. Who should help if not the Church of Christ? His hearers begin making excuses: they know few of their fellow townsmen and wouldn't know how to go about distributing gifts in a fair way. But Ephraem undercuts these arguments by saying that he will himself collect the donations and see to their equitable distribution. Once more, through the initiative of one man, a large relief work comes into being. Strangers from far-distant areas pour into the city and are provided for. Eventually Ephraem manages to provide beds for three hundred sick people under one roof. His last years are thus spent in a living demonstration before his congregation of that which he had taught them all his life, namely, the way of love and discipleship. The founding of the Basileiad may well have exerted an influence on Ephraem, for tradition has it that he and Basil knew each other.

Constantinople affords another example of similar work. Here the patriarch John Chrysostom begins in 398 to build a number of "hospitals." His chief aim was to "help the poor, who must spend their nights half naked and maimed in the streets and public squares, even though hunger and cold make them cry out." Five thousand needy persons are regularly supported by him. He manages again and again to attract new volunteers to his broadly conceived mission of mercy, workers who perform their difficult tasks zealously and faithfully.

Meanwhile, a similar movement is growing in Italy. In 398 the distinguished Roman Pammachius builds a hospice at the mouth of the Tiber and takes care of the sick himself. Excavations in the nineteenth century at the site of Ostia have uncovered this hospice. Wards and storerooms are arranged around the "quadriporticus," a large quadrangular area circumscribed by a colonnade and having a fountain at its center. To the east is a basilica with three naves, and next to it the quarters for the deacons and hospital workers. The fountain bears the inscription: "Water in abundance flows here for all who are thirsty."

Also renowned in those days, and probably similar in appearance, was the hospital of Nosocium, donated by the Roman noblewoman Fabiola. And there is Dionysius, the Roman deacon and physician, who follows Pammachius's example and whose epitaph testifies that he "granted the sick who came to him everything without charge." In fact, hospitals are now being built everywhere, persuasive evidence that there is no lack of persons who are serious about the commandment to love their neighbor.

But individual help is often not enough. Conditions in general need to be improved, and this may require a forceful approach to the responsible authorities. Thus in the second half of the fourth century we find Bishop Ambrose of Milan, the venerated teacher of Augustine, denouncing the high-handed practices of municipal authorities who regularly hustle all needy strangers out of the city in times of want. His reproach actually produces results: the practice is discontinued. One of his sayings might well be addressed to all men of all times: "The wild beasts regard the fruit of the soil as common to all; they are also helpful, each to his kind. But man would live in enmity."

Ambrose, by the way, is one of those princes of the church who, in times of severe hardship, sell off a number of sacramental vessels in order to aid oppressed debtors and prisoners. There are similar accounts of Bishop Paulinus of Nola, who lives a few decades later. Little by little he gives away all his possessions to help the poor. What makes his action all the more noteworthy is that Paulinus obviously comes from a family of considerable property. It is said of a relation of his named Melanie that her possessions reached from North Africa to England. Nor is Melanie outdone by Paulinus. Gradually she too sells everything she has, in some cases against the will of her relatives. The entire proceeds of an estate worth millions are given to the poor.

Severinus and the Care of Refugees

In this same period lives a man whose life gives flesh and blood to the parable of the Good Samaritan. His name is Severinus, and his home is in Noricum, between Vienna and Passau. In this remote border-province of the Roman Empire, the rule of the emperor is threatened. Germanic tribes make periodic raids, looting and robbing. It is the time of wholesale tribal migrations, and in the confusion of these endless skirmishes law and order are increasingly eroded. The soldiers are poorly armed, poorly paid, and almost without supplies. Only behind the solid walls of the larger cities can they still hope to stand; and one by one these cities are falling. The soldiers flee from stronghold to stronghold; the people flee with the soldiers; and both are pursued by the armies of the Germanic tribes. An entire people lives in constant flight, and these refugees fare no differently from refugees of all times: they are beset by hunger and want.

Severinus goes to work in the midst of this chaos. Of obscure origins, having neither rank nor mandate from church or state, Severinus is simply there, as if he had happened along the way. Like the Good Samaritan, he sees the need and does something about it. He travels with the refugees in order to give them moral support. He approaches the few people who have managed to hold onto their possessions, and so stirs their hearts that many of them volunteer to give a tithe of all that they have. Severinus collects food and clothing for those who need them, as well as money for the captives, often having to follow the latter for considerable distances before overtaking them and their captors. He negotiates with the opposing military commanders, and since he finds Christians on both sides he is able, in the midst of the carnage of war, to speak plainly to those military leaders who have not yet perceived the implications of their faith. He advocates charity in all things, but he can also speak very pointedly, warning and castigating when the occasion requires it. Severinus becomes the protector of an entire people.

When a siege of the plague is added to the horrors of war, he remains undaunted, although the daily demands made upon him are sapping his strength. His mission now becomes that of caring for the plague-stricken and burying the dead, and he performs it without complaint. Untiring, undespairing, he traverses the whole provincial borderland along the Danube—inadequately clothed, barefoot even in winter, but with a burning heart and healing hands. No glory comes to Severinus for his sacrifices. He dies unnoticed and unknown in the confusion of the times. A few years later the emperor yields the province to the Germanic tribes. Did Severinus labor in vain? Were his efforts wasted? No: Severinus was neither politician nor soldier. He fought neither for Rome nor for Constantinople, nor against the Germanic tribes. His cause was solely the need of the individual; his enemies were hunger and fear, plague and misery. He helped to build where others knew only to destroy; his is the ultimate triumph.

The life of Severinus not only reminds us how necessary the individual act of mercy becomes in times when all human order is about to disintegrate; it also shows us how terribly hard it can be to do good. The person who walks into human snake pits in order to rescue his fellowman is exposing his own life to grave danger. Only the man of faith can stand here. But if, at the moment of crisis, even such a man should waver, who would presume to sit in judgment upon him?

Islands of Mercy

For many Christians living in these times the risks are too great. They feel their faith is too weak to weather the many temptations. Often they see no way at all to maintain their testimony in a milieu that mocks God's order for this world. So they flee the world, flee testing and temptation, flee the dangers they have no confidence of withstanding. They become monks in sequestered monasteries, they withdraw to hermitages, where they hope to live in righteousness before their Lord, Jesus Christ. It is as if the community comes to stand in the stead of the individual. Where the individual has failed, the community becomes a source of new strength. For these monks and hermits know one thing: their retreat from the world must not become a retreat from their neighbor. And so the monasteries become little islands of mercy.

There is hardly a monastery that does not maintain a hostel or hospital. In the lonely lands of the Euphrates, Thalassius and his monks gather and shelter blind beggars; in the desert of Scete, solitaries build a house and provide work for strangers; in Egypt, monks build their hostels at the foot of the pyramids.

In the fifth century, Apa (Father) Shenute, the abbot of the White Monastery of Atripe in upper Egypt, institutes a truly comprehensive relief ministry. At this time the Nubians, invading from the south, attack the land, murdering and pillaging. The people are in panic. Whoever can do so flees. But where is one to go? The Nubians move quickly, and anyone who cannot stay out of range becomes a target for their bows and spears. Then Apa Shenute opens the gates of his monastery. It is an extensive complex, with numerous outbuildings and storerooms and spacious courtyards. It is also unusually well fortified. People stream in by the thousands. Shenute himself describes the event, noting that twenty thousand people find refuge within his gates. Among them are many women and children, as well as many aged and sick people.

Shenute puts the whole monastery on "alert." The monks, who are used to spending their days in silent prayer, suddenly become housefathers, orderlies, emergency relief workers. Only very old or sick members of the community are excused from duty; everyone else is put to work by the alert abbot. He himself hardly pauses to rest. Day after day he is busy seeing to it that the massive relief operation proceeds smoothly. Enormous amounts of food must be procured in order to feed the refugees. Shenute raids his own storehouses, and when the monastery's supplies are exhausted he sends monks to buy all the provisions they can. In a single week 25,000 copper drachmas are spent on vegetables alone. Shenute also gives the refugees money, so that they can fend for themselves as much as possible. Once he notes that 500,000 copper drachmas have been given out in this way.

Seven doctors are on hand to treat the sick and wounded. The relief program lasts three months, during which time fifty-two children are born and twenty-four persons are buried within the monastery walls. But even after the terrors of the Nubian invasion have passed, there is plenty for the courageous abbot to do. He now tries to ransom the captives. He writes, "In the same years we ransomed one hundred prisoners of war, so that they suffered no lack; each prisoner for 400,000 copper drachmas, not including the money that we spent for clothes, food, and ferriage for the duration of their journey home."

From Arabic sources we learn that the Tabennês and Pbow monasteries in Egypt carried out similar relief programs. Later, however, the sources of outreach in the eastern cloisters begin to go dry. Spiritual offices are given more and more attention, physical labor is accordingly deemphasized, and poverty and decline soon follow. The monasteries of the West, however, are becoming real examples of the Christian's love for his neighbor. The foundations are laid by Benedict of Nursia, who is known as the father of Western monasticism, and whose guiding rule is *ora et labora,* "pray and work." He gives monastic life its discipline, a balanced Rule of work and prayer, spiritual exercises and productive activity. Mercy is understood as the unquestioned duty of every monk. Benedict's principles prove themselves in the very first days of the monastery founded by him on Monte Cassino. When a famine strikes Campania, Benedict opens his well-stocked larders and granaries, thereby saving thousands of people from sickness and death.

Martin and the Beggar

Anyone searching for works of love in these centuries cannot fail to be drawn to another figure, whose name is renowned as are few others: St. Martin. To this day, the honor accorded St. Martin is almost without parallel, and it is understandable that such mass veneration and popular affection have woven a colorful garland of legends around his life. But, even allowing for a certain amount of exaggeration, his is still the life of a man of peace and goodness, a true warrior of Christ, so different from the lives of most men who bore the sword.

For a time, Martin did bear a sword; he was a soldier in the army of the Roman Empire, as was his father. The latter was a captain when Martin was born around the year 316 in Sabaria (Hungary). Following in his father's footsteps, and in response to an imperial edict, the son enters the army as a conscript and is assigned to Gaul. Because of his bravery he is soon commissioned an officer, but the glory of war does not cause him to forget what he learned during baptismal instruction. Though not yet baptized, he lives the life of a Christian. As the saying goes, he served his slave more than his slave served him. During his tour in Gaul there occurs that encounter with the beggar: the story that has moved the hearts of men and inspired artists to portray it in stone and bronze. His biographer, Sulpicius Severus, writes:

> He was not as yet born anew in Christ. But he was, in a manner, by his good deeds, qualifying as a candidate for baptism; by tending the sick, succouring the unfortunate, feeding the hungry, clothing the naked, and of his pay reserving for himself only what sufficed for his daily bread. Even then he was not deaf to the Gospel teaching; for he took no thought for the morrow.
>
> One day when Martin was garbed only in his armor and his military cloak—in the middle of a more than usually severe winter, which was moreover so stormy that many were dying of cold—he met at the gate of the city of the Ambiens (Amiens) a poor, naked man. The unfortunate creature implored in vain the pity of the passers-by, but none took heed of him. Then the man

of God, perceiving that none had compassion, knew that it was for him to succour the beggar. But how was he to do so? He had with him nothing but the *chlamyde* he was wearing, for he had already parted with all else in the cause of charity. Quickly then, he seized his sword and cutting his cloak through the middle, he gave half to the beggar and girt the remaining portion round himself. Some of the bystanders mocked him thinking that he presented a grotesque appearance thus draped in his spoilt cloak. But many others who were wiser, groaned within themselves that they had not done likewise, knowing that since they were in possession of all their garments they would have been able to clothe the beggar without entirely stripping themselves.

The following night, during his sleep, Martin beheld Christ robed in the half of the *chlamyde* with which he had covered the beggar.

Martin later becomes a monk, founds a monastery, and is called to Tours as bishop. But he always remains a kind and simple man who wishes nothing for himself and looks only for other persons whom he can help. What sets him apart from many of his contemporaries is preeminently his tolerance, as in the case when Priscillian, later Bishop of Avila, becomes involved in a doctrinal controversy with two Spanish bishops. Priscillian is eventually convicted of heresy, and his accusers demand that he be put to death in order to protect the church from false doctrine. The demand accords perfectly with the temper of the times, as any number of examples could prove, for heresy merits no indulgence. But when Martin learns of the affair, he immediately communicates with the two leading accusers, penetrates their defenses with eloquent words, and exhorts and adjures them. In the end he is actually successful: the two ecclesiastics withdraw their complaint and Bishop Priscillian is saved.

The church, says Martin, may not shed blood for the sake of the faith. It is the tragedy of this man and of the whole church that the mercy shown the beggar at Amiens was loudly praised, while Martin's words about the shedding of blood were soon forgotten—so soon in fact that Priscillian was eventually put to death after all.

3. From Charlemagne to Saladin

For centuries the memory and example of St. Martin live on in Gaul. The idea of the charitable endowment (which in this case means money set aside for the building and maintaining of hospitals and hostels) becomes a trend; and the trend shows how deeply rooted in Christian thought is the idea of the indivisibility of body and soul. A good example is the hospital of Bishop Caesarius of Arles. Caesarius has the buildings laid out in a way that permits the patients to see and participate in the worship services without getting out of bed. It is clear that invalids need something beyond care for their diseased bodies. Care must include the whole man.

The Middle Ages have their share of social problems, and the reformers of the day sometimes seek to cope with them in strange ways. An especially critical problem is that of unwed mothers and their babies. It has long been maintained that abortion—condoned by Plato in his day—amounts to infanticide, and that to abandon newborn babies is no better than murder. But babies continue to be born out of wedlock and then abandoned; and their number is not small, the moral climate of the fifth and sixth centuries being what it is. What can be done? Eventually someone has the idea of putting marble basins in front of the churches. The word is spread that babies may be left in them with no questions asked; the church will assume responsibility for them and bring them up in parochial homes or convents. Not an ideal solution, certainly, but it is still a way to help unfortunate children who are not to blame for their situation; and it is also a way to help the mothers, who are oftentimes no less unfortunate and who are thus spared the torments of conscience that would otherwise assail them. It is perfectly lawful to entrust one's child to the church; and above all there is the certainty that such a child will receive a proper upbringing.

Charlemagne's Efforts to Relieve Poverty

The promising start that the Frankish church makes toward a well-planned poor relief program is lost again during the civil wars that begin in 683. A lone exception is the ministry of St. Odilia, who around the turn of the eighth century cares for the poor and the sick on what will later be called the Odilienberg near Strasbourg. But then both church and state are reorganized almost at the same time. Charles Martel puts the empire in the hands of the Carolingians; Pepin wears the Frankish crown. Supported by the Carolingians, St. Boniface, the Anglo-Saxon monk who is called the "Apostle of Germany," reorganizes the Frankish church. Then, at the zenith of Frankish power Charlemagne brings about an epochal change in the history of Europe. As the first Holy Roman Emperor, he forges the bonds between Empire and Papacy—bonds that are not always felicitous but that endure for five centuries and impart to the Middle Ages its dominant characteristics.

It is inevitable that Charlemagne, whose practical turn of mind helps him to construct a well-ordered state, should consider poor relief an important part of this state order. Consequently, the practice of doing good is reinterpreted during his reign. Previously charity was largely dependent on the initiative of individuals or monasteries—or at most on the authority and good offices of a bishop. Charlemagne sees the care of the needy as an affair of state, and he launches the first full-fledged poverty program since the days of ancient Rome. His church-state poor relief is an improvement on the Roman system: aid is no longer doled out with cold efficiency; genuine concern is shown for the poor person receiving it.

The emperor spells out the individual's responsibilities toward his neighbor in a series of capitularies or decrees. Feudal lords are bidden to render all necessary aid to their subordinates, servants, and vassals. In the capitulary of A.D. 805 we read: "Everyone shall support his own people to the limit of his capacity, and he shall not sell his grain dearly." As to the crown estates, Charlemagne goes a step further, stipulating precisely how much food is to be given to the needy, so that no one must go hungry or beg. He also sets ceiling prices on grain, oats, barley, and rye; and since the crown estates control a large share of the market, he is able to hold down prices and to curb, if not fully eliminate, profiteering. He thus takes a number of measures not unlike those in use today for regulating the economy.

In times of emergency Charlemagne applies stricter sanctions. In 779, a year of severe famine and plague, he orders the richer bishops, abbots, and abbesses to contribute a pound of silver toward the support of the poor. Less wealthy monasteries are assessed half a pound, and the really poor ones five *solidi.* (These were considerable sums in the currency of the day; a pound of silver, for example, would buy an entire knight's estate.) Counts and feudal lords are similarly assessed during the same period. This poverty tax—which is what it amounted to—permits the state to assist those whose lords are not able to do so, and even those needy persons who serve no lord.

Again and again Charlemagne charges the clergy to give alms regularly and not to neglect doing the works that are required in loving their neighbor. He orders gifts for the poor to be distributed publicly four times a year: before Easter, Pentecost, Christmas, and on a specified day in the summer. Other laws govern the rearing of illegitimate children, the care of strangers and travelers, and particularly the care of widows and orphans. The emperor himself takes pains to see that these last two groups particularly are not unjustly treated and that their property is not touched.

Charlemagne's own good works are unstinting. Einhard, his biographer, complains that hordes of beggars regularly collect in the courtyard and are never sent away. On the contrary, Charlemagne protects them by having his own inspector see to it that no frauds sneak into their ranks. It is true that Charlemagne may be the richest man that ever lived; when his estate is parceled out among the endless list of beneficiaries named in his will, each

This twelfth century manuscript portrays Charlemagne as the lawgiver. The text shown is the beginning of his capitulary of March, 779.

person receives a fortune. Riches alone, however, have never been an incentive for philanthropy. On the contrary, they have often choked philanthropic impulses. But Charlemagne's conception of mercy is clearly shown in the capitulary of 802, the *admonitio generalis,* which says, "Love your neighbor as yourselves and give the poor all the alms you can. Receive strangers into your house, visit the sick, show mercy to those in prison." Clearly, the emperor has found the basis for his edicts in the commands of the Bible. He may also be said to act in an ecumenical spirit. He has love-offerings sent to the Anglo-Saxon churches, he supports the Christians in Carthage and Alexandria, and he collects money with which to found and support a hospital for German merchants and pilgrims near the Church of the Holy Sepulcher in Jerusalem.

Charlemagne's wars, particularly the terrible Saxon wars, have tended to obscure his active social concern. In his military policies he may differ little from other mighty men in history, and without question he was responsible for a dreadful amount of bloodshed. But the extensive poverty relief program he incorporated into the legislative structure of his great empire sets him above other kings and emperors. He anticipates by centuries the broad social reform movements that only in modern times have gradually been gaining acceptance and spreading beyond the borders of a few nations to embrace whole continents.

The Monasteries and the Poor

But Charlemagne is to share the fate of other men who are ahead of their time. Even in France, the period of genuine social progress he inaugurates is only an interlude. Under his successors the commandments of mercy gradually lapse into oblivion. When the empire is divided, many of the institutions disappear in the resultant turmoil: notably those hospitals that are independently operated and supported by relief funds. Once more, the burden of caring for the poor and the sick is left chiefly to the monasteries.

Charlemagne's son, Louis the Pious, establishes at the Council of Aachen (817) a general rule modeled on the Rule of Benedict and applicable to all monastic communities. Spiritual offices are balanced with practical work. The monasteries will thereby avoid the risk of financial ruin or of total dependence on charitable foundations. Under the new rule the monasteries may also be reasonably required to set aside a certain portion of their income for assistance to the needy. During Louis's reign every monastic community gives a tenth of all its income for charitable purposes, in addition to whatever other works of mercy it is engaged in.

To be sure, in the chaotic decades of the mid-ninth century, many monasteries neglect these commandments, grow morally lax, and fall into worldliness. However, as numerous contemporary chronicles attest, there are other monasteries in which the works of mercy are practiced as before. The activities of such monasteries are largely determined by their location. Those near cities usually have a kind of welfare hostel, the *hospitale pauperum.* Medical care is also strongly emphasized. The less strategically located monasteries concentrate more on serving travelers, and they become perforce the automatic choice of every wayfarer looking for lodging: merchant and vagabond, clergyman and beggar. In some regions a minimum capacity is prescribed for such lodges: at least forty beds for men and thirty beds for women. To provide facilities for this number involves quite an outlay in itself. Food must also be provided, along with provender and stables for the horses of the gentry, and emergency medical supplies.

The Prüm abbey in the Eifel mountains of Germany invests the total proceeds of one of its farms in the abbey hospital, so that "Christ's poor there may be refreshed and cheered." In the hospital of the abbey of Corbie on the Somme river (France), forty-five loaves of bread are consumed daily. Made from mixed grains, each loaf weighs three-and-a-half pounds. The "New Corbie" or Corvey, a sister abbey on the Weser (Germany), has to secure even larger amounts of food to feed the hungry who come to its doors every day. In addition, almost every monastery takes regular care of a certain number of poor people. In early times the number is usually twelve, presumably harking back to the twelve tribes of Israel and the twelve disciples.

The Cluniac Reforms

In the tenth century the practice of good works shows a marked upswing. Everywhere a new trend toward the ascetic life is apparent, its most visible expression being in the Cluniac reforms. The Benedictine abbey of Cluny, founded in 910 by Duke William of Aquitaine, achieves a position of major importance under its very first abbot, Count Bruno, and exerts a powerful influence on other monastic communities. Under Bruno's successors, Odo and Odilo, Cluny becomes the nucleus of a movement that spreads to monastery after monastery and eventually accomplishes a reform in the whole church.

The Cluniac reforms are initially concerned with the general restoration of monastic discipline and a strict monastic Rule. The monasteries also disavow the sovereignty of their bishops and declare themselves answerable directly to the pope. Finally, the reform movement is concerned with the acquisition of more land and with securing the monastic holdings against the predatory attacks of the secular knighthood. The new, strict monastic rule includes as self-evident the commandment to love one's neighbor, every neighbor. Cluny itself has a large hospice or lodge, as well as a *hospitale pauperum*, the welfare house. In addition to a supervisor, the latter requires six servants to take care of the guests. Every needy stranger who knocks at Cluny's doors receives a pound of bread and, when he leaves the next morning, another half-pound to take with him. Cabbage, peas, and beans, even meat and wine are also served; and there is a special, fine-quality bread for widows, orphans, cripples, and the blind. Besides its day-guests Cluny also shelters eighteen poor people on a regular basis and, at Christmas, gives them shoes and clothing. When a monk at Cluny dies, his daily ration is continued for a month and given to a needy person. And once a week the brothers who serve in the lodge for the poor carry baskets of bread and meat and jugs of wine to the sick and needy in the surrounding villages. Cluny is said to have cared for some 17,000 poor people annually. The pork consumption alone required the slaughter of 150 pigs a year.

But the Benedictines of Cluny are not only committed to helping the individual. In 1031 they are able to advance significantly the cause of peace, a cause that has fared badly throughout the land. When the Carolingian reign comes to an end, the small feudal lords grow bolder and bolder, and the pugnacity of the knights vents itself in unceasing feuds. "Empty are the cities," laments Hervaeus, archbishop of Rheims, "the monasteries ravaged and burned, the fields turned to wasteland. Immorality, adultery, sacrilege, and murder are rampant in the land, blood is mingled with blood, the laws are of no effect, the decrees of the bishops are flouted. Everyone does as he pleases. The consequences are now before us: throughout the whole world the poor are robbed."

The abundant harvest of 1031 makes up for the lean years preceding it; as a result, the monks of Cluny are able to conclude with the robber-knights an agreement: the *Treuga Dei* or Truce of God. Hereby it is established once and for all, and sworn to with sacred oaths by the knights, that from Wednesday evening until Monday morning of every week all feuding shall stop. Under the protection of God and the church, the people are to have peace during that time. Such an arrangement obviously precludes any large-scale pillaging and fighting, permitting the land a measure of peace.

The example set by Cluny has a powerful effect, reaching far beyond the monasteries. The principle of showing brotherly love toward one's neighbor penetrates to the household of the emperor. Adelaide, wife of Otto the Great—who after her husband's death assumes the regency in the stead of her son and her grandson and saves the empire from dissolution—retires in her declining years to the Convent of Saints Peter and Paul, which she had herself founded at Salz in Alsace, and serves the poor there in workclothes and apron, just as the humblest servant-girl.

Kunigunde, wife of Emperor Henry II, is not unlike her. Henry, who is later canonized, is able to find no rest during the short span of his reign. Though frail and in poor health, he must repeatedly defend his empire by armed force. Kunigunde accompanies him on all his campaigns. While her husband is wielding his sword to make the land secure Kunigunde trudges over the battlefields, tending the injured. She braves combat and prolonged exposure in order to dress the wounds of those who have fallen, bring food to the hungry, and slake the thirst of the fever-ridden. She also does whatever she can for all who suffer injustice, who are oppressed or persecuted. Because of the press of state affairs, the emperor can do no more, even in peacetime, than assist the church and the monasteries by numerous endowments and gifts. Meanwhile, his wife is busy with her works of mercy—an indefatigable "Red Cross nurse" of the early Middle Ages. After Henry's death she too, like Adelaide, retires to a convent she had herself founded at Oberkaufingen, near Kassel. Here she exchanges her crown and purple robe for the black habit of the Benedictines and serves the sick as an ordinary nun for the rest of her life.

Henry and Kunigunde are buried in Bamberg. A century later, about 1125, in a time of bitter controversy between emperor and pope, the resident bishop at Bamberg becomes a real man of peace. He is also remembered as the organizer of extensive relief work. Following the Cluniac pattern, Bishop Otto initiates a foresighted program of food storage. One year a late snowfall brings on a disastrous famine in the area, and Otto, the Joseph of his day, opens his granaries and has bread baked for all. The bread is regularly distributed in Bamberg's marketplace, and contemporaries report that the scene was "like a fair." Otto knows enough about human nature to realize that bread without price could lead to idleness and mendicancy, and so he distributes not only bread but also sickles and other tools. This helps the needy to help themselves, and it also provides for next year's harvest.

But let us return to the monasteries, whose importance for the cultural and spiritual life of the Middle Ages cannot be overestimated. Not only are good works and mercy practiced behind cloister walls; the arts and sciences are cultivated here as well. Ancient manuscripts are translated; the sacred scriptures and the works of classical philosophers are read, studied, and copied. And in the monastic schools the church takes great pains to pass on its theological and philosophical canons. What we know as natural science, including medicine, does not yet exist, of course, but by studying the ancient Greeks and Romans the monks find much that can be applied to the care and treatment of the sick.

One of these monastic schools produces a graduate who can be called with some justification the first woman doctor in Europe: Hildegard von Bingen. Born the tenth child of a "burgrave" or castle lord living at Böckelheim on the Nahe, a tributary of the Rhine, Hildegard is sick during much of her early childhood. When she is eight years old her parents, who have dedicated her to the service of God, send her to the monks' school on the Rubertsberg, a mountain not far from the mouth of the Nahe. Here she is taught to read and write, she learns the classical languages, and she begins to study the structure and the functions of the human body. She reads all the pertinent literature she can lay her hands on, organizes what she finds, draws her own conclusions, and finally writes her own book about the forces of nature. The book establishes her reputation as a scholar and writer. When she later becomes an abbess, her fame is such that emperors and popes seek her advice. She writes innumerable letters in which she tries

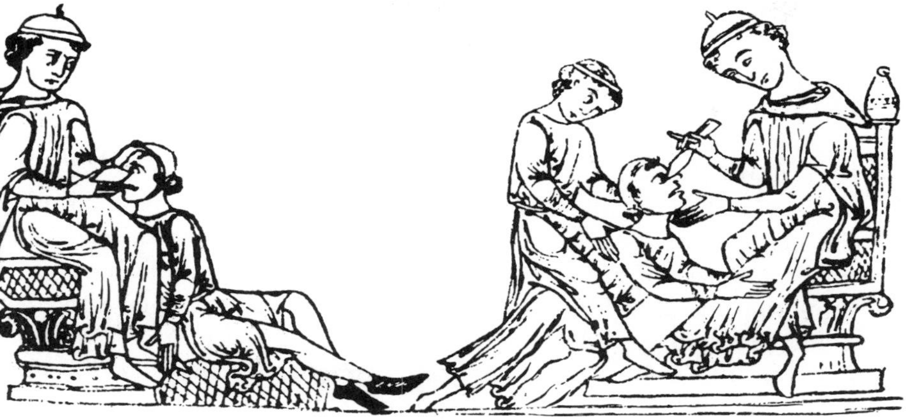

Eye "surgery" in the Middle Ages. A miniature from a French manuscript on surgery, circa 1250.

to help, cheer, or counsel. But never from an ivory tower. Together with her nuns she also operates a hospital which becomes famous for its numerous healings. In an age of widespread faith in alchemy and magic, Hildegard is concerned with thoroughgoing, objective research. Because of her work, age-old knowledge and experience is rediscovered and preserved for future generations.

The practice of medicine in the Middle Ages does not owe its major impetus to Hildegard von Bingen alone, of course. Incentive also comes from a quarter that is considered the archenemy of all Western civilization: Islam. The healing arts are in full flower among the Arabs, and contact with Arabian doctors results in important advances for the Europeans. The contact is brought about by the Crusades.

It is admittedly difficult to consider the Crusades exclusively in terms of the works of mercy they called forth, which is here our present concern, for they were also full of inhumanity. To be sure, they may have given rise to a variety of forces and developments; but essentially they were war and nothing but war. The almost two centuries of savagery, tribulation, and terror involved in fighting for the Holy Sepulcher created more misery than could possibly be offset by all the good works of the monasteries and monastic orders taken together.

The Hospitalers

The hospices and hospitals of the Holy Land are older than the Crusades. In Jerusalem they go back to Charlemagne's time, as we have noted; and the larger the crowds of believers streaming to the tomb of Jesus, the more lodging houses must be built along the main roads. Because of the long marches, the unfamiliar climate, and the often severe privations, the pilgrims succumb to numerous diseases. Epidemics often break out as well, their spread being hastened by totally inadequate sanitary provisions.

It is at this point that we see the emergence of a number of hospitaler orders, that is, groups of devout men who, while not living under a strict monastic rule, undertake to work in the lodging houses and hospitals—no easy life. Such orders are established chiefly in places where some devout benefactor has founded a hospital. An example is the hospital established in Jerusalem about the middle of the eleventh century by an Italian merchant named Amalfi. Run by a lay order under the leadership of a "master," it is secured financially by property deeded to it in southern France.

The city of Jerusalem remains in the hands of the Mohammedans until 1099, but the influx of pilgrims seems hardly diminished on that account. Trade with the Arab peoples continues to flourish, and the number of people visiting the Holy Sepulcher grows from year to year. The first Crusade is mounted anyway (in 1096), probably for two main reasons. First, there is the inspiring vision of liberating the tomb of the Redeemer from the followers of Mohammed, an idea powerful enough to unify the whole of European knighthood. Second, there is the natural counterreaction to the unprecedented, devastating sweep of the Arabs, who have set out to conquer the world by fire and sword for Allah and to convert it to the true faith. Seven Crusades are undertaken with varying degrees of success, and it is not long before the lofty ideals upon which they were launched are buried under a mass of political and economic rationalizations as well as the crusaders' personal lust for adventure and rapine. Brutality mounts on both sides. Disease, misery, and destitution among the ranks of the crusaders and travelers alike grow to terrifying proportions. This crisis produces the first great hospitaler order, whose sole objective at the outset is that of aiding pilgrims and knights who are sick or in distress.

Those who form the order are themselves knights. The first Crusade has fulfilled their hopes, and they can think of no nobler way to continue their service than by taking care of the sick in the name of their Lord. They begin their work in the hospital founded by Amalfi, now administered by Master Gerhard. Gerhard's successor, Raymund de Puy, gives the brotherhood a new Rule, and since de Puy is building a second hospital near the Church of St. John the Baptist, the whole order is given the name of the "Knights of St. John."

At first these knights do only two things; they treat the sick and aid the pilgrims. Since their activities both come under the heading of "hospital" work, they are dubbed the Knights Hospitalers. The conquest of Jerusalem turns out to be a precarious victory, and when the fighting breaks out again, these knights rearm themselves. But not, initially, for battle. Their intention is rather to form a kind of protective escort for the pilgrim caravans, to ward off the attacks of bandits. Not until later do the Knights of St. John join the battle against the Mohammedans.

Meanwhile they are making remarkable progress in the field of hospital work. The demand for their services is so great that their one hospital soon becomes several. Male and female patients are treated in separate wards. Often there are more than 2,000 people a day to feed. The knights also move to extend their ministry beyond the institutions they serve. They give alms and visit all who are in need, particularly the sick. Four doctors are employed, for whom exacting standards are set: they must prove themselves good diagnosticians, and they must not only prescribe the right treatment for their patients but also know how to prepare the medicine themselves. Routine patient care is handled by members of the order on a rotating basis. One of the regulations stipulates that the beds are always to be made with clean sheets—which, in those days, was nothing to be taken for granted. Another regulation, equally remarkable in its setting, mentions a special diet for patients on the critical list. Mothers-to-be and young mothers are also provided for, and the delivery room is equipped with cradles.

The large number of carefully considered regulations and the

In the age of the Crusades, hospitals generally had their own pharmacies, where the doctors and members of the hospitaler orders would prepare their medicines. A French miniature, circa 1250.

abundant testimony of contemporaries make it clear that the Knights of St. John are never content simply with making do. Their hospitals are model institutions in every way. No wonder, then, that their example is quickly followed. In 1150 the leprosarium of St. Lazarus is founded, the Hospitalers of St. Lazarus borrowing heavily from the Knights of St. John. In the decades that follow, as the hardships of the crusaders mount amid the vicissitudes of war, Count Adolf von Holstein lays the foundations of yet another hospitaler order called the Teutonic Knights because most of the members come from German territories. Von Holstein begins his Samaritan ministry to the sick and wounded in the tents which the crusaders have pitched before Acre. A hospital is founded, and the order is established a few years later. Under the fourth master, Hermann von Salza, the Teutonic Knights mount a military campaign on Germany's eastern borders. But their other mission of caring for the sick is never wholly forgotten.

The era of the Crusades also refocuses the attention of Christians with particular urgency upon the privations of captivity. As the war rages back and forth, thousands and tens of thousands of knights, knights' squires, and pilgrims fall into the hands of the Mohammedans. Almost without exception it is their fate to be sold as slaves in the markets of the East. It is a dreadful sentence, particularly for the women and girls, who are shamefully abused. There is only one recourse: the captives must be ransomed. Relatively little can be accomplished by scattered individuals, although a number of men do contribute their entire fortune toward the liberation of slaves. But in the face of such a great number of captives, the only effective aid is organized aid. Consequently several orders are now founded that are dedicated to the one cause of freeing captives. They serve with conspicuous success over a long period of time.

There are, for example, the Trinitarian orders founded by two French hermits, St. John of Matha and Felix de Valois, who in 1198 receive the official blessing of Pope Innocent III upon their ventures. Their mission is carried out in two ways. The obvious one is to collect large sums of money and use it to ransom the captives directly from the slave traders. The more roundabout way is to buy Mohammedan prisoners and exchange them for captured Christians.

Their work is a stunning success. Over the years the number of ransomed captives mounts to well over ten thousand. Often the Trinitarians are able to carry out their plans only by risking their own lives. John of Matha himself once ends up in a very precarious situation in Tunis when he tries to ransom 220 captives and runs out of money. Offering himself as an exchange-prisoner, he suffers gross mistreatment. On other occasions the Trinitarians are double-crossed, imprisoned themselves, or murdered by the Mohammedan slave traders. For all that, the zeal of the Brothers does not flag.

A similar order is founded in 1240 in Spain by St. Peter Nolasco. Peter has already given to the poor a large estate he had inherited as a young man. The members of his order devote themselves to aiding persons taken captive in the war of the king of Aragon against the Moors; and here again, thousands of prisoners are saved from a life of despair.

Deeds of Kindness in Islam

Most contemporary accounts of the Crusades imply that the Mohammedans were cruel and inhuman. It is true that the followers of the Prophet were fanatical about spreading their faith, and that fire and sword were considered legitimate means for doing so. But after all, Christians also resorted to arms in the Crusades. And when we find crusaders and Mohammedans confronting each other, neither side is innocent of atrocities. The longer these wars last, the more grimly they are prosecuted—particularly on the part of the Christians. The armies of the crusaders spread terror wherever they go, and the personal behavior of their captains and generals often lacks any trace of human feeling. Conversely, Saladin, the Egyptian sultan and the undisputed leader and hero of the Arabs, frequently displays a not inconsiderable element of magnanimity, which in itself shows how responsibly this ruler lives his faith.

The student of the Crusades cannot help feeling that it would have been quite possible to clarify the issues through peaceful negotiation and resolve them by mutual agreement. This is clearly borne out, in fact, by the treaty between Hohenstaufen Emperor Frederick and the Egyptian sultan Malik al-Kamil during the Sixth Crusade (1228-29). But theirs is the only attempt at a negotiated peace, possibly because the crusaders are not motivated by Christian ideals as much as is sometimes asserted. They are moved also by the spirit of adventure, the warrior's zest for his trade, political considerations, personal greed, and vengefulness.

Even when proselyting is the real objective, we can observe evangelistic fervor and political expediency joined in strange alliance, and this is true on both sides. It is precisely because of such alliances of religious zeal and fanaticism with political and personal ambition that the Crusades are characterized by inhumanity and cruelty. On the one side we have Christians, swords drawn, aglow at the thought of liberating the Tomb of the Redeemer; on the other side the Mohammedans, their swords likewise in hand, are burning to spread belief in Allah throughout the world. But because both Mohammedans and Christians do have this religious motivation—in addition to all the other ones—we find on both sides examples of a willingness to show love to the neighbor, to help, and to be merciful.

The place Islam accords to deeds of kindness is no small one. While we possess no written records of the daily life of the Mohammedans, the Holy Scripture of Islam, the Koran, is replete

LIBERALITATIS

Historiæ & Miracula.

Das ist:

Historien vnnd Miraculn der Freygäbigkeit/gegen den armen Notdürfftigen: wie GOtt solche Tugent zeitlich vnd ewig belohnet: mit kurtzen Annotationibus moralibus erklärt.

Sampt angehengten Historischen Spiegel von den Miraculn deß Geitzes vnd Wuchers/ wie solcher hergegen gestrafft wirdt.

Durch

VALENTINVM LEVCHTHIVM

S.Th.D. Prothon. Apost. & Com.Pal.Cæs.

Gedruckt in der Churfürstlichen Statt Meyntz durch Balthasarum Lipppin Verlegung Nicolai Steinij.

ANNO 1594.

"Stories . . . of liberality to the poor . . . including a historical pano-
Valentine Leucht . . . printed by Balthasar Lipp in Mainz . . . 1594."
rama of . . . greed and usury and how such are punished. . . . By

Bildarchiv Foto Marburg

with commandments to show mercy. Almsgiving is stressed again and again. The universal rule of Mohammed is the *zakat*, the levy for the poor exacted of everyone who is not poor himself.

In the second *sura* of the Koran we read: "Righteous is he who . . . giveth his wealth . . . to kinsfolk and to orphans and the needy and the wayfarer." And "Lo! Allah is Seer of what ye do." And in the same *sura:* "O ye who believe! Spend of the good things which ye have earned, and of that which we bring forth from the earth for you, and seek not the bad (with intent) to spend thereof (in charity) when ye would not take it for yourselves." A warning immediately follows to the believers not to boast of their good deeds: "If ye publish your almsgiving, it is well, but if ye hide it and give to the poor, it will be better for you."

To him who has sinned the Koran assigns a good work as penance. He who has promised to marry a woman, and then breaks his word, shall free a prisoner from bondage or feed sixty poor people—thus commands the fifty-eighth *sura*. In addition to good works, the Koran enjoins friendliness and kindness toward all: "Be ye kind to parents, kinsmen, orphans, the poor; to your neighbor, whether he be near or far from you; to the friends of your heart, to every wanderer, and to your slaves."

He who does good, promises the Koran, will be richly repaid by Allah. In the fourth *sura* we read: ". . . those who pay the poor-due, the believers in Allah and the Last Day. Upon these [shall be bestowed] immense reward." And in another passage: "Whoso doeth good and believeth, whether man or woman, shall gain paradise and never suffer the slightest injustice."

"Whoso doeth good works . . . whoso believeth . . ." these are recurrent themes in the Koran. Actually the one is equated with the other. No one can be a believer without giving evidence of good works. A section of the thirty-third *sura* says that "men who believe and women who believe . . . and men who speak the truth and women who speak the truth, and men who persevere (in righteousness) and women who persevere, and men who are humble and women who are humble, and men who give alms and women who give alms . . . Allah hath prepared for them forgiveness and a vast reward."

Almsgiving as a visible sign of faith is typical for the whole system of Islamic doctrine. Anyone who knows the fervor with which the Mohammedan dedicates himself to follow the commands of the Koran may justifiably conclude that deeds of kindness and loving one's neighbor have played an important part in the Arab world.

4. The Works of the Great Saints

Brother Francis

At the foot of Monte Subasio in the Italian Apennines lies Assisi, a little town of no great importance. Since the ominous tension between Emperor Henry IV and Pope Gregory VII has grown into a major dispute over temporal and spiritual power, however, even the most obscure hamlet is caught up in the turmoil. Raw passions and virulent animosities sweep the land. Men seem to live only for war. The large cities deem themselves independent and sovereign as never before. They maintain their own militia. Even the small communities summon their citizens to arms and organize their own civilian and military defense corps. Local trade rivalries may turn the most peaceful cities into archenemies. Raids, melees, and actual warfare become the order of the day.

Toward the end of the twelfth century the battle lines grow increasingly confused: emperor against pope, Guelph against Ghibelline, free citizen against nobleman, and city against city. Anathemas and excommunications are hurled at enemies, treaties are made and broken, friends are betrayed. The princes of the church have become political overlords; voluntarily or involuntarily they play a role that travesties their spiritual office and mission. The cloisters, including the Cluniac monasteries, have grown wealthy, and the wealth breeds luxury and immorality. Spiritual exercises are neglected, mercy and charity are forgotten.

Whole groups of Christians, bewildered by the church and the times, begin to look around for a new Canaan of faith. In the

Piedmont and southern France some of them renounce the church and set out as poor wanderers. The Cathari, the Albigenses, the Waldensians travel throughout the land, seeking true piety.

In this age of confusion and upheaval, a son is born (circa 1182) to the wife of a wealthy Assisi textile merchant named Bernardone. The son is called Francis. Intelligent, talented, rich, and well-bred, the young Francis is lionized by the elegant crowd made up of the sons of Assisi's first families. He develops a passion for epics and chivalric romances and turns troubadour. He is also the gallant, kindhearted benefactor of his friends. Those without means he fits out lavishly with his father's money. Bernardone, who is actually something of a miser, tolerates this largesse because the son's growing reputation for nonconformism is good for business.

War is still raging, and Francis enlists along with his contemporaries, for he dreams of glory and valiant deeds. When the citizens of Assisi rise up against the ducal fortress of Zwingburg, and when they go to war against their hated sister city of Perugia, Francis joins them, proud to show his mettle as a warrior. But the glamour is short-lived. The enemy wins the day, and the swashbuckler is reduced to the ignominious status of a prisoner.

Upon his return from captivity Francis succumbs to a mysterious fatigue, a wasting disease that takes with it all pleasure in his former style of life. The wassails and bacchanals are over, displaced by a genuine fervor for the cause of the Holy Father. Francis decides to enlist in the army of the pope.

But sickness intervenes once more, and it is upon the sickbed that he receives his real call, an event not unlike the experience of Paul on the road to Damascus. Overnight, Francis is a different person. Against his father's wishes he gives away all his possessions and takes up the life of a penitent. Furious, convinced that his son has lost his mind, Bernardone has him locked up, but Francis's mother gets him out again when Bernardone is away. Upon his return Bernardone files a complaint against his son with the city authorities, but they refer him to an ecclesiastical court, as Francis maintains he is in the service of God. The case then comes before the bishop. The father demands the return of all the money his son has given away. Francis renounces his father. The last of his possessions—the clothes he is wearing—he throws at his father's feet and stands naked before the court. The bishop covers him with his own robe and takes him in his care.

Francis leaves his birthplace and sets out with no particular destination in mind. Before long he comes upon the little chapel of St. Mary of the Angels, also known as the "Portiuncula." The chapel is falling apart, but he rebuilds it and turns it into his hermitage, living there the life of a pious recluse. He is not to remain alone for long, however; he is joined by like-minded companions who wish to share with him the life of poverty. The first of these comrades is Bernhart, from Quintavalle. Next comes Peter Catani, a lawyer. The three adopt the plain habit of the shepherd, a simple cowl tied with a cord. Opening the Bible they read: "Go your way. . . . Carry no purse, no bag, no sandals. . . . Whatever house you enter, first say, 'Peace be to this house!' " Then they read: "If any man would come after me, let him deny himself and take up his cross and follow me." "That will be our Rule," says Francis, "and that our life!"

So they set out, barefoot, without staff or purse, like the poorest beggar. They accept no money and no more bread than they need for themselves. At first they are laughed at, but the people soon become aware of the power issuing from these men as they preach in the streets and city squares. The sermons of Francis and his companions are not somber calls to penance; instead they radiate a holy enthusiasm and joy. The people dub Francis *il poverello*—"the little poor man."

Their number soon grows to ten, twenty, fifty, a hundred. All of them lay aside their clothes and other possessions, put on the cowl of Francis, and travel through the land as mendicants. They preach to the people they meet along the way, proclaiming the joy that has become theirs through faith in God's omnipotence and goodness. They hate nothing more than despondency; melancholy is for them the cardinal sin. The happy songs they sing can be heard all around them. They are glad for the sun and the flowers, and for the wind and rain as well. But they do not live in self-satisfied inwardness; they keep their eyes open for any need they might encounter. Francis himself is drawn to the lepers. He kisses their hands and tends their sores. No matter how little he has, he always finds something to give to others as poor as himself. It is only for the sake of the poor that he too has become poor. "I would not be a thief," he says. "We rob the great almsgiver in heaven if we do not give something to those needier than ourselves." On one occasion he is seized by robbers. When they find that their victim, who has literally nothing on his person, is even poorer than they are, they grow very angry. Francis hastens to put himself at their service, fetching what they demand and thinking to himself that they must have had some grievous reason for becoming robbers. His behavior has an unexpected effect. The men are so shaken by this incomprehensible gentleness that they renounce their trade and join Francis.

The example set by the "poor man of Assisi" becomes a movement, and the movement grows. People come by the hundreds, by the thousands, to join him. Pope Innocent III confirms the order, which is now known as the *fratres minores* or Friars Minor. At the same time Innocent confirms the sister order of the "Poor Clares," founded by a disciple of Francis, Clara Sciffi. These men and women love poverty because they love the poor, and their love is without reservation or discrimination. Nothing shows this more clearly than a passage from a letter written by Francis to a member of the order: "There must be no brother in the world, no matter how dire his sin, who after looking into your eyes has to depart without having found mercy."

Francis opens the order to all applicants. No one is excluded, and no one has to undergo a trial period. But the thing that sets him preeminently apart is his love for all of God's creatures. He loves animals with the same devotion and self-giving dedication that he shows to men, and he looks after them in whatever way he can. Francis is one of the few great figures in the history of Christianity whose ethic extends beyond the human sphere to include the whole of creation. This alone is enough to preserve his memory, for seldom has anyone shown such compassion for animals as he did. Animals are God's creatures, as man is, yet man has repeatedly sinned against them.

Soon thousands of Friars Minor and Poor Clares can be found on all the main roads of Europe. Francis himself marches along with them, although his health remains delicate and he is easily

Mendicant friars travel through the land, following the example set by Francis of Assisi.

fatigued. His zeal carries him all the way to the Holy Land and to the crusaders. But he has not come to fight unbelief with the sword; he seeks only to proclaim the Good News with a thankful heart. In the attempt Francis is not very successful. He is appalled to find how far the Christian crusaders have strayed from Christianity. The healing orders are now full of knights who are more interested in covering themselves with military glory than in serving their neighbor. Their customs are frightful, their way of life godless, their actions self-centered.

To these great disappointments is added another. A friar who has set out after Francis in secret finally overtakes him here, and his message is a sad one: the order is in danger of forgetting its Rule and abandoning the law of poverty and love.

Francis hurries back to Italy and succeeds in restoring the old discipline of the brotherhood. His influence is so great that even today, despite the many intervening changes and the numerous lapses into mediocrity and error, it is still discernible in the order that bears his name, the Franciscans. Even beyond the order itself, whose seven centuries of Christian discipleship have produced a million members, the effect of this one life, so plainly and simply lived, is remarkable indeed. Francis of Assisi died in 1226, but he remains a supreme example of active love and totally committed discipleship. His life is like a bright shaft of light from another world, shining on his own dark time and beyond it into our own. Again and again it has inspired men to "go and do likewise" for the sake of God and their neighbor.

Princess Elizabeth, the Humble Servant

Among those who dare to follow St. Francis without reservation, perhaps none is as well known as Elizabeth, the young Hungarian princess who became the wife of Louis of Thuringia and the most beloved of the German saints. Elizabeth is born in 1207 to Andrew II, King of Hungary, and his wife Gertrude of Andechs-Meran. At the tender age of four she is betrothed to the young son of the landgrave of Thuringia and taken to the landgrave's court at Wartburg Castle, where she is brought up. Even if we disregard the countless legends that folklore has woven around her life, Elizabeth remains an unusual child. From her earliest youth she inclines to deep piety. At the same time, so far from being wrapped up in a mystical haze, she is high-spirited, often unruly, effervescent, and unfailingly cheerful. And her childlike joy is never greater than when she is able to do something for someone else.

Cheerfulness remains her dominant trait, despite the tragedies that shadow her early life. She is six when her mother is assassinated by Hungarian magnates, and nine at the death of her future father-in-law, Landgrave Hermann, who is devoted to her.

There are scores of tales describing little Elizabeth's joy in giving. Some of these are legends, but many are reliably authenticated. Coming out of church one day, she gives her coat to the first beggar-woman that comes along; her golden circlet she gives to a cripple; once she raids the castle kitchen and passes her plunder along to the poor.

As she grows older, her whims are viewed with increasing disfavor at court. The complaint is that she is too liberal with the landgrave's possessions. And when the promised dowry from Hungary fails to materialize, there are open demands that she be sent back to Pressburg (Bratislava), the former residence of the king. But the opposition has reckoned without Louis, her fiancé. Louis and Elizabeth, who were brought up together almost as brother and sister, have grown to love each other dearly, and when Louis is knighted at the age of twenty and comes into his father's estate, he and the barely fourteen-year-old Elizabeth are married.

It is hard to imagine a happier marriage. The two are hardly ever apart. Whenever she can, Elizabeth accompanies her husband on his trips. For his part, Louis gives his young wife complete freedom to do the good deeds on which her heart is set. The young landgravine becomes the motherly provider for the whole land. She has hospitals built and makes no secret of tending the sick herself. She takes the orphans under her patronage, sees to it that they are properly fed and brought up, and plays games with them. Twice a day she is supposed to have made her way down the mountain (some 1,500 feet high) on which the castle stood in order to look after the poor and sick in the village of Eisenach.

When she is fifteen Elizabeth bears her husband the first child of their marriage. She names the boy Hermann after her father-in-law. Two years later Sophie is born. During these years the Franciscan movement becomes ever more widely known, and Elizabeth is strongly attracted to the ideals of its founder. The Franciscans' combination of piety, simplicity, cheerfulness, and compassion is in keeping with her own character; and, above all, their ideal of living in poverty awakens in her a great longing to do likewise. Mindful, however, of the obligations of a landgravine, she stays where she is, despite her dreams of a life of poverty, simplicity, and contentment at the side of her husband.

At court festivities she continues to play the role she has always played. Tradition tells us that her zest for dancing and other diversions stays with her. But an early incident sets her distinctly apart from her courtly milieu. During the famine of 1225-28 she adamantly refuses to touch any food that does not come from her own lands. Her conscience will not let her sit down at a well-laid table to eat and drink what properly belongs to her starving

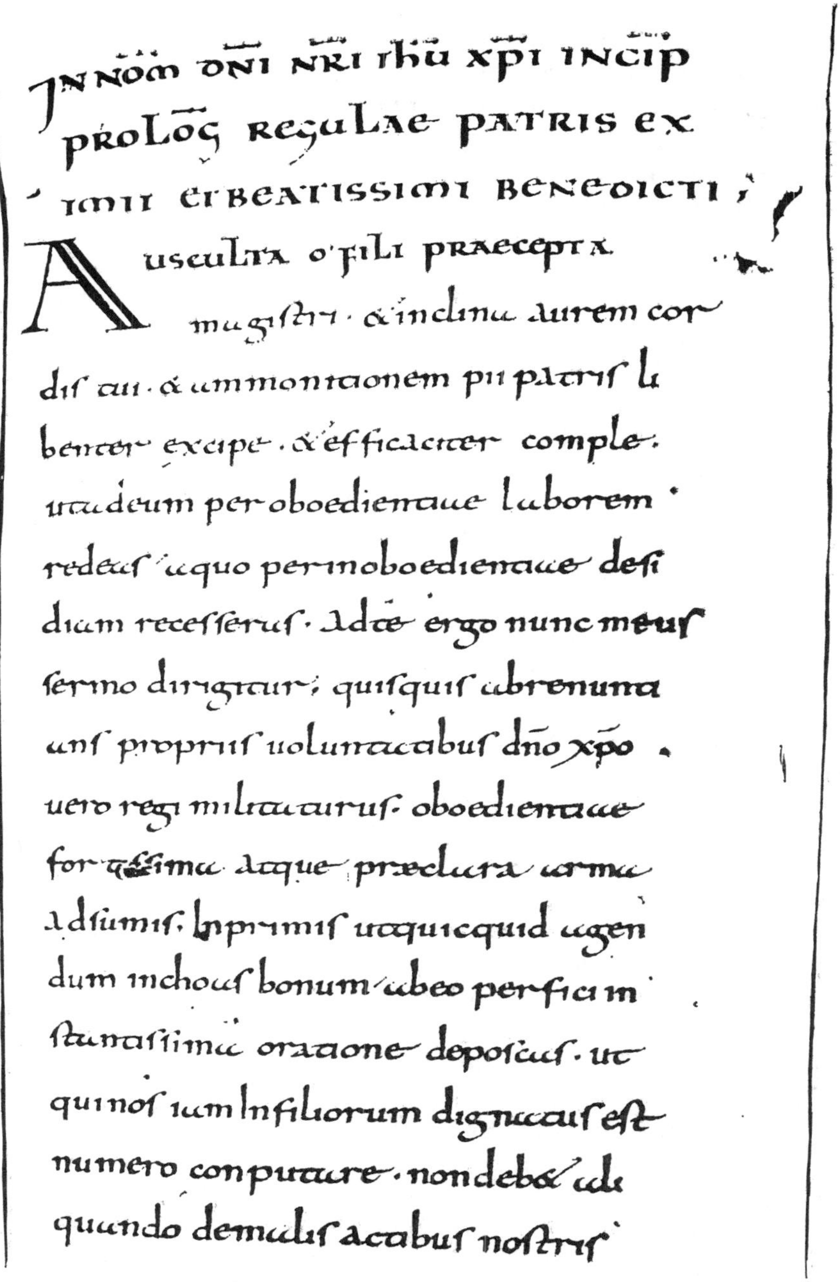
IN NOM DNI NRI IHU XPI INCIP
PROLOG REGULAE PATRIS EX
IMII ET BEATISSIMI BENEDICTI;
Ausculta o fili praecepta
magistri. et inclina aurem cor
dis tui. et ammonitionem pii patris li
benter excipe. et efficaciter comple.
ut ad eum per oboedientiae laborem
redeas a quo per inoboedientiae desi
diam recesseras. Ad te ergo nunc meus
sermo dirigitur; quisquis abrenuntia
ns propriis uoluntatibus dno xpo
uero regi militaturus. oboedientiae
fortissima atque praeclara arma
adsumis. In primis ut quicquid agen
dum inchoas bonum ab eo perfici in
stantissima oratione deposcas. ut
qui nos iam in filiorum dignatus est
numero conputare. non debet ali
quando de malis actibus nostris

Besides the heroic efforts of individuals in the face of want and misery there were official acts, such as this writ of a reigning prince-bishop-abbot, making provision for the poor.

people. This resolve, self-imposed and strictly maintained, is not only for conscience' sake, however, it is also a public reproof of unprincipled courtiers to whom the plight of the people matters nothing as long as they themselves live well.

Elizabeth also knows how to pilot the ship of state with a steady hand, as she proves in the plague year of 1226. Louis is summoned by the emperor to Ravenna, and his departure puts the whole burden of government upon the shoulders of his nineteen-year-old wife. She turns out to be an able administrator. When the plague devastates the land and the crops are ruined Elizabeth, like the bishop of Bamberg in his time, opens the granaries of the palace estates and distributes bread and grain to the people. She also sees to it that scythes and sickles are given out. On his return Louis finds nothing to criticize and ratifies all the measures she has taken.

One of Elizabeth's closest advisors during these years is her confessor, Conrad of Marburg, a man of dubious qualities. He no doubt counsels her wisely and supports her actively during these times of crisis; he gives intelligent guidance, reminding her that her first concern is the welfare of the people and that she must not let herself be carried away by romantic notions of a life of poverty. Only later do his disciplinary methods border on cruelty.

In 1227 Louis takes from the hand of the bishop of Hildesheim the Crusader's cross and strikes out southwards. His departure is a heart-rending experience for Elizabeth. She dons mourning garments which she is destined to wear for the rest of her life. In the fall, word comes from Italy that Louis has died of an epidemic infection in Otranto. Bereft of her one source of earthly happiness, Elizabeth is inconsolable. Eventually she rallies, resolving to devote the rest of her life to loving and serving her neighbor.

She leaves the Wartburg for Marburg, the residence to which she is entitled as the landgrave's widow. But instead of settling at the castle she moves into a modest cottage on the banks of the Lahn. Here she opens a hospital and spends her days caring for the sick and needy. Assisted by two simple servant-girls, she herself waits on the patients, cooks their meals, washes their clothes, and makes their beds. Nonetheless she is still a rich woman, as her inheritance is substantial. She wants to give all her money away, virtually at random, but Conrad intervenes, arranging for it to be distributed in small amounts to the needy. Large numbers of beggars make pilgrimages to the little house of mercy on the Lahn, and no one goes away disappointed.

Elizabeth is not only a rich woman; she has remained a celebrated beauty. One day Emperor Frederick II conveys a proposal to her. Elizabeth refuses him. She does not covet the emperor's crown, but chooses instead the gray habit of the Franciscans, desiring nothing else than to spend the rest of her life wholly in the service of her neighbor. When envoys from the Hungarian court at Marburg arrive to take her home, they are sent away. Elizabeth wants to remain what she now is: a simple maid who serves her Lord in voluntary humility and self-abnegation by making herself available to the poorest of the poor. No records are kept of how many people Elizabeth helps, but the news of her work spreads throughout the land. When she dies peacefully at the age of twenty-four, people come by the thousands to crowd around her deathbed; they kneel there as if she had already been canonized.

One of the most beautiful of the German cathedrals, the early-Gothic *Elisabethkirche,* is built over her grave by the Teutonic Knights; and the emperor himself, barefoot and dressed in penitential garments, carries her body into the golden shrine prepared for it. For three centuries this grave and shrine are the cynosure of countless pilgrims, more of them visiting Marburg than any other shrine in the world except the Holy Sepulcher. It remains to Philip the "Magnanimous" in 1539 to desecrate the grave of his ancestor and to scatter her bones. Philip succeeded in putting a stop to the pilgrimages, but he was not able to destroy the memory of this great woman. Her memory is still fresh today, showing that the acts of one human being, even of a frail young woman, may continue to bear fruit for centuries by serving as an inspiration and a challenge to others.

Hedwig, Mother to a Nation

The house of Andechs, from which Elizabeth's mother comes, gives the world another great benefactress, the beloved Duchess Hedwig of Silesia. Long before Elizabeth is born Hedwig is wedded to young Duke Henry of Silesia, and at the time Elizabeth is canonized by the church Hedwig is still active in her role as mother to a nation.

In 1201 Hedwig becomes a duchess at the side of her husband. Not long afterward, the tragic murder of King Philip of Swabia plunges Hedwig and her family into misfortune. The murderer is Otto of Wittelsbach, a frustrated suitor of her daughter Gertrude. Philip, knowing Otto to be unpredictable and given to fits of rage, had warned against the alliance. Otto, having learned of the king's letter, promptly flies into one of his rages; concluding that his honor has been impugned, he resolves on bloody vengeance. On the day the duke of Meran is to wed Beatrice, the emperor's beautiful niece, in Bamberg, Otto breaks in, bared sword in hand, and charges at the king, fatally wounding him. As Philip lies dying in the palace of the bishop of Bamberg, the murderer and his henchmen escape. But the reprisal is terrible. Otto is charged with regicide and the ban of the empire is pronounced upon his head. He is an outlaw. The ban also applies to Hedwig's brothers, who belong to Otto's faction. The palace of Andechs is demolished and the father dies, grief-stricken. Hedwig is alone at the funeral. Her daughter Gertrude, on whose account the murder was perpetrated, enters the convent of Trebnitz, later to become its abbess.

Trebnitz, which had been founded by Hedwig, is also Hedwig's usual residence when Duke Henry is out of the country. Here she has her own private ministry to thirteen needy people, whom she personally attends each day, honoring in this symbolic way the Lord and his twelve disciples. The custom is widespread in the Middle Ages, revealing something of the attitude in which the poor are held: It is Christ himself who lives in the poor, and the poor are needed—their existence is needed—so that a man may test and retest his love for and mercy to his neighbor. A wealthy lady of the upper classes never goes out of her house without distributing coins all around. The alms-purse is just as much a part of one's clothing as belt or shoes. Liberality toward the needy is a kind of touchstone of true Christianity, an infallible sign of whether the Christian is serious about obeying the commandments of his Lord.

And in the Middle Ages, he is indeed serious about it. Medieval man is terribly concerned for the salvation of his soul. The extremes of hedonism and licentiousness of which he is capable are matched by the extremes of his zeal in the quest of salvation.

Care of the sick includes the soul as well as the body. Bedside intercession is here represented in a 1512 woodcut by Nicolaus de Graeve.

Bildarchiv Foto Marburg

Throughout the entire Middle Ages God is seen more as a stern judge than as a loving father. Man must pass God's inspection; hence the good works on behalf of the poor. The belief in justification by works is gaining more and more ground, works being seen as an instrument for bargaining with God: "Because I go about doing good, you have to save me."

Elizabeth and Hedwig and their spiritual kindred are conspicuously different. By measuring their motivation against the prevailing medieval norm, we see that the strength for their own ministry is drawn from deeper resources. Their lives are utterly committed to the service of their neighbor. Indeed, they are consumed in that service, because God so wills it. This is the reason they are venerated, and the reason they have lived on for centuries in the memory of the people.

Upon her arrival in Silesia Hedwig is faced with circumstances far different from those confronting Elizabeth in Thuringia. Nearly all of Hedwig's subjects are poor. They have no land and no education. The duchess is not upset to find that most of them are of Slavic descent, for she knows no barriers of nationality: the people are dependent on her protection, so she must take care of them. And she does more than princesses have ever done. In the numerous convents founded by her, the needy are provided for in decently furnished hospitals and poorhouses. Hedwig shows genuine concern for everyone who comes to her, whatever their need. She sees to it that debtors are excused from paying exorbitant interest. She personally cares for expectant mothers in straitened circumstances, and she takes steps to ensure that pregnant women and young mothers throughout the duchy are given whatever help they need. She also intercedes for the Silesian priests, many of whom are practically destitute. Of particular concern to her is the evangelization of the land, which for the most part still clings to its Slavic deities. She does everything she can to bring about the conversion of her people to Christianity. When a large number of Breslau residents lose everything they have in a great fire that sweeps the capital city, she sets up an emergency relief center on a nearby estate where thousands of the disaster victims are fed and provided for every day. Many poor people find shelter here for extended periods.

In spite of all her efforts, however, Hedwig is not able to raise the general standard of living in the duchy. She therefore advises Henry to invite German settlers into the land. These also receive the active support of the duchess. The wisdom and foresight of this move would be revealed a hundred years later, when the totally impoverished land has grown to a thriving province, its prosperity shared equally by Germans and Slavs.

In 1241 Hedwig's work is threatened from a new quarter. All the efforts on behalf of the welfare of the land are in danger of being swept away in the wake of the Mongolian invasion of Silesia. True, Genghis Khan—before whom all Asia had trembled and whose barbaric atrocities had multiplied until somewhat checked by the influence of the Chinese scholar Yeh-lü Ch'u-ts'ai—is no longer on the throne. But his successors have overrun Russia and are now preparing to trample central Europe under the hooves of their horses. Emperor Frederick II does not lift a finger to defend the eastern borders of the empire; he leaves that task to his princes. Duke Henry, the son of Hedwig, who has now succeeded his father, marches against the redoubtable enemy with a small army of Germans and Poles. At Liegnitz the duke's army, which has fought bravely, makes its last stand. Henry himself falls. Now there is nothing to stop the marauders of the Tatar Steppes from continuing their victory sweep. Europe lies open before them. But suddenly, as if by some miracle, they turn the heads of their shaggy-maned horses to the East and ride away. They are recalled to their Asian homeland by the death of their khan.

When Hedwig learns that Henry is slain, she and her daughter-in-law wander over the battlefield looking for the body of their loved one. And here Hedwig, whose life has been wholly committed to love of neighbor, adds to her ministry the "seventh work" of mercy. She sees to it that the dead are buried. No fallen soldier is denied the loving service she had intended for her son. Although her own grief is great, she takes time to visit the mothers, the widows, and the orphans of those others who gave their lives. Two years later the beloved "mother" of the Silesians dies, but she is remembered to this very day, and not only on the banks of the Oder.

Hospitalers and City Welfare Programs

It is not only the aristocracy who care for the poor and practice the other works of mercy. As early as the thirteenth century, the structure of society begins to change, and with it the pattern of social welfare. Gradually the serfs and bondsmen of the towns become burghers, free citizens, and with their enfranchisement is laid the groundwork for free trade and commerce, which develops rapidly. At the same time, artisans in the cities organize themselves into guilds, and the cities themselves win their independence from their princes and bishops, either by tedious negotiations or bloody battles. Patricians and guildsmen govern these free cities together. The old agrarian economy gives way to an economy dominated by trade and commercial enterprise. Currency replaces the barter system, new social classes and conventions replace the old ones. The urban influence gradually infiltrates the church as well. We have already noted that St. Francis is the son of a merchant in one of these prosperous towns.

The new era brings new challenges to the work of Christian charity. The rural serf, though living in total subjection to his lord, got support and protection from that lord when he needed it. The newly enfranchised townsman, on the other hand, has no such recourse when trouble strikes. He is completely dependent on the charity of those who have managed to hold onto their material possessions in good times and bad. Thus the responsibility for the welfare of the unpropertied townsman comes to rest on the shoulders of the well-to-do citizens, who as a class show that they are aware of their responsibility.

Hospitals and hospices spring up everywhere, founded and maintained solely by the landed burghers. The guilds later join the movement by incorporating welfare provisions into their bylaws. The guild (one might well say: the group) takes the place of the feudal lord (the individual). The guild establishes rules, exacts compliance from its artisan-members, maintains strict discipline within its ranks, and does not hesitate to expel dishonest workmen. In return it offers its members protection. As early as the fourteenth century there are guilds that impose a kind of insurance premium upon their members and use the funds to support the widows and orphans of prematurely deceased guildmasters.

But there is no escaping the fact that the sick are not properly cared for in this era. Some effort is made in the city "hospitals," but the general backwardness during these times is alarming. Most of those engaged in hospital work form orders or groups resembling orders. The hospitaler orders of the rising middle class originate in this way, but their members are monks and nuns first

Lepers, forced to live in primitive shelters outside the city gates, always carry a rattle with which to warn others of their presence.

and nurses and orderlies second. There is no lack of goodwill, but there is a decided lack of know-how and experience. Doctors are almost nonexistent. Most of those who style themselves doctors are no better than quacks. The result is that the care given the sick is about the same as that given the poor: they get a bed and something to eat. Wounds and external ailments are treated in primitive fashion, simply because no one knows how to do the job better. In most hospitals, even the city institutions, the emphasis is on a spiritual ministry.

A peculiar and—from our perspective today—incomprehensible phenomenon of the age is the general attitude toward lepers. Their number is considerable, and in the Middle Ages it increases in many places. Lepers have always come to know at firsthand how far Christians are prepared to go in their pursuit of good works. Francis goes very far; Elizabeth actively intercedes for them; and when Hedwig is canonized by Clement IV, the papal bull bears record that she did not recoil at the sight of the lepers' running sores. But the historical context against which these works of love stand out so clearly is something else again. The leper is an exile from the human community. Society considers him beyond the pale. He can no longer earn his own livelihood, he possesses nothing, he is driven out of the cities. Little shelters are built outside the city walls, and here the lepers are required to live in complete isolation. They are the living dead. Indeed, the banishment of a leper is sometimes preceded by an actual funeral ceremony. This clearly shows the extremes in thought and action of which medieval man is capable.

The flowering of the cities and of urban commerce automatically brings an increase of traffic on the main roads, which in turn means that more and more lodging houses are necessary. Clemens von Brentano, the romantic poet, quotes an old pilgrim song describing these hospices or inns, most of which are run by monks:

> And as we hike through Switzerland
> A godly welcome they extend
> And give us meat and bread.
> They cover us warm in proper beds
> And tell us the roads ahead.

Especially well known are the hospices in the Alps, for example, those at the Great and Little St. Bernard passes where for centuries the monks, assisted by their faithful St. Bernard dogs, undertake the rescue work in the area. Other orders are said to have assumed responsibility for maintaining the roads and paths and bridges. Unquestionably, all of these things have a direct bearing on the growing importance of the cities.

City hospitals without a healing order of their own sometimes employ "Beguines." This semimonastic community, whose origins are obscure, is made up of women who unite for a common vocational purpose and are paid for their work. They are repeatedly referred to as nurses and welfare workers.

In 1459 the city of Frankfurt, which is at war with nearby Hanau, presses the Alexian Brothers into service. Their mission is to bury the dead and care for the wounded, and the service they render can be considered an early instance of a lay ministry to the military. It is worth noting that the name of the Alexians appears most often in connection with acute crises such as wars, epidemics, and other disasters. They might be called a kind of medieval Red Cross corps. A lay brotherhood rather than a monastic order, they are also known as the "voluntary poor," or the Cellites. Most of them are potters, brewers, or weavers by trade; their burial work is performed in addition to their main duties. Later they broaden their ministry to include working with the mentally ill (whose plight in those days was wretched indeed), and they also undertake outpatient care. Still active today, the Alexians pursue a mission exclusively to the insane.

The Bubonic Plague in Europe

All the orders, hospitalers, nurses, and poverty relief workers are powerless against the formidable enemy that invades Europe from the Black Sea between 1340 and 1350: the bubonic plague. Wholesale migrations have always had the effect of unleashing epidemics. The Crusades brought leprosy to Europe, the disease of which so many crusaders died, and with leprosy came yellow fever, malaria, scurvy, and dysentery. But none of these is so dreadful as the plague, which becomes the scourge of nations. No land is spared, no house is safe. Its victims include young and old, rich and poor.

Within a few years of its emergence in Europe the plague is taking the life of one person in three. Death reaps its harvest everywhere, and nothing can be done to stop it. Panic and superstition drive some people to make hideous charges; blame for the plague-epidemic is often put on the Jews, for example, and as a result they are slaughtered without mercy. Even in times of plague, however, there are men who prove their faith by volunteering to care for the victims and to help in whatever way they can. The problem is that such "help" is not very effective. When the plague has touched a person, he is as good as lost. The healing arts know no effective remedy, and consequently the communities limit their efforts to seeing that the dead are buried. Each city and village has a platoon of workers to push the rumbling death-cart and hurry the victims into their mass graves, often without benefit of clergy. In all likelihood such measures for burial are inspired by fear rather than compassion. During sieges of the plague, real love of neighbor is active in other directions. Obviously, once a person is infected, he will die. Therefore, since the bodies of the dying cannot be saved, there remains at least the prospect of helping them to find salvation for their souls. Hence the ministry of love to those infected with the plague becomes primarily a spiritual ministry. Priests and monks, nuns and laywomen accomplish more in this area than can ever be recorded, and often enough they pay for it themselves with infection, suffering, and death.

History has preserved the names of a few of these men and women. Those we mention may stand as representative of many others who also risked their lives in times of plague.

In 1348, when the plague kills 16,000 persons in Strasbourg, an ordinary Dominican monk goes from house to house to comfort the dying and alleviate suffering and hardship. His name is Johannes Tauler, one of the quiet Christians who have long outgrown a blind adherence to the external practices of their church. Tauler is a grass roots kind of preacher who uses plain German rather than Latin in his sermons. During an interdict, when bells and organs are silent and only the dying may be attended, Tauler carries right on and administers the sacrament, incurring the enmity of his bishop and other clergy. Tauler also refuses to shut his eyes to the need of others when the plague strikes. He prays with the flagellants who travel through the land, chastising themselves in hope of averting calamity. But Tauler's hands are not always folded in prayer. He knows that busy hands can help make hard circumstances easier. All idle contemplation is alien to him. "Works of love are more pleasing to God than great contemplation," he says. "The man who does not go out and serve his neighbor usefully will have much to render account for."

Thus Tauler comforts the living in a time of death. He has compassion on the dying, stands by them in their last hour, and personally escorts their bodies to the cemetery outside the city gates. One thing alone is his great consolation: the redemption of man through Jesus Christ, whose coming he celebrates in an advent hymn still sung today: *Es kommt ein Schiff geladen . . .* "There comes a galley sailing. . . ." Only those who are familiar with those times, the time of the interdict, plague, and death, will truly appreciate the words of Tauler's hymn:

And he who would this child embrace
And kiss him joyfully
Must first with him taste bitterness
And pain and agony.

Twenty-six years later a Dominican nun living in a tiny Italian town called Siena becomes a plague relief volunteer. Neither derision nor base ingratitude cause Catherine to waver in her work of love. In the sick and the abandoned, who can do no more than wait for death, she sees the Lord Christ himself. By serving them she would serve him.

It is not only during the plague years that Catherine proves herself. In 1369, when she is barely twenty-two, she enters the jail where Niccolò di Toldo is imprisoned. Toldo is raging like a trapped animal. He has been sentenced to die, and he is terrified of death. Catherine subdues him by the power of her faith, prays for him, and so comforts him that he puts his trust in God and, when the time comes, is able to walk calmly to the gallows. Catherine herself serves him his last meal and stays with him until the end.

Later Catherine becomes one of the great peacemakers in an age of turmoil which sees the lower classes rise up against the aristocracy, the cities against the princes, and ultimately one pope against another. At the behest of the city fathers of Florence, she tries for years to induce the pope, who is in residence in Avignon, to return to Rome. In numerous letters she exhorts princes and cardinals to pursue peace and gentleness, and eventually she is summoned to Rome by Pope Urban VI and asked for advice. She dies at the age of thirty-three, and it is not until four decades later that her untiring work on behalf of the unity of the church bears fruit and the division of the papacy ends.

Another Catherine, Catherine of Genoa, also proves herself an effective relief worker during the plague years. She is in charge of the large hospital and foundling home in her native city. Cooperating with her is the Confraternity of the Misericordia, which is founded in the 1400s and one of whose chief works is the care of the sick. Her "spiritual son," Ettore Vernazza, later founds a home for the chronically ill in Genoa and a brotherhood in Naples called "Albi" whose members work with prisoners condemned to death. Vernazza becomes fatally ill and dies in 1528, evidently of an infection incurred during his hospital work.

For centuries the plague remains the scourge of the peoples of Europe. In the sixteenth century, for example, it is recorded of Martin Luther and Johann Bugenhagen that during a siege of the plague in Wittenberg they remain with the sick and the dying, despite pleas from all quarters not to risk their lives by staying on in the city. In 1542, Constance, the native city of the reformer Ambrosius Blarer, is hit by the plague. Blarer, who becomes active in volunteer work in Constance after leaving the University of Tübingen, joins forces with his sister Margarete in ministering to the sick. Like so many volunteer relief workers, Margarete succumbs to the disease she has so staunchly fought. The same is true of Johannes Zwick, the writer of the hymn, "Each morning brings us fresh outpoured . . . " (*All Morgen ist ganz frisch und neu . . .*).

It is worth noting that some hymnwriters of the age composed their most beautiful and comforting songs when their outward circumstances were the bitterest. Two of these may be mentioned here.

In the fall of 1597, the plague sweeps the Westphalian town of Unna. Hundreds have succumbed; and one day the infection spreads to the rectory. The pastor, Philipp Nicolai, remains at his post, however. He has the dead brought to the churchyard behind his house, often twenty or more in a single day. And in the midst of these dark times he writes some of the most beautiful songs in Christian hymnody: "O morning star how fair and bright" (*Wie schön leuchtet der Morgenstern*), and "Wake, awake, for night is flying" (*Wachet auf, ruft uns die Stimme*). These hymns of praise celebrating the promise of eternal life are composed in a world of nightmare, and in an age when life had never before appeared so fleeting.

The chorale "Farewell I gladly bid thee . . ." (*Valet will ich*

Funeral customs are quickly adapted to prevailing conditions. During sieges of the plague, the clergyman is often the only person to accompany the cart bearing the corpse. A 1522 woodcut, from Petrarch's treatise on happiness, Augsburg, 1532.

dir geben), is written at the height of the plague by Valerius Herberger, who lives in the tiny Polish town of Fraustadt. In 1613, two hundred of the town's residents die in a few weeks' time. Everyone who can scrape together enough money hastily moves out. But Herberger stays on with his flock, caring for the dying by day and by night, not hesitating to enter plague-infested areas, struggling to overcome his revulsion and horror at the sight of the grotesque human disfigurement he encounters. When some of Herberger's closest relatives become infected, he still refuses to give up. He decides to stay where he is, no matter how many others leave. Sometimes he is all alone as he makes his rounds, striding through the empty streets at the head of the "plague-cart." Since he himself has been spared, he feels all the more keenly his responsibility toward those who are not so fortunate. As he says, "The believer must not lose courage or yield to despair in these times of death, even though every second his life may hang by a silver thread."

Pastor Johann Valentin Andreae is engaged in similar work in Calw, a town in the Black Forest of Württemberg, as is Friedrich von Spee in Trier. Von Spee is fatally stricken while treating victims of the plague.

From the Middle Ages to the seventeenth century the black death continues its march through towns and villages, depopulating entire areas and spreading terror and despair. But from the Middle Ages to our own times there have been men and women brave enough to defy it. Were there hundreds? Thousands? We know only a few of the names. But however severe those plague years were, they were times in which the power of believing love was proven over and over.

The Martyrdom of the Jews

We cannot end this chapter without recalling the ordeal of those whom the Bible calls God's Chosen People. Any picture of these times would be incomplete and one-sided if it focused on the successes and failures of active Christian love and omitted what was endured by the Jews.

Israel begins its wandering course through the nations and through the centuries in A.D. 70 when, six hundred years after the return from exile, the Jews again lose the land of their fathers. Now they are utterly homeless. Many flee to the West where they live in peace during the early centuries of the Christian era. Even those who live under Mohammedan rule do not fare badly. Christians and Jews are still aware of their common heritage, and the Mohammedans prove quite tolerant of their religious beliefs, recognizing that a good deal of the Old Testament is common to all three faiths.

Then the Christian church in the West falls into terrible error. The Jews, so runs the inhuman dictum, must be brought to judgment as the killers of Christ. This thesis is widely accepted, even though any Christian could find in his Bible the clear teaching that Christ's command of love to neighbor applies to Jewish neighbors no less than to other neighbors, and that no Christian can be anti-Semitic without at the same time denying Jesus. Nevertheless, the insane notion seduces the minds of men: first the uneducated classes, and later the intelligentsia as well. Pope Innocent III is led astray—as is Martin Luther.

The great martyrdom of the Jews begins in the century of the Crusades. When Christian knighthood bands together in 1096 in order to raise its standard against the crescent, a large group of the crusaders join forces independently (before the main forces are mobilized) under William the Carpenter and proceed to march on the Jews. Their aim is to destroy the "enemies of Christ" in their own land before setting out to take the Holy Sepulcher. William the Carpenter is French, and since the Jews in France are protected by the people in power, he turns to the Rhineland. With Emperor Henry IV far away, no one is there to protect the Jews, and so a large-scale campaign of persecution is launched, beginning in Trier. The frightened Jews turn to Bishop Egilbert, but the bishop is himself as benighted as the French crusaders. He demands that the Jews become Christians in return for his protection; anyone who refuses is an outlaw. Many Jews commit suicide that year rather than deny their faith. In Speyer, however, Bishop John does give them aid and comfort. He shelters the Jews in his castle, calmly confronts their pursuers, and pronounces a severe judgment upon some of them.

The Jews also look for help to the bishop of Worms, and initially he does in fact accommodate them in his palace. But then he tells them that they must become Christians and that anyone who refuses to be baptized will be delivered over to his pursuers. The Jews ask for time to think this over, and the request is granted. But when the day of decision arrives, the bishop finds only dead bodies in his palace. The Jews have chosen to take their own lives rather than live in the company of Christians who profane God's commandment to love their neighbors as themselves.

William's murdering horde falls upon the city of Mainz, killing over a thousand Jews. But in Cologne Bishop Hermann intercedes for the Jews in his bishopric and grants them asylum. At his request many of Cologne's citizens also hide the fugitives in their homes. The marauders continue their march until judgment finally overtakes them in Hungary where Christian peasant-farmers rise up and slaughter them to the last man.

The main forces of the crusaders, under the command of Godfrey of Bouillon, do not take part in these outrages, but after the Mohammedans are defeated, the butchery is renewed in Jerusalem. Moslems and Jews are cut down with equal abandon.

No less infamous is the persecution of the Jews in London under Richard the Lionhearted. The attacks first occur in 1189, his coronation year, and then rapidly become a systematic liquidation. Adding to the shame of the murders is the motivation of the murderers. Some kill Jews simply in order to get rid of their creditors (many of the crusaders being heavily in debt to Jewish moneylenders). Others, looking for instant wealth, seek out a rich Jew to strike down. Perhaps the supreme irony is that the money obtained in this way is not infrequently used by the crusaders to finance their holy wars.

One of the few laudable exceptions to such folly is Emperor Frederick Barbarossa. No one can accuse him of ulterior motives for his crusades. Moreover, he puts a stop to the persecution of the Jews. He has his own Rhenish castles opened to them, so that they can hide from the advancing crusaders. He also makes it a capital offense to kill a Jew. In one of his proclamations he sets an example of tolerance all too rare in those times: "It behooves the imperial majesty, it is sanctioned by justice, and it is demanded by reason that all of our subjects—not only those who venerate the Christian religion, but those who dissent from our faith and live according to the traditions of their fathers—should be assured of the safety of those things to which they are fairly entitled; that their customs be preserved, and that their persons and their goods be left in peace." Frederick is responsible for much bloodshed too, in Germany and particularly in Italy, for often enough he was a ruthless politician and military tactician; but his achievements, especially on behalf of the Jews, must not be forgotten. His edict of tolerance gave them at least a few years of respite.

Soon the more familiar pattern reasserts itself. It becomes popular all over Europe to blame the Jews for any and every catastrophe. Jews are blamed for the plague in the fourteenth century, for example. They are said to have poisoned wells, springs, and rivers. They are accused of murdering Christian children and devouring their hearts at the Feast of the Passover. Everywhere

Jmpator redit dans Judeis legē moysi i rotulo.

Since Jews do not enjoy equal rights with gentiles, certain "privileges" must be granted them anew by each new sovereign, in this case Henry VII.

they are persecuted out of superstition, ignorance, hate, and envy; they are condemned without a trial, cruelly tortured, and hounded to death. Ultimately the Jews are totally disenfranchised and imprisoned in ghettos where they are doomed to vegetate for the rest of their lives—human beings second-class.

The extent of the dreadful persecution in Spain is almost indescribable, and this after Jews, Christians, and Mohammedans had coexisted peacefully for centuries, and together had brought about the flowering of Moorish culture. Those Jews able to escape are aided by the king of Portugal, until persecutions erupt in that country as well and thousands more are killed. Some of the survivors set out on an arduous trek through North Africa; the others follow the Danube to the Slavic regions of eastern Europe. But here, too, respite is denied them. They are soon being hunted down again and exterminated; and they will be the targets of all the countless pogroms that have continued to the present day During one six-month period in the seventeenth century over 200,000 Jews were murdered, a figure exceeded only by the grisly statistics of our own century.

And no one helps. In any case the feeble efforts of the few never grow into an effective campaign to save an entire people. The suffering of the Jews through the centuries is a grave warning, an appeal to the conscience of our times. In the last analysis, human nature today is exactly what it was a thousand years ago. We are horrified by the brutality of which man is capable. We also wonder at the compassion that, despite everything, shines through again and again. We must allow our horror at the one and our wonder at the other to hone our vision—and our conscience—and thus lead us to do justice and love mercy.

5. The Age of the Reformation

The Fuggers' Housing Colony

In 1519 Maximilian I, Holy Roman Emperor since 1493, dies, and for a time the question of his successor goes unresolved. Since Frederick the Wise (the German elector of Saxony) declines, King Charles of Spain is elected to the throne. The election is financed, and thus ultimately decided, by the Augsburg merchant family of the Fuggers.

The Fuggers are the real power brokers of the empire. Even Maximilian in his time lived on their money and favor. Their riches are legendary, their influence enormous. The common people, so many of whom barely eke out an existence, refer with bitter contempt to the *Fuggerei* of the rich. But however controversial the Fuggers may be as merchants and kingmakers, beginning in 1521 there is another kind of *Fuggerei* that the poor do not scorn—for it benefits them and them alone—and that is a housing settlement for the underprivileged which bears the family name.

In this settlement are long rows of pleasant-looking houses, whose rental prices are minimal. A large endowment makes it possible to guarantee that the rents will never be raised. And they never are, even when a series of currency fluctuations reduces them to the status of a token payment. Although the Fuggers are thoroughgoing capitalists, in their housing program they actually anticipate the great social reformers of future generations.

In all other cities the poor are badly housed, and in some areas there is an urgent housing shortage. The affluent citizen builds his

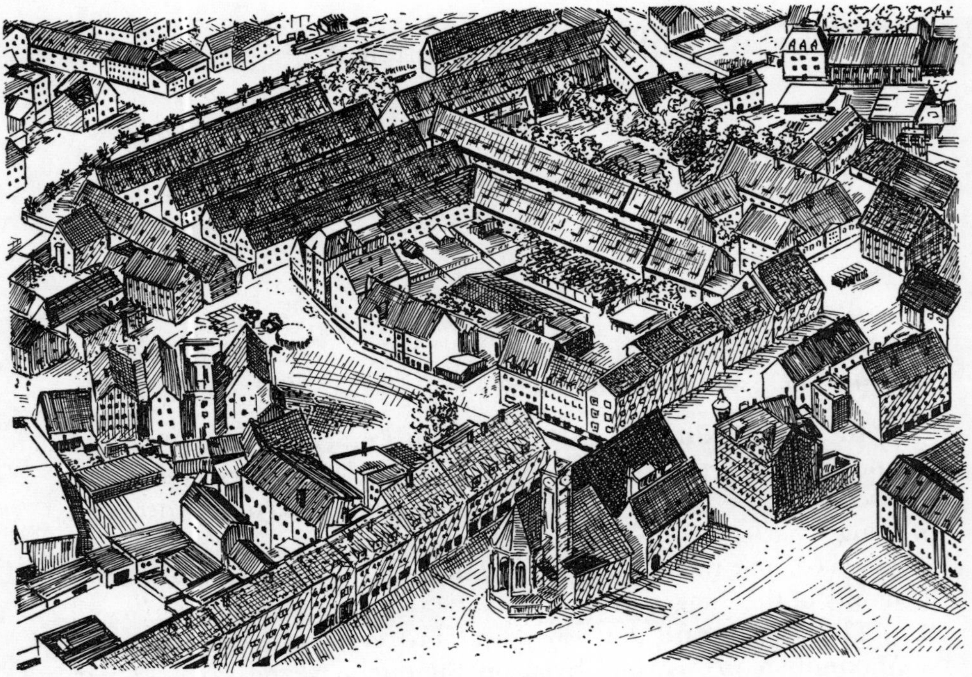

The Fuggerei *in Augsburg, the oldest existing settlement for the poor, is still maintained by the princes and counts of the Fugger family. The annual rent today for an apartment with three rooms and a kitchen is 1.72 marks (less than half a dollar), exactly what it was 400 years ago.*

own house, of course, and medieval European cities still pride themselves today on the stately homes of their first families. But the elite are not at all willing to throw open their homes to strangers—to say nothing of poor people. And all the while urban poverty is becoming an acute problem. Even before 1500 a regular proletariat is emerging in the cities of Flanders, Italy, and Germany. It is made up of textile workers (chiefly in Flanders), foreign laborers who cannot find jobs, and indigent burghers about whom no one bothers. How can such people, who are either underpaid or out of work, find a place to live? Finding no welcome in the homes of the upper classes, they are forced to retreat to the city walls, which are soon lined with squalid hovels: breeding grounds for a variety of diseases.

The enfranchised city-dweller who has established himself and secured an entrée into a merchant's or artisan's guild is better off, of course. Guild brothers stand by each other; welfare funds are raised by members for members; and here and there we see the beginnings of municipal welfare programs. But by and large these community programs prove inadequate. They fail utterly to cope with the problem of begging, which is getting out of control. The beggar is still living on his medieval status: he is inviolate, under God's special protection. One gives him alms to save one's own soul.

Then too, in these pre-Reformation decades men's thoughts are ranging further and further afield. Amazing inventions and discoveries, adventurous land and sea expeditions have awakened new hopes and dreams; and more crises, hardships, and disappointments are accepted as the price of their fulfillment. The wealth of far-off lands and peoples lures the mind and diverts the eye from the misery at home.

World conquerors and aspiring world conquerors especially are bedazzled by the prospects of exotic wealth and treasure. They are blinded to the social conditions of the peoples they encounter overseas. Seldom indeed has the Christian Occident recognized and properly appreciated the social achievements of other cultures. This tragic state of affairs is conspicuously illustrated by Francis Pizarro's conquest of the Inca Empire of South America.

The Land Where No One Is Poor

What Pizarro's small army finds on the plateau of Peru has no counterpart anywhere else in all the world. It turns out to be the purest form of socialism. The socialism of the Incas, of course, has nothing to do with Christian charity. Neither does it resemble the ordered system of ancient Egyptian government. In Egypt there was still room for individual philanthropy whereas the Indians of Peru have everything organized according to rigid procedures and laws. And the Indian does not seem to have the intellectual awareness of the Egyptian; he is more easygoing and—secure in his socialist system—more apathetic. He is content to

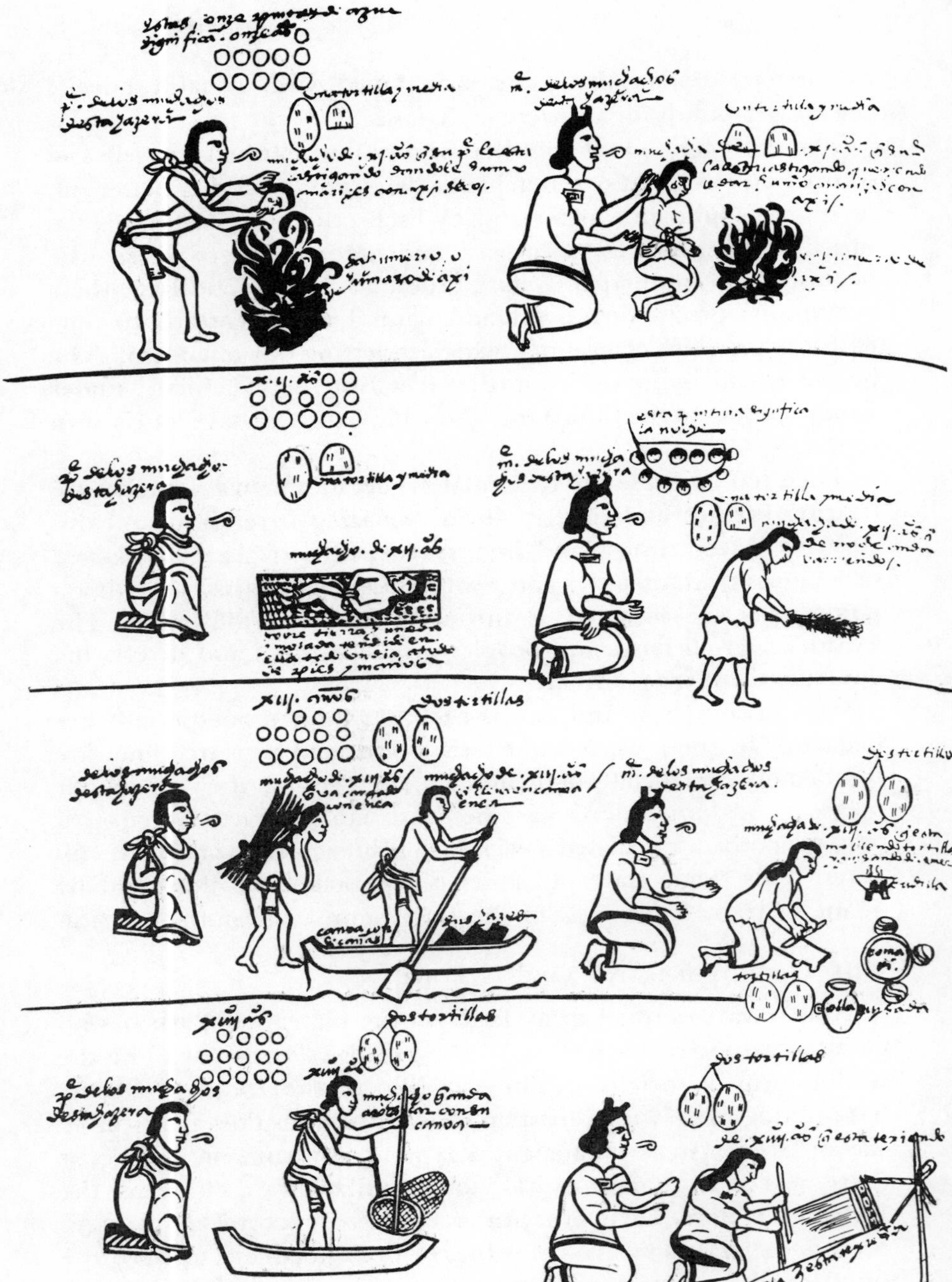

Like everything else in the Inca state, the upbringing of children is well organized. For some misdeeds there are drastic penalties such as being held over the fire, or being made to fast. The upper portion of this drawing by an Inca child illustrates the penalties; the lower portion shows children being taught how to do a variety of tasks. It is interesting to note how the tortillas are apportioned in each case.

let himself be cared for; and cared for he certainly is. The burden of care is borne solely by an elite class which controls and parcels out all property. As with the Egyptians, the preeminent responsibility is borne by the divine king, the Great Inca. The elite are a class unto themselves, of course. They live in palaces whereas the ordinary Indian's house is plain and small. But in the Inca Empire there are no really poor people. Beggars are unknown.

When frost ruins the crops, the state provides food from its reserves for all who have suffered losses. There is a standing compensation arrangement whereby surpluses are reapportioned among those whose fields are frozen or unproductive. Wartime property damages are offset by reconstruction aid. When earthquakes or epidemics strike, the state steps in again to lift the burden from the shoulders of the individual. The state hands out the rations and allotments; it cares for everyone. Its officials plan so far ahead that the stockpiled food surpluses available at any one time are sufficient to feed the needy for up to ten years. Surpluses that are perishable are distributed before they spoil and become unusable. When the Spaniards invade Peru they find on all the main roads government warehouses packed full with all kinds of food. On these same admirably finished roads they also find shelters for travelers.

The *conquistadores* move in on this model state without gaining any insight whatever into its social structure. They live on the food in the warehouses, they marvel at the provisions, but they learn nothing. Because their hearts and minds are set on gold, and because their greed is insatiable, they do not see the real riches of the land. In barbarian fashion they set about destroying this prosperous state and its social institutions. The gold they extort from Atahualpa, the Inca, becomes their great pride; but in addition to robbing the nation of its gold they also strip it of its social and economic foundation. Thus the encounter of the Christian powers with the remote and very different world of the Indians leads not to a fruitful exchange but to oppression and destruction—all in profanation of the name of Christ.

It is true that the European states could not have adopted the socialism of the Incas outright; but it would have been humane—to say the least—to let the people keep the system they

Social welfare in the Inca state is also well organized. Here an overseer of the granaries renders account to the sovereign.

were used to, and on which in fact their life depended. The basis for a useful future exchange between practical socialism and applied Christian charity would thereby have been established; and much of what had been tried and proven in Peru could have been carefully studied and tested in Europe.

No such exchange of experience and learning, however, is allowed to happen. It will take several more centuries of uphill toil before the nations of the old world advance beyond the traditional, scattered, *ad hoc* operations to new, coordinated social programs covering the whole field of human need. And in South America to this day, the nations later established on those ancient Indian territories lag far behind Europe and North America in terms of social progress.

Another thing the Christian has to relearn, after esteeming it so lightly for centuries, is the joy of work—which, no doubt, comes rather naturally to the Incas. To be sure, when Christ told his disciples, "The poor you always have with you," what he said was true, and it remains true for all time. But the beggar does not exist simply as an occasion for others to go about practicing their works of mercy. It is not enough merely to give alms to the poor or the beggar, however much these alms may in fact alleviate a specific need. In the long run the only help that really helps the beggar is job training and employment. For it is in working that a man gains a sense of dignity and learns to have faith in himself. What the Incas took for granted, that in working according to his capacity each man benefits both himself and society, has by many Christians not yet been seen to be a part of the command to love their neighbor.

It should be pointed out, of course, that the first mendicant friars did not become beggars because they could not or would not work, but because their voluntary poverty enabled them to give themselves more completely to the service of their Lord. In the age of which we are speaking, however, idleness is not a matter of that kind of religious integrity. On the contrary, it is the product of an economic situation and a popular attitude which Eberlin von Günzburg, in one of his many incisive broadsides, describes as follows: "The peasant wants to outshine the nobleman, the nobleman the count, the count the prince. Everyone wants to get by on little or no work; no good will come of that. The strangest thing is that one man has to do the work of fifteen while the others go idle: Four are too young, four too old; then there are the sick, the slothful, the parsons, monks, and nuns, the students and playboys at the universities, also the many back alley tycoons who live on usury and profiteering and all kinds of disreputable and dishonest schemes, and then the many unprofitable workmen who make playing-cards and illumine documents, and the petty tradesmen who sit and bait their shameful traps in shameful idleness, luring the money from the pockets of the unsuspecting and gullible." There is no doubt but that the prime evil lies in the mistaken notion of man's natural task. This is why all the laws against begging accomplish nothing. What is needed is a new understanding of work, and that means a rethinking of the value of "good works."

According to the medieval notion of good works, almsgiving is a meritorious deed, and a meritorious deed is first of all a point in favor of the salvation of the doer; consequently, works of love in this age are performed at random and consist of a great number of isolated, one-time ventures. Hundreds of people are helped, often in a measure far exceeding their basic needs, while thousands of others go on starving. What is lacking is comprehensive, organized, and systematic relief programs. With things as they are at the beginning of the sixteenth century, the "hallowed" custom of begging appears—and has long appeared—as a general plague.

The Reformation and Charity

The sixteenth-century Reformation, while it arouses the peoples of Europe and opens their minds to new ideas, does not solve the problem of begging. In fact, in the early stages, illustrations of a Christian love of neighbor are conspicuously lacking. But students of the history of the period will not be surprised by this. The Reformers, beginning with Martin Luther, are concerned above all to restore purity of doctrine, the unadulterated gospel. Their reform program centers on the tenets of the faith. They have little time left over to reorder the Christian life. They proceed on the unquestionably correct assumption that all attempts at reform will fall short of the mark if a new foundation is not laid first.

From the outset, the Reformers *are* at pains to reexamine the whole relationship between faith and works. Martin Luther knows that man is justified by faith alone. Luther does not reject good deeds as such, but he does reject any suggestion that they are a kind of merit badge. The truth for Luther is not that "he who does good works will be saved," but rather that "he who is saved will also do good works." Faith alone produces the love that expresses itself in good works. In restoring this doctrine in all its purity, the Reformation also reestablishes the works of charity on

Beggars crowd the marketplace.

the firm foundation laid by Christ himself. And thus Luther can say, "What matters to God is not good works but obedience."

Obedience means a new way of life. The man who obeys God becomes a different man, a new man. The essential quality of his new life is not this or that specific work of love but a radically transformed existence. Good works no longer come in grades or sizes; instead, the total transformation of the person is revealed in every act, however trivial. Above all, forgiveness is not measured by the number of good works or the amount of the gift; rather, the assurance of forgiveness makes the person as such thankful and merciful. This is what Jesus taught, and this is how he lived; this is what Francis applied in his life, and it is what Luther teaches here.

Out of this perception arises a new understanding of work. Work is not something man does naturally, a duty that is performed as a matter of course; work is rather a matter of love-in-action, for work that is honestly and carefully done benefits the neighbor. Everyone who can work should work, so that he does not become dependent on his neighbors. Their help should be reserved for those who are unable to work. At the same time, the honest workman creates the foundation for a social order which will be of equal benefit to everyone.

Here, of course, Reformation thought is advancing along the lines of social reform, the implications of which will be seen in the social legislation to be enacted centuries later. During the age of the Reformation itself, these ideas remain largely in the realm of theory. To be sure, there are attempts to put them into practice—Calvin's efforts in Geneva for example—but no trends follow in their wake. The criticism leveled at the Reformers, that in many ways their thinking is better than their doing, cannot be brushed off. But we must not fail to see that the great need at the time was precisely for such rethinking of the questions. A new way of life cannot be generally assimilated overnight any more than the Christianizing of a people is able to eradicate in a moment all the vestiges of heathenism. Then too, some of the political sovereigns of the time did more mischief than the Reformers could ever have prevented. Thus if Martin Luther does not follow up his often dramatic campaign against the works-righteousness of the medieval church by erecting an enduring edifice of charity based on his own ethical principles, that is regrettable but understandable: he is fully occupied in buttressing and finishing that work on the foundations of the Reformation to which he has been driven. Even so, whenever time allows, Luther does devote himself to the service of his neighbor, showing as he does so that love of neighbor has its proper setting not in some sacred economy of salvation but right in the middle of the Christian's life in the world.

Thus we find Luther the man always hospitable, compassionate, and ready to help. His wife Katie often complains that his generous giving to others hardly leaves her the wherewithal with which to run a household. He remains in Wittenberg during the plague because of his deeply felt obligation to stand by his neighbor without regard for his own life. Luther's prayer for Tetzel when this archenemy is fatally stricken is by no means a matter of mere outward show or form; and the last thing Luther does on this earth is to mediate between two feuding counts, the brothers Albrecht and Gebhard von Mansfeld, in such a way as to bring peace to the land.

It is also a perfectly consistent move on the part of Luther and the other Reformers when they make the secular powers share in the responsibility of caring for the poor and the sick. It is Luther in particular who aids the civil authorities wherever he can, especially in the matter of setting up municipal ordinances for caring for the poor. Indeed, such poor-laws are hardly possible prior to the Reformation and the intellectual and spiritual emancipation that it brings.

But the idea of replacing sporadic almsgiving with systematic parish programs for relief of the poor is not very well implemented in the lands adopting the Reformation. One innovation that is widely adopted is the "Common Chest." Introduced primarily through the efforts of one of Luther's companions-in-arms, Johann Bugenhagen, the Common Chest is meant to become the central collecting point for the alms of the parish. However, it never does become the focal point of the parish's love-in-action. With the social upheaval produced by the Peasants' Revolt, the charitable activity of the people at large slips back into the old pre-Reformation mold of meritorious works. Luther's new insights are not lost, however. They continue to operate, and their influence is evident even in the Roman Catholic Counter-Reformation. They also flourish in the Reformed church of John Calvin, and among some Anabaptist groups which later become known as Mennonites, after Menno Simons.

Katharina Zell and the Refugees in Strasbourg

During this struggle for a new and comprehensive systematizing of Christian love, there is no lack of examples of individual sacrifice on behalf of one's neighbor. For an outstanding illustration of compassion in the Protestant sphere during Reformation times, we might look at the work of Matthäus and Katharina Zell in Strasbourg.

The former professor and rector of the University of Freiburg, Matthäus has been living as a lay priest in Strasbourg since 1518. In 1522 he marries Katharina Schütz, the daughter of what we would call middle-class parents. The Zells establish the first Protestant parsonage in Strasbourg. Although anathematized by the bishop, Zell has the support of the council and the populace of the free city. His parsonage in the Bruderhofgasse quickly becomes a haven for needy and persecuted people. And persecution in these times is common. The citizens of a neighboring hamlet in Breisgau are denied entrance into their own town for religious reasons: when their pastor had been expelled by the government, they had accompanied him. Now as they approach the city walls, soldiers bar their way back to their own homes and families. In their distress they turn to Strasbourg, where they are admitted. Katharina Zell takes care of fifty to sixty refugees every day in her home. She also helps other refugees find food and shelter, and she writes reassuring letters to their wives.

The next year the peasants in Alsace band together and revolt against their noble overlords. In vain Zell tries to mediate a settlement. Open fighting breaks out, and the peasants' army is annihilated. The wives and children flee in great numbers to the security of Strasbourg. A comprehensive relief program must now be launched, on hardly any notice; and again it is Katharina Zell who takes the operation in hand. Some three thousand refugees are housed in emergency quarters in the Franciscan monastery, but there is still the problem of feeding them. Katharina appeals for aid, collects provisions, and sees to the distribution herself. Nor does she forget the dying. The city records of Strasbourg recount how she stands by those who are fatally stricken. Ten weeks before her own death, already too ill to walk, she has herself carried to the cemetery where she conducts a funeral that no clergyman in Strasbourg would conduct, because the deceased was not of their faith. For Katharina, tolerance is one of the hallmarks of the Protestant way of life. Wherever she can, she tries to reconcile, appeal for peace, and spread cheer.

Matthäus Zell's Strasbourg parsonage is the prototype of the Protestant parsonage that will bear such abundant fruit in centuries to come. Again and again the drive and vigor of the pastor and the compassion and concern of his wife combine to produce works of mercy. Three hundred years later, parsonages in Kaiserswerth and Bethel will become wellsprings of love-in-action.

The Congregational Diaconate

The century of the Reformation produces still another application of Christian love-in-action. Besides the cities' provisions for poor relief and the cooperative ecclesiastical-civil campaigns on behalf of the poor, there arise the congregational ministries of serving love.

It is well known that in times of persecution churches are more united, more ready to make sacrifices, more willing to help. Dutch refugees form such a congregation in England, where Edward VI is granting asylum to the victims of persecution. One day a Polish nobleman named Jan Laski turns up in this church. A refugee for the sake of the gospel, Laski has been driven out of his Catholic homeland, as well as out of the Frisian city of Emden where he had been active as a Protestant pastor.

Laski gives the "foreigners' church" in London a new set of bylaws. He uses earlier precedents, but his system also clearly shows the independent spirit of the Pole. Great stress is put on care of the poor; for, says Laski, this ministry is an essential element of all congregational life. If Jesus commanded the church to care for the poor, Laski continues, then the church must act on the command. The congregation should take it upon itself to name deacons or deaconesses who will dedicate themselves totally to serving the needy.

Upon Edward's death Laski and his congregation are forced to flee the England of Bloody Mary. After a long period of wandering about, he eventually returns to Emden. Here too he leaves behind him a set of bylaws stressing provision for the poor. He is subsequently called back to his homeland, where he devotes himself to promoting a union of the Lutherans, the Reformed, and the Bohemian Brethren.

In Emden the congregational diaconate which he instituted takes root and thrives. The basis for its work is articulately stated in a report dated 1594: "Since God has made man body and soul, he has also, in his divine wisdom and grace, provided and prescribed the framework and the needs of each part. Hence, there is ordained and commanded in the Old and New Testament, besides the preaching office, the *diaconiae pauperum* or ministries to the poor." Consequently there are in Emden "many diverse, regular, and public ministries to the poor." There is, first of all, the lodge erected on the grounds of an abandoned monastery for discalced (barefoot) friars; three times a year funds for it are collected from among the congregation, and once a year a kind of white-gift offering is made. In addition there is the house-to-house mission to the poor: thirty-two deacons visit needy people in their homes. The city is divided into six districts, and every Saturday afternoon the deacons meet, parcel out the assignments, exchange experiences, or deal with complaints that have been brought before them. All income and expenses are carefully recorded. It is also recommended that all beggars who knock at the doors of the lodge be referred to the appropriate deacons. Many townsmen take underprivileged young boys into their homes in order to give them an education in school or to apprentice them in a trade; and the townspeople also get together and hire a barber-surgeon to doctor the sick. The third ministry of the congregational diaconate is to seamen. This relief work is not only for the needy sailors living in Emden but also for all shipwrecked sailors who may "land" at Emden. The lodge maintained by the congregation is always open to old seamen.

Finally, the Reformed congregation of Emden takes special care of all strangers, especially brother Protestants who have been expelled from their homes. These strangers and refugees are cordially welcomed and sheltered and fed. Thus there emerges, in 1558, a full-fledged congregational diaconate serving the "indigent strangers within Emden."

Laski's principles take firm hold especially in the Reformed churches of the lower Rhine area. Aid to the poor is also prescribed in the ordinances of the Reformed (Huguenot) church of France, which is undergoing severe persecution and testing. Even the persecutors must repeatedly acknowledge "how the heretics stand together, how each watches out for the welfare of the other, how they help each other in times of need, how their poor are provided for, how they visit their sick."

In France, the prince of Sedan, Henri-Robert de La Marck founds the society of the "Maids of Charity" for the care of the poor, the aged, and the sick. Although not deaconesses in the sense of an order bound by vows, they call to mind Vincent de Paul's "Daughters of Charity" and the deaconesses of Kaiserswerth.

In the Netherlands the congregational diaconate is especially quick to blossom. Substantial financial resources are available here, of course, for commerce and shipping have made the land rich. Nearly every city has its organized ministries of love, and model facilities are being built everywhere: there are orphan homes, homes for the aged, hospitals and mental institutions—and workhouses and penal institutions as well. In Amsterdam, where a city orphanage has been in existence since 1579, a "spinnery" for women and a "house of correction" are founded, the latter for the compulsory occupational training of beggars.

It is typical of Amsterdam, even in those days, to support the diaconate and its welfare institutions by lotteries. But even apart from such revenue, the contributions that come in from Amsterdam's citizens show an astonishing degree of sacrificial commitment. Twice a year collections are taken up for the many welfare institutions in the city, whether Walloon-Reformed, Dutch-Reformed, Mennonite, or Lutheran. The total proceeds of the two collections are enough to support all of the institutions for an entire year—and several of the orphanages house as many as 1,500 children! The deacons are assisted by deaconesses, who are chiefly in charge of supplies, meals, and laundry in the various institutions but also put in additional hours as nurses. The churches also send visitors to the hospitals to look after the patients' spiritual needs. The Amsterdam diaconate even has its own bakery. All in all, this is a well-planned ministry providing effective help for everyone in need.

The influence of these congregational ministries of love is reflected in England in the Poor Law of 1601 instituted by Queen Elizabeth I, upon which the entire English system of poor relief is built. Elizabeth orders that "overseers of the poor" shall be named to take charge of precisely defined districts, two to four in each district. These overseers are to see that work is provided for the beggars, that children of needy parents are given a regular education, and that the unemployable, the blind, the disabled, and the aged are given adequate assistance.

Originally the English system of poor relief is built around the local parishes. Gradually it is taken over by the state, but the Protestant principle—vocational training for poor people who can work, financial assistance only for the unemployable—is preserved. Thus a part of the program involves providing the necessary jobs and working materials. Flax, hemp, wool, and metals must be secured for processing. The law is a model one, but the immediate results in seventeenth-century England are negligible.

Mercy during the Counter-Reformation

Meanwhile, changes in poor relief programs are impending in the Roman Catholic church as well. Two forces are converging: first, the intellectual undercurrents of humanism and the Renaissance, which stress the role of the individual; second, the precedent of Protestantism, which acts as a stimulus and perhaps also as a challenge. The Catholic poor relief movement grows with surprising rapidity and, in turn, provides further stimulus to the Protestant movement. Thus at this early point a healthy trend toward interaction is emerging, even while the leaders of the church are locked in a bitter struggle and the Counter-Reformation is presenting the world with the spectacle of an inquisition. The resurgence of charitable endeavor does not originate in Rome, however, but in Spain.

Here at the beginning of the sixteenth century a Portuguese named Juan Ciudad, who has lived a life of adventure and dissipation, is converted by an evangelist. Seeking peace of heart through excessive self-mortification, he overtaxes body and mind. Eventually he is committed to a hospital as a mental patient, where he experiences firsthand all the misery and cruelty of such institutions. Upon his discharge, a wise confessor counsels him to practice mercy himself. That is the better way to reconciliation with God, says the confessor. So Juan rents a house in Granada and opens it to sick people who are unable to pay for medical care. He supports them by working or begging. The superior facilities he builds up and the individual attention provided for the patients make this institution exemplary. It is unlike anything that has gone before it. With Juan Ciudad, later to be called St. John of God, begins the history of the modern hospital.

Juan quickly gathers a group of brothers around him to assist in caring for the sick. When he dies in 1550, his first co-worker, Anton Martin, reorganizes the society into a full-fledged order, one that is exclusively dedicated to works of charity. That is something new. The institutions it maintains are not primarily concerned with spiritual ministry—they are not cloisters filled with hospital beds. Instead they are real hospitals. Thus the society Juan founds, which becomes known as the Brothers Hospitalers or Brothers of Charity, ushers in a new era of hospital care and comes to exert an influence that spreads far beyond its environs.

In the Spanish world of chivalry and dalliance emerges a brave young officer who eventually becomes one of the greatest warriors of the Catholic church: Ignatius of Loyola. The Jesuit order, founded by him, is not devoted to good works—the charter he gave it was missions. But Loyola himself never forgets the needy. He is active on behalf of young people who are exposed to temptation, especially girls who have either fallen into vice or are in danger of doing so. Thus, in order to save the daughters of the elite courtesans of Rome from the sordid way of life of their mothers, he founds a home for them, the Casa di S. Marta. Ever since Ignatius's time, the ministry to young people in or close to trouble and that of moral "rescue operations" have been an important part of the Jesuits' mission.

But the outstanding figure in the history of Catholic charitable endeavor of the sixteenth century is probably Carlo Borromeo, archbishop of Milan. Quite early in his life he becomes strongly impressed by the work of Bishop Giberte of Verona who—himself born out of wedlock—directs his concern toward the victims of social evil. He finds regular work for the unemployed, secures loans for impecunious farmers, and above all mounts a vigorous attack on the vicious custom of abandoning newborn babies. Borromeo also begins his work of mercy at this point. He finds accommodations and nurses for foundlings in order to save them from certain death. He also founds a mental institution and a home for girls who have fallen into prostitution. But he soon realizes that prevention is better than cure. He sees that many girls are driven to prostitution by the brute fact of poverty. They are unlearned, unskilled, and simply do not know how to earn an honest living. Education and vocational training are the key to saving such girls from a career of vice. Thus he gives all possible support to the new order of the Ursulines, whose mission is the education of underprivileged children.

But Borromeo is not content to let it go at that. At the outbreak of a famine in 1570, he immediately organizes a relief program, buying up provisions, selling them at noninflationary prices, and thus preventing much hardship and profiteering. When Milan is hit by the plague six years later, and the prosperous citizens, led by the governor, flee for their lives, he stays on in the beleaguered city, even when the epidemic has taken the lives of 25,000 persons. He has six barracks-hospitals erected outside the city, and he himself goes out daily to visit the plague victims there. Here again he proves to be a man of vision and foresight. After the plague has spent itself, he convenes a provincial council which takes up in detail the matter of emergency regulations during outbreaks of the plague. Instructions on sanitation are issued and contingency provisions set up in order to prevent unnecessary fear, confusion, or panic. In addition, guidelines are worked out to ensure that those who become infected will receive all possible physical and spiritual care. Borromeo also issues penal laws in his capacity as bishop, and he renews an old agreement aimed at providing the poor with medicine and medical care. Thanks to his initiative Milan is also provided with welfare and poverty legislation that is exemplary in the whole Catholic world.

That Borromeo's multifarious service in the cause of charity is performed so unstintingly is all the more noteworthy when it is remembered that the archbishop lives in the period dominated by the Counter-Reformation. Since the time of the Council of Trent, the conversion of heretics has been deemed the first and foremost mission of the Catholic church, even taking precedence over the ministry of charity. Not for Borromeo, however. He helps where help is needed, and he sees first the suffering man, whether heretic or not.

Germany has its counterpart to Borromeo in these times. He is Julius Echter, Bishop of Würzburg, who in 1576 establishes the Julius Hospital, a complex with extensive facilities, where only those who are really poor and sick are admitted. Echter's personal physician, a Dr. Upillo, is put in charge. The regulations, which have quite a modern sound to them, stipulate that the hospital doctor shall visit the patients twice a day. Echter makes improvements in hospital administration throughout his whole diocese. He also initiates a new system of almsgiving.

9.

Discurs/ ober deß Hospittals Gebäw/ vnd deroselben sonderbaren guten Commoditeten.

Wiewolen sonsten die Italianer/ von bald zorniger/ vnd ernstlicher Natur/ daher gewachsen seynd/ so haben sie jedoch gegen den Armen/ Krancken vnd Nothleidenden Menschen/ gleichsam mehrere Erbarmung/ vnd Milttthätigkeit/ als nicht zum theil/in vnsern teutschen Landen geschihet/dieselbige nit nur schlecht hinwegk/wie das thumme Vihe hingehn zulassen so lang es kan oder mag/ sonder sie lassen jhnen gar eyferig angelegen seyn/ Hülff/Rath/vnd gute Mittel zuverschaffen/die trostlose von der Welt verachte Personen/wol vnd recht zuversorgen/ einigen Mangel nit zu leiden/damit vnd nach dem Willen Gottes/ sie widerumben zu jhrer Gesundheit gelangen mögen.

Zu welchem Ende/ so werden allda/ mit grossen vnd mercklichen Vnkosten/ manicherley Hospitäler vnnd Gottshäuser auffgebawet/ (massen dann in meinem/ deß 1627. Jahrs in den Truck gegebenen Itinerario Italiæ, daselbsten an folio 23. 24. zu lesen ist. Was gestalt in der so mächtigen Statt Mayland/ ein sehr Pomposisches Hospital gefunden wird/darinnen den dürfftigen lobwürdig außgewartet. Nicht weniger/ vnd vermög deß obangedeuten Itinerarij, an folio 121. so befindt sich in der grossen Statt Rom/ auch ein nit viel geringers Hospital/ neben noch viel andern dergleichen angenemen Gottshäuser mehr/ alles zu Gottes Lob vnd Ehr/ vnd dann zu nutzen deß Nechsten angesehen) damit jedes Gebresten absonderlichen könde curiert werden. Vnd

Erstlich für die Statt vnd Landleut/als da seynd gar alterlebte/ außgearbeitete/matte Personen/denselben eine Pfründ zuverordnen/da dann etwan ein altes paar Ehevolck/ oder aber ein Mann/ so wolen ein Weib/noch ein stücklein Gelts in jhrem Leben ersparet/mit der guten

C ij Inten-

Extract from a 1655 monograph by Joseph Fürttenbach on hospital construction.

But at this point, as the Protestant-Catholic controversy grows increasingly polemic, and frequently infected with a combination of secular politics and human lust for power, the work of charity suffers a decline that reaches its appalling depths in the Thirty Years' War.

Vincent de Paul and the Daughters of Charity

Then in France an ordinary priest from the peasant-farmer class precipitates a wave of Christian charity whose effects are still felt today. The priest is Vincent de Paul, the St. Francis of the seventeenth century. In 1604 Vincent, then twenty-three and already admitted to the priesthood, goes on family business to Bordeaux and Marseilles. He is returning home when (according to one version) his ship is seized by Tunisian pirates, whose forays in those days took them as far as the French coast and beyond. Before Vincent realizes what is happening, he is sold as a slave in Tunis. After years of slavery and unspeakable misery, he is finally able to escape on a small and precariously pitching boat. Vincent is now a different man; his sufferings have borne the fruit of human kindness.

Returning home, he assumes the duties of chaplain to the family of Count de Joigny (Philippe-Emmanuel de Gondi), General of the Galleys. To be chained to the galleys—and abused by cruel overseers—is still a common sentence for criminals in these times, and it is a thoroughly wretched existence. Count de Joigny is a Christian, and he does what he can to make the life of galley slaves more bearable. He appoints Vincent Chaplain General of the Galleys, and together the two men are able to alleviate much suffering and to bring cheer and relief to many.

They are aided in their efforts by the Lazarists, a society of missionary-priests founded by Vincent himself and dedicated to spiritual renewal in primarily rural areas. Hospitals for prisoners are built in Marseilles and Paris, and hospitals for slaves in Tunis and Algeria. In addition, over a period of years more than twelve hundred slaves are ransomed.

The count's charitable ministry paves the way for Father Vincent's own extensive work. Societies for the care of the poor and the sick are founded. The first of these, the Confraternity of Charity (founded in 1617 in Chatillon-les-dombes, near Lyon) soon proves to have its imperfections. The fashionable ladies who belong to it are not very anxious, for social reasons, to visit the sick in their homes; they would rather send their servants. Hardly satisfied with this, de Paul hits upon the idea of training young girls and enlisting them in the society. He succeeds in finding a simple country maid who is willing to go to Paris and take nurse's training. This girl, the first of the Daughters of Charity, dies at an early age from an infection incurred while treating victims of the

Since the time of Vincent de Paul, the Daughters of Charity have been active all over the world. This picture from an 1864 issue of the "Leipziger Illustrierte" shows them at work in the war which Prussia and Austria fought against Denmark in 1864.

plague, but she is followed by others who form a small order of charity. But this is still not enough for the zealous Father Vincent. He wants the girls better trained, and he wants the order more tightly knit, so that it will become a real team of relief workers.

At this point he is approached by Louise de Marillac, who volunteers to undertake the training of the girls. The idea is suggested to her by Francis de Sales, who in 1610, together with Frances de Chantal, founded the charitable order of the Visitandines (Daughters of the Visitation). In 1633 Louise de Marillac begins training four girls. Soon there are other candidates, and Louise throws herself unreservedly into her new task. She becomes Vincent's most loyal and reliable sister worker. Later Vincent gives the new order its Rule, which is officially recognized by both church and state. The Daughters of Charity differ markedly from all earlier hospital orders, including the Visitandines. Instead of being permanently attached to one hospital, they belong to their motherhouse, which trains and commissions them. They find their work everywhere: in hospitals, churches, prisons, even on the battlefield. It is reported that after the Battle of Dunkirk in 1658, Vincent sends four of the order to Calais to care for the sick and wounded. When two of them come down with a contagious disease, twenty of their sisters volunteer to carry on their work.

An incident in Poland shows how deeply the Daughters of Charity are committed to the poor. In 1662 a number of them are sent for the first time beyond the borders of France to work in several Polish cities. The queen of Poland hears of them, meets them, and expresses the wish to have one of them remain at court to attend her. The Daughters' answer is characteristic: "We have given ourselves to God to serve the poor." Their place is in the hovels of the wretched of the earth, not in the palace of the queen.

The order finds it has not exhausted the list of needs; new challenges keep arising. One day Vincent de Paul has a profoundly shaking experience. He happens to be walking along by the city walls of Paris at dusk one day when suddenly he hears a series of dreadful cries and comes upon a beggar about to mutilate a child in cold blood. This grisly custom is more widespread at the time than the unsuspecting populace realizes. Beggars pick up foundlings, gouge one of their eyes out, cut their hands off, or inflict hideous wounds upon them. These infants are then used to arouse the pity of the public, from whom the beggars hope—not without justification—to receive large gifts. It is also customary, by the way, to conduct regular business with these foundlings: twenty sous for a baby is the going rate. The misery in store for these children is beyond imagining, and the mutilation is often the least of the evils they suffer.

Father Vincent snatches the baby from the beggar, carries it off, and takes it to a foundling home. In Paris there are a number of these homes, for in this city of two hundred thousand people more than four hundred babies are abandoned each year. But even in such homes the children live in misery. The care is more than indifferent, the food totally inadequate; frequently the babies die a few days after arrival. Those that do survive are later sold.

Vincent feels challenged to do something about this shocking situation. But again, he does not gallop off in all directions; his action is well-considered and practical. First he collects the children from the streets and alleys and commits them to the charge of the Daughters of Charity, who once more set to work where others have failed.

But on that evening by the city walls of Paris, it was not only the plight of the foundlings that was driven home to Vincent; it was also the plight of the beggars. Beggars and begging still represent a national plague, and in the turmoil of the Thirty Years' War the practice threatens to get completely out of control. The dreadful statistics show that one out of every five inhabitants of Paris goes begging. The beggars have formed their own organization and live in several camps outside the city. The largest of them can hold up to three thousand people. Every evening wondrous "healings" take place in these camps (which are accordingly dubbed "miracle" camps). During the daytime, the lame, blind, and deaf beggars who live here arouse the sympathies of the populace by displaying their grievous ills. In the evening, when the time has come to squander the spoils, the beggars recover their sight, their hearing, and the full use of their limbs. No ban has been able to put an end to this scourge. The police do not venture into the miracle camps, nor does the church send its representatives into such perils.

Vincent tackles this problem as well. He uses a large anonymous donation to build a hospital (he calls it the hospital of the Name of Jesus), which becomes a kind of monastic workhouse. Paris learns with astonishment that he has managed to rehabilitate forty men and women he has brought there. Louis XIV, in a characteristic gesture of generosity, adopts the cause as his own, and in 1655 founds the General Hospital, which can hold thousands of beggars. Its workshops are so extensive that fifty-two master craftsmen are employed as supervisors. The government's venture into the field may have been too hasty. At any rate, the initial success of the operation is soon followed by reverses. Not even the nationwide scope of the campaign is able to wipe out begging; it flourishes throughout the eighteenth century. One of the lacks in Catholic regions is the active involvement of the local church in welfare work, to supplement the extensive care provided by institutions. (By contrast, parish involvement is gradually being built up in Protestant regions.)

But the extraordinary power of Vincent de Paul is even more compellingly demonstrated in the general emergencies of those unsettled times. In Lothringen the priest and his associates, with the backing of the queen, already supplied a whole province with provisions when the land was still in ruins. He is also on hand in the regions of Picardy and Champagne. In 1640 he stands before mighty Cardinal Richelieu and calls upon the state to stop its war-making: "Peace—have pity on us, give France peace." But the state ignores the plea and the war goes on. Vincent wastes no more time in futile petitioning; he throws himself into the relief campaign, and France soon has a "minister of national charity." For the hungry, Vincent institutes the public dole: the "oeuvre des potages économiques." These "economy soup" kitchens save the lives of thousands of people. Anyone can buy a bowlful of soup for a sou. The recipe is Vincent's own: twenty-five pounds of bread, seven quarter-pounds of fat, four liters of peas or beans, herbs, salt, and five buckets of water; break the bread into pieces, put everything into a pot, and cook—serves one hundred.

During this time civil war is threatening in Paris. Cardinal Mazarin's intrigues after the death of Louis XIII had driven a wedge between the court and the people. The masses are in revolt. Soldiers march on Paris and besiege it. Once more a severe famine ensues, and once more it is Father Vincent who comes to the people's aid. He risks delivering a petition to the queen, despite the fact that on the way to St. Germain he is forced to splash through the swollen waters of the Seine on horseback. What does it matter to him that his health is critical, that he has exhausted himself prematurely in his steadfast pursuit of the welfare of others? He has never asked whether his sacrifices are appreciated, and it is just as well, for the thanks he gets is meager indeed.

The peace agreement that Mazarin is forced by parliamentary pressure to make has the effect of demolishing Vincent's work

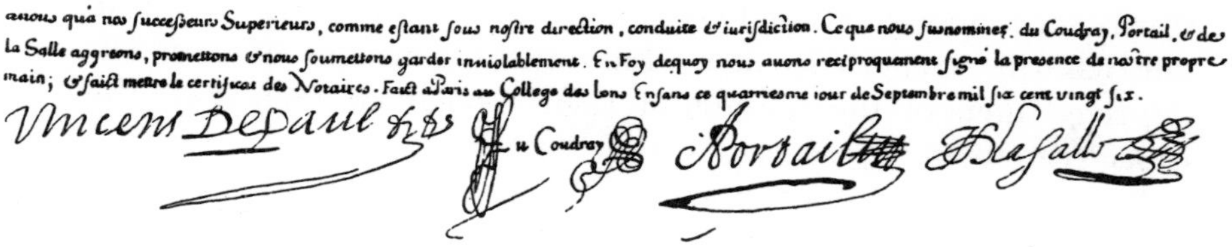

anous qu'à nos successeurs Superieurs, comme estant sous nostre direction, conduite & iurisdiction. Ce que nous susnommez. du Coudray, Portail, & de la Salle aggreons, promettons & nous soumettons garder inuiolablement. En Foy dequoy nous auons reciproquement signé la presence de nostre propre main; & faict mettre le certificat des Notaires. Faict à Paris au College des bons Enfans ce quatriesme iour de Septembre mil six cent vingt six.

Vincent Depaul · du Coudray · Portail · Delasalle

The signatures of Vincent de Paul and several associates on a contract in which they agree to "instruct the poor people of the provinces in the catechism."

Echter-Verlag, Würzburg

with a single stroke. Vincent is suddenly called a traitor, his charitable foundations are seized and plundered. The greatest of France's "caring people" is left to live on the despoiled estate of Orsigny, destitute and forsaken by all. He spends his days as he did in his youth, before he had ever met the Franciscans: he herds sheep on the barren plains of Etampes.

But France cannot get along without him after all. Vincent lives to see a dramatic reversal of his fortunes. Anna, the dowager queen, recalls him: "Your work of mercy must not die . . . all France needs you . . . !" This gives Vincent a few more years of ministry. And in the history of charity he lives on, his only real peer being the son of the Assisi textile merchant. Yet Vincent is more than simply the recipient of a tradition; he is also the precursor of future movements and works of love.

The Thirty Years' War

Meanwhile in Germany, the times seem inimical to large-scale charitable efforts. The terrors of the Thirty Years' War are such as to extinguish organized Christian charity everywhere in the land. Suffering produces prayer, it is said; and there are ample illustrations of congregations who draw especially close together in times of crisis. But the suffering may also produce cursing; and when the suffering exceeds the limits of human endurance men may become indifferent, unfeeling, driven to despair. The closest, most intimate ties may snap. Unconcerned, neighbor watches neighbor lose everything he has. Unconcerned, believer watches believer sink into ruin. Unresisting, men look on as their wives are raped and their children abused. Farmers who have fled to the cities sink slowly into their squalid labyrinths. No one volunteers to help: no one has the strength to help. The crushing weight of pain has deprived men of the noblest of their God-given capacities, the capacity to love.

Rich today, poor as a churchmouse tomorrow—thus H. J. C. von Grimmelshausen's *Simplicissimus* pictures the man of the age. He takes things as they come without thinking, drains to the dregs the pleasures of the moment, and perhaps the next day is ruined. Men and women succumb to brazen immorality, pursuing the fleeting pleasures of lust. The children, who simply grow up without really being brought up, follow the law of the jungle until in the end they have destroyed both body and soul.

Suffering may indeed produce cursing. And suffering is itself a curse, a scourge upon mankind. Johann Valentin Andreae finds out the truth of this in Calw, before the war has begun its real work of destruction there. Andreae comes from Herrenberg and is the son of a Swabian dean. In Geneva he has been introduced to the strict discipline of the Calvinists, and he is so impressed by it that he resolves to start a similar regimen in the district he oversees. In a period of strict Lutheran orthodoxy he is one of the few men to complain that there is more *science* than *conscience* in the Lutheran churches, more emphasis on knowledge and learning than on compassion, a superfluity of words and a dearth of works. Beginning with his first pastorate in Vaihingen, Andreae tries to counteract the moral decline by a thorough program of youth education and training, as well as strict ecclesiastical discipline, but his plan founders on the divisions within the church. When he becomes superintendent in Calw, his eyes are opened to the dreadful effects of war, even though his region is initially spared from becoming a battlefield. Inflation, a by-product of the war, brings about the collapse of all civil order. Honorable citizens become gamblers and drinkers, reducing their families to begging. Andreae boldly intervenes, trying to cope with the crisis and the threat to morality. Inspired by the Reformers, he introduces a weekly almsgathering, out of which grows the foundation he calls the *Färbergestift*. The assets of the foundation are used to help anyone who is in need, including young theologians, needy schoolchildren, and apprentices in the trades.

Andreae actually succeeds in turning the city of Calw into a little enclave of order amid the surrounding turmoil.

But eventually, enemy troops invade Andreae's district as well. After the battle of Nördlingen the citizens of Calw are forced to flee. They hide in the surrounding forests and try to appease their gnawing hunger with bread made from acorns and tree bark. Less than half the town survives the rigors of this existence, and when the rest are able to return, barely four thousand strong, the plague descends upon their devastated city and takes the lives of two thousand more.

Andreae sticks by the remnant of his flock. He helps as best he can with the few resources left to him. He also makes innumerable appeals for help: one goes to the duke of Württemberg, who has fled to Strasbourg and is living in comfort there; others go to Frankfurt, Ulm, and Augsburg. Eventually his efforts are rewarded and help comes from the outside. By the time it arrives, Andreae has already given away everything that he owns. Had it not been for him, scarcely anyone in Calw would have survived.

Only a few accounts of those bitter years tell of achievements comparable to Andreae's work. Notable among his contemporaries is Pastor Martin Rinckart, composer of the hymn, "Now thank we all our God." After the battle of Lützen, Rinckart and his congregation are forced to flee their homes in Eilenburg, Saxony. The courageous pastor leads the refugees as far as the city gates of Wittenberg, where they are forced to make camp for several days until they find accommodations within. Then the plague breaks out, killing every clergyman in Wittenberg except Rinckart; and he is thus left to shoulder the pastoral responsibilities for the whole city. He conducts the last rites for over four thousand men and women, including his wife. When the epidemic is over, it is followed by a famine so severe that people fight even over the body of a dead crow. Rinckart scrapes together his possessions, sells everything that is saleable, buys flour with the proceeds, and has it baked into bread. Like a father surrounded by his children, he distributes the bread to the hungry.

In fact, whenever trouble threatens, he is on hand. A Swedish army commandant tries to extort thirty thousand talers from the totally despoiled city, and Rinckart himself goes to the enemy camp to bargain. But all his supplications are useless; the Swede will have his money, otherwise he is going to burn the city down. Whereupon Rinckart says, "God will hear us, even if men's ears are deaf." He calls his congregation to prayer. It is a matter of record that the enemy suddenly moderates his demands; and in the middle of the protracted and inconclusive negotiations that follow, commandant and troops suddenly take to their heels, having got neither money nor spoils.

By the end of the war Germany is a shambles, and it is not until many years after the peace treaty of 1648 that the works of mercy prosper again.

Witch-Hunts

Meanwhile one of the darkest chapters of the Christian West, that of the witch trials, is written into history. These trials give us a bloodcurdling view of a mass hysteria that is almost incomprehensible to us today.

In surveying the centuries of the witch trials, one gets the impression that the dominant faith of mankind is superstition. Christianity has assimilated too many heathen elements into its thinking. Man has become trapped in a tightly woven web of unreason, the most grotesque instance of which is belief in witchcraft. This notion is not confined to the masses; men of learning, with theologians in the lead, work out detailed apologias arguing the existence of witches and justifying the witch-hunts. A witch is an abomination that consorts with the devil and that is invested with malignant powers in return. For exercising these evil powers witches must be punished by death. Thus they are seized by the religious vigilantes of the day, cruelly tortured, and usually executed.

Little status is enjoyed by the married woman of this age. The woman with status is the virgin, and supreme among her ranks is the nun. If a married woman presumes to exalt herself above the low esteem accorded her sex, she is summarily pronounced a witch and accused of being in league with the devil.

Legal opinion readily goes along with public opinion in this case, and the papal bull of 1484 officially recognizes the charge of consorting with the devil, which is tantamount to passing the death sentence upon the helpless and unfortunate "witches." The Dominicans, well known as leaders of the Inquisition, compose

Ein erschröckliche geschicht/so zu Derneburg in der Graffschafft Reinsteyn-am Hartz gelegen-von dreyen Zauberin-vnnd zwayen Mañen/Iñ etlichen tagen des Monats Octobris Im 1 5 5 5. Jare ergangen ist.

DJe alte Schlang der Teüffel/dieweyl er Got/vnd zůuoran den Sun Gottes/vnsern Herrn Jesum Christum/vnd das gantze menschliche geschlecht/fürnemlich vmb vnsers Haylands Christi willen hasset/hat er sich bald im anfang/vnd kürtzlich nach der erschaffung vmb dz weibsbild/als vmb die/welcher same seinen kopff zertretten solt/angenom̃en/dieselbigen durch sein hinderlist vnd lugen/zů dem jämerlichen fal/deß vnglaubens vñ vngehorsams wider Got gebracht/Darauß das gantz menschlich geschlecht/in ewige verdamnuß vñ verderben komen were/so Christus vnser Hayland/den zorn des Vatters nicht weckgenom̃en/vnd das gericht wider vns auffgehaben het. Nu behelt der alte Feind gleichwol alten haß wider Christum/vnd vns/für vñ für/vnd helt auch sein alte weyse/er setzet sonderlich dem weiblichen gschlecht hart zů/als dem schwecheren werckzeug/damit er sie von Christo wegreysse/vñ in ewige verdamnuß füre/vñ wie er zů Eua sprach/sie wurden werdē wie die Götter/Also bläßt er noch das gifft in der weyber hertzen/lernet sie zaubern/auff das er sie klůg mache/das sie mehr wissen dann andere leüt/vnd also den Göttern gleich werden/damit macht er sie jm anhengig/vnd zů Teüffels dienerin/ja auch zů Teuffels breüten/wie dise jämerliche geschicht/welche warhafftigklich also wie vnden angezaiget/am Hartz ergangen ist/Die derhalben also gemalet vñ geschriben/im druck auß gangen. Auff das doch die rohelose welt/zů Gottes forcht erwecket/vnd von dem Gottlosen wesen abgeschreckt werden/ Dann Gott der allmächtige derhalben solche Exempel vns sehen laßt/das er damit vnsere harten hertzen durch dise erschröckliche exempel / zur forcht Göttliches gerichts/vnd straffe erwecke/man mag es malen/predigen/singen vnd sagen/vñ wie man jm̃er kan den leüten einbilden/damit der laydige hauffe ein wenig zů Gottes forcht/gehorsam/vnd zucht gezogen werde/besonder zů disen letsten zeyten/in welchē der listige Sathan/dieweyl er mercket/das der tag des gerichts sich nahet/gar raffend toll vnd vnsinnig ist/vnd bede durch sich vnd seine gelider/ grewlicher weyse/wider Christum vnd sein armes heüfflein wüttet/Die ellende welt aber dargegē so frey sicher in allem můtwillen dahin lebet/als ob der Teüffel vor langst gestorben sey/vnd kain Got/kain gericht oder straff/verhanden were/Der Almächtig Got vnd vatter/vnsers Herrn Jesu Christi/wölle dem grimigen feinde wehren/sein armes heüfflein vor jm vnd seinen glidern schützen vnd handthaben/seinem vnd der seinen wůtten vnd toben/einmal ein ende machen/durch Jesum Christum Amen.

¶ Folget die geschichte / so zů Derneburg in der Graffschafft Reynstein am Hartz gelegen/ergangen ist/ Im October des 1 5 5 5. Jars.

AVff den Dinstag nach Michaelis/den ersten Octobris/seind zwů Zauberin gebrandt/die eine Gröbische/die ander Gißlersche genañt/ vñ hat die Gröbische bekandt/das sie Aylff jar mit dem Teüffel gebůlet habe/vñ wie man dieselben Gröbischen zů der Fewrstat gebracht/vnd an die saul mit Ketten geschlagen/vnd das Fewr angezündt/ist der bůle/der Sathan komen/vnd sie in lüfften sichtigklich vor yederman weckgefürt. Am Donerstag/nach dem die Gröbische vñ die Gißlerschin am Dinstag zůuor seind gerichtet worden/das ist den 3. Octobris/seind dise bede Frawen auff den abend in der Gißlersche hauß komen/vnd der Gißlerschen man zur thür hinauß gestossen/das er nider gefallen vnnd gestorben ist/welches ain Nachbaur gegen vber gehöret/vnd zů gelauffen ist/durch die thür gesehen/das zway weyber bede eytel fewrige/vmbs fewr gedantzet/der Gißlerschin man aber/lag vor der thür vnd war todt. Am Sonnabendt nach Dionisij/das ist der 12. Octobris/ist der Gröbischen mañ gerichtet worden/vmb der vrsach willē/das er bey seines weybs schwester geschlaffen hat/welche er zůuorn zum weybe gehabt/vñ darnach die Gröbischen genom̃en/Des Montags darnach/das ist der 14. Octobris ist ain weyb die Serckschen genandt/auch verbrandt worden/der vrsach/das sie des Herrn Achacius von Veldthaym des Stiffts Halberstat Hauptmans weybe vergeben hate/ vnd ainem mañ zů Derneburg ain Krotten vnter die Schwöllen gegraben/daruon der man erlamet/vnd jm das vihe vmbkomen ist.

¶ Hie sihet man wañ der Teüffel an ainem orth einnistet/vñ begundt zů Regieren/wie wůst er mit seinem gifft vmb sich stichet/wie vil personen komen hie vmb/in wenig tagen/vnd soll vns solch grewlich exempel billich raytzen zur bůß/vnd zur forcht Gottes/auff das wir vns mit dem wort Gottes vnd gebette/wider den gemelten feynd schützen/vnd mag dise Historj den sichern gotlosen Epicurern vnnd Zaubrern/wol ain erinnerung sein/dieweyl sie sehen/das der Teüffel noch lebt/vnd das daß Hellische fewr noch nit erloschen ist/Der Almechtig Got wölle sie auch zur bůsse bringen/vnd vns alle inn/vnd bey seinem raynen wort erhalten/vnd mit seinem hayligen Gayst regieren/ auff das wir leben inn aller Gottseligkayt/Zucht vnd Erbarkayt/zů ehren seinem hayligen Namen/Durch vnsern Herren Jesum Christum/ AMEN.

¶ Getruckt zů Nürnberg bey Jörg Merckel/durch verleg Endres Zenckel Botten.

One of man's most ghastly mistakes: torture and witch-burning. Extract from a 1555 tract.

the infamous "Witch Hammer," a polemic whose title itself suggests the severity of the persecution. The "Hammer" is especially cynical in its description of the alleged sexual activities of the "devil's paramours" and coaches the torturers in the main points of their unblushing inquiries. For two hundred years the judges, Protestant and Catholic, mete out sentences for the practice of witchcraft. Often the charge is used merely as a pretext for disposing of undesirables. During the Counter-Reformation, for example, many a witch trial serves to mask the persecution of a Protestant. The total number of women who are accused of witchcraft is estimated at over a million. During the eight years of Adolph von Ehrenreich's tenure as bishop of Würzburg (1623–31), more than nine hundred "witches" are burned at the stake; and in Quedlinburg in 1589, one hundred thirty "witches" are executed in one day. In Austria, witch trials continue on into the nineteenth century.

Very slowly—and for the most part very timidly—men begin to speak out in defense of the victims of these witch-hunts. The first man to do so is Johann Wier, a doctor living in the lower Rhine area during the Reformation period. Wier attacks superstition and the prevailing obsession with the supernatural. His particular target is the witchcraft mania, but he is unable to give any direct help to the countless victims of those times. There are scattered reports of other courageous men who recognize the mania for what it is. But they cannot outshout the chorus of eminent scholars who brand the witches as heretics—any more than they can prevail against the superstitious notions of the uneducated and unreasoning masses. The jurists of the times ignore all objections to the trials; the matter is one that requires their special competence, and they will tolerate no meddling by outsiders.

In the seventeenth century too, voices are raised against the witch-trial tactics in particular and the witch-craze in general, but again to no avail. Several of these critics are worthy of note, however: Balthasar Bekker, a Protestant who is influenced by Descartes; and two Jesuits, Adam Tanner and Friedrich von Spee. All three agree that confessions extracted under torture are invalid—a nicety that goes unperceived by jurists until several centuries later.

Chiefly known to posterity as a baroque poet, Friedrich von Spee is a Jesuit priest who becomes attached to the bishopric in Würzburg. One of his responsibilities is the spiritual care of women who have been sentenced to death as witches. He learns of the torture inflicted upon them, and although he is unable to unshackle himself from his own belief in witches, he does see the inhumanity the women are made to suffer at the hands of the law; and in his *cautio criminalis* he attacks it. Justifiably concerned for his life, he publishes the indictment anonymously. *Cautio criminalis,* which comes straight from its author's heart, creates a considerable stir, but in the end it accomplishes nothing. Von Spee dies in Trier of an infection incurred while treating victims of the plague.

Christian Thomasius, a Saxon jurist, is the first to crack the sheer wall of legalized superstition. He chooses what is perhaps the only effective means of bringing his colleagues to their senses: ridicule. In 1701 he publishes *De crimine magiae,* which has the effect of making a laughingstock out of any jurist who persists in believing in witches. His tactics are successful. As no one likes to be made a fool of, there is an immediate decline in witch trials. Frederick the Great of Prussia writes aptly of Thomasius, "He so exposed the witch-judges to ridicule that from then on people were ashamed of such trials." By this time, in fact, Prussian law does not recognize the term "witch."

Thomasius is also able to refute the theological arguments: he proves that the belief in witches is not of biblical but pagan origin. It is a sad fact that he is sharply opposed at this point by a great many Protestant theologians. But all counterattacks are short-lived. Thomasius has already demolished them with biting sarcasm and unanswerable logic. The last witch trial in Prussia takes place in 1728, the year of his death.

To be sure, Thomasius is not at heart a Christian, nor are his motives essentially Christian. But his name should not be missing from any list of the great benefactors of mankind. He helped rid the world of a vicious evil, and the fact that in so doing he incurred the enmity of many theologians is a judgment on the theologians, not on him.

6. To the Ends of the Earth

Francke's "Sizable Sum"

August Hermann Francke, a pietist, is not popular among his fellow pastors. In Erfurt they hound him with threats and drive him out of town. He takes a pastorate in Glaucha, on the outskirts of Halle, and begins his new duties with great vigor even though the pastors of Halle also try to arrange his downfall. Glaucha is the kind of ground on which only a fully committed Christian can stand. Francke quickly sees that the Sunday sermon is going to be only a small part of his ministry; there are other challenges to be faced. Of the two hundred houses in Glaucha, thirty-seven are taverns. Here the solid citizens of Halle while away their evenings with alcohol and gambling, recuperating from the virtuous lives they lead. Is it any wonder that such an environment breeds vice—from begging to all sorts of worse evils? Unquestionably it is the children who suffer most, particularly the orphans, who must grow up in more than dubious surroundings without proper education or home training.

Francke does what he can. Every Thursday he distributes bread and soup to the poor. As man does not live by bread alone, Francke also invites the beggars into his house and gives them the word of God. His is a grim fight against appalling ignorance and moral degradation and wickedness. He experiments, trying first this idea and then that. He risks money on his ventures, begins to make financial appeals to the prosperous, and is soon forced to give it all up again.

Teacher, assistant, and pupils. A woodcut dating from 1500.

At the beginning of 1695 a new idea strikes him. He puts a collection box in his living room. What he finds in it he uses to meet the needs in the community as best he can. But he doesn't find a great deal. During the first three months the box yields no more than a trickle. Then one day a "certain person" puts four talers and sixteen pennies (the equivalent of almost fifty dollars) into the box. An unheard-of event! Francke writes, "As I took the money in my hands, I said rejoicing in faith, 'this is a sizable sum; it ought to be used for something worthwhile. I know what I'll do with it. I'll start a school for the poor!' "

This is how Francke's work in Halle gets its start: the beginnings are small and humble indeed. Francke buys a few books, gives them to underprivileged children, and hires a student to tutor them. The initial plan is to have two hours of classes a day, but little comes of it, for most of the books rapidly disappear.

Francke takes the rest of his capital and buys more books—which are kept in the schoolroom and given to the children only during class. This method works, and the little school begins to grow. Soon there are more than fifty boys and girls attending.

Francke sees how little his school can do for parentless children who have to return to their grubby milieu as soon as class is over, and so he decides to assume full charge of his orphans. His pedagogical innovations—which include a balanced and coordinated program of instruction, prayer, and work—put him far ahead of his time. The number of his charges grows, and soon Francke needs a whole house, an orphan home. So he begins to build. Where he manages to get all the money he needs is an insoluble mystery to many people. He must have hidden resources, they say; rumor has it that piles of gold are being shipped to him from somewhere. The truth is that Francke possesses virtually nothing. His work is the work of a man who relies entirely upon God's providence. Every time he seems to be in real trouble, donations arrive from unexpected quarters. Whenever the increasing attacks from outside grow particularly venomous Francke is also likely to find a new helper and loyal friend.

From its humble beginnings the work grows to surprising proportions. The first house is followed by others; the day comes when Francke enrolls his two-thousandth ward. A doctor has to be hired to examine the children, and the doctor needs medical supplies; so Francke sets up his own pharmacy, which grows into a regular pharmaceutical plant. The medicines prepared there are sold at high prices, and once more he incurs the ire of his critics. But he remains faithful to his principles: charge only the customers who can afford to pay; the needy are served free.

A printing press and eventually a regular publishing house are added to the growing facilities. Bibles, New Testaments, pietistic books, pamphlets, and hymnals are printed and shipped in great numbers; outside contract work keeps the presses from standing idle and assures a steady flow of income.

These, then, are the dividends accruing from that "sizable sum": a whole city with its own unique character, a city like none before it. It is possible that the Basileiad outside the gates of Caesarea in Cappadocia was one of the models from which Francke worked; but the two cannot really be compared. The radically new element in Francke's case was that one man built a whole city, without aid, without capital, relying solely on God's help. There is no foundation backing him, no trust fund; and yet Glaucha is neither an experimental model nor a flash in the pan; it is an enduring achievement. Seen in true perspective, it could not be anything else, for its foundation is firm: Francke built on faith alone.

Enemies continue to badger him until the end of his life. When he begins work on his first building with no funds in sight, the derisive comment is that he is building a wall from which to hang himself. Others charge that he is shamelessly exploiting the children in his orphanage by using them as workhorses. These are malicious allegations. Later, the same charges will be leveled at Pestalozzi. We may disagree today with many of Francke's educational methods, but from the perspective of his times he is a trailblazer. As far as he is concerned, children are created by God; they are not objects for exploitation by man.

Francke's pietism also provokes a lifelong antagonism on the part of orthodox Lutherans, to whom he is a constant gadfly. Many of the recriminations against him are justified, but they cannot gainsay the significance of a lifework that springs exclusively from faith, that faith which

> does not ask whether good works are to be done but before the question is asked, it has already done them, and is constantly doing them.

His own good works have an impact that reaches far beyond the walls of his city. The numerous divinity students at Halle carry the spirit of Glaucha back to their own parishes; and many of the "graduates" of the orphanage, following the example of their teacher, found similar works in other places. Glaucha also exerts an influence upon a Saxon count named Zinzendorf.

Gradually, then, an active ministry of caring develops in Protestant Germany, where not long before the prospects for such ministry seemed bleak. Orphanages are founded in dozens of cities, all of them modeled on the Halle prototype and run according to Francke's principles.

In Bunzlau (Boleslawiec), Silesia, an institution is founded whose dimensions approach those of the Halle complex. Near Weissenfels an ordinary farmer establishes an orphanage. At Wernigerode Countess Christine champions the cause of the poor, in her will explicitly commending them to the care of her heirs. Under Henry (Reuss) the XXIV, the city of Bad Köstritz becomes a refuge for the oppressed. In many places, prison conditions are being improved as well; sunlight is permitted to penetrate to the prisoners' cells, and heating stoves are installed during the winter—amenities that are previously unknown.

A revitalizing stream of Christian love begins to flow from Glaucha through the lands still recovering from the devastation of the Thirty Years' War. Unfortunately, the results of the new impulses are neither enduring nor widespread. Perhaps the country has simply been too impoverished. The still irreconcilable class distinctions and class polarities also tend to inhibit any systematic approach to the works of love. It is small wonder, then, that many of these spontaneously initiated works soon die out. Only Francke's institution stands the test of time. The work of this great man endures long after his death and into our own century.

The Beginnings of Ecumenical World Service

Francke's influence is extensive in space as well as in time. It reaches beyond Germany's borders halfway around the world and fosters an ecumenical outlook that will be a major force, several centuries later, in our own day.

In 1706 Frederick IV of Denmark appeals for missionaries for South India. Two men from Halle named Ziegenbalg and Plütschau immediately respond and are sent out. After an arduous journey they land in Tranquebar and, by dint of selfless labor, establish a full-fledged mission. This mission is directed by Francke, in close consultation with the king and a group of English backers. German missionary-doctors, among them Kaspar Gottlieb Schlegelmilch, bring medical supplies to combat the host of diseases prevalent in the region, particularly among the people living in abject poverty. Love-gifts and donations from the countries of Europe are collected in Halle and sent to India in order to

Pope Gregory I, circa 600, dividing his robe. A twelfth-century representation.

G. S. Wegener

Clothing the naked is one of the "seven works of physical mercy" practiced in all ages. Above: St. Martin and the beggar. From a fourteenth-century illuminated manuscript.

Bildarchiv Foto Marburg

Abbé Pierre, the organizer of a relief effort in Paris to assist the homeless, makes frequent visits to his shelters in order to keep in direct personal touch with the needy being served there.

DPA

A valuable cargo bound for America: Africans on a slave-ship. From a contemporary engraving.

Sanssouci-Verlag, Zurich

A sheik of our own times—and his sl

Erwin Rei

Following the example of St. Martin, Francis of Assisi gives his coat away to a poor man. This Giotto work (1297) is in the Church of San Francesco in Assisi.

During the Franco-Prussian War of 1870–71, the Montrouge Church in Paris is turned into an emergency first aid center.

International Committee of the Red Cross, Geneva

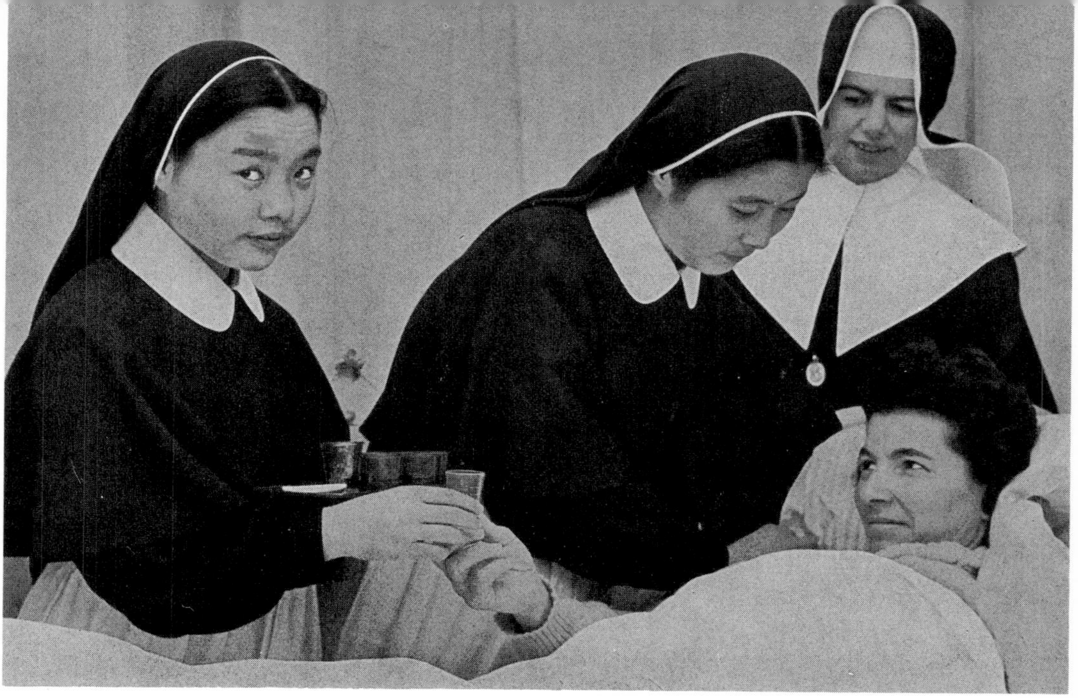

With the barriers of race and barbed wire removed, young Korean women take their nurses' training in the West before returning home to work in their chosen profession.

DPA

Pestalozzi taking leave of his orphans. Engraving by Th. v. Oer.
Historisches Bildarchiv Handke, Bad Berneck

The poor of the world today challenge us to follow the example of St. Elizabeth. Milk for children in Honduras.
Food and Agriculture Organization of the United Nations

Rice for the hungry in Hong Kong.
Food and Agriculture Organization of the United Nations

St. Elizabeth gives her money to the poor. Detail from the shrine of St. Elizabeth in Marburg.

Bildarchiv Foto Marburg

Healing the sick and burying the dead—ministries for which men of all ages and all social classes have volunteered. Above, "Healing of the Leper," from a twelfth-century Salzburg lectionary.

Bildarchiv Foto Marburg

Below, "Mass Burial" during the plague year of 1349, from a fourteenth-century French miniature.

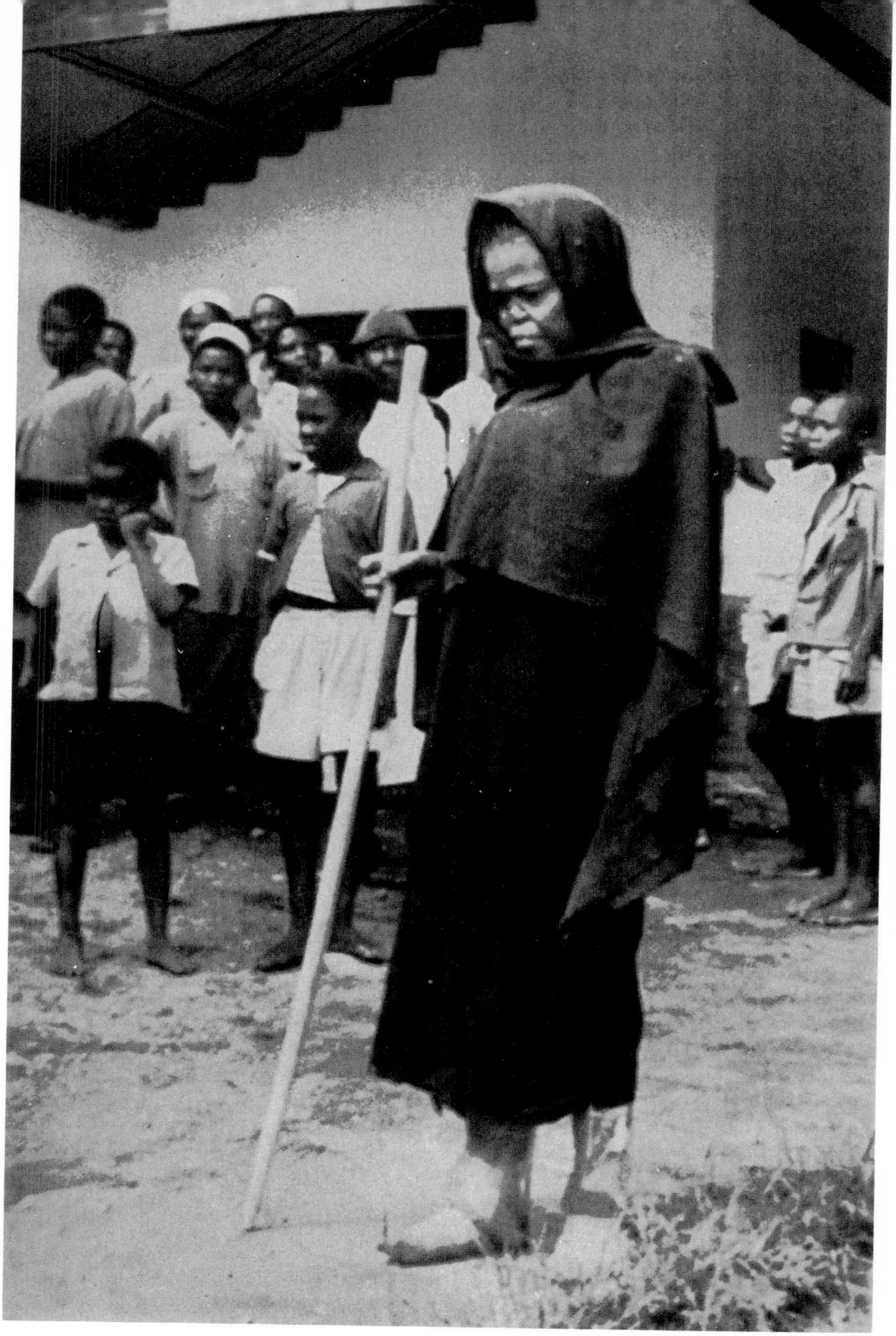

1960: Inhabitants of a leper colony in Tanganyika waiting to be treated at the polyclinic.

Ursula Namgalies

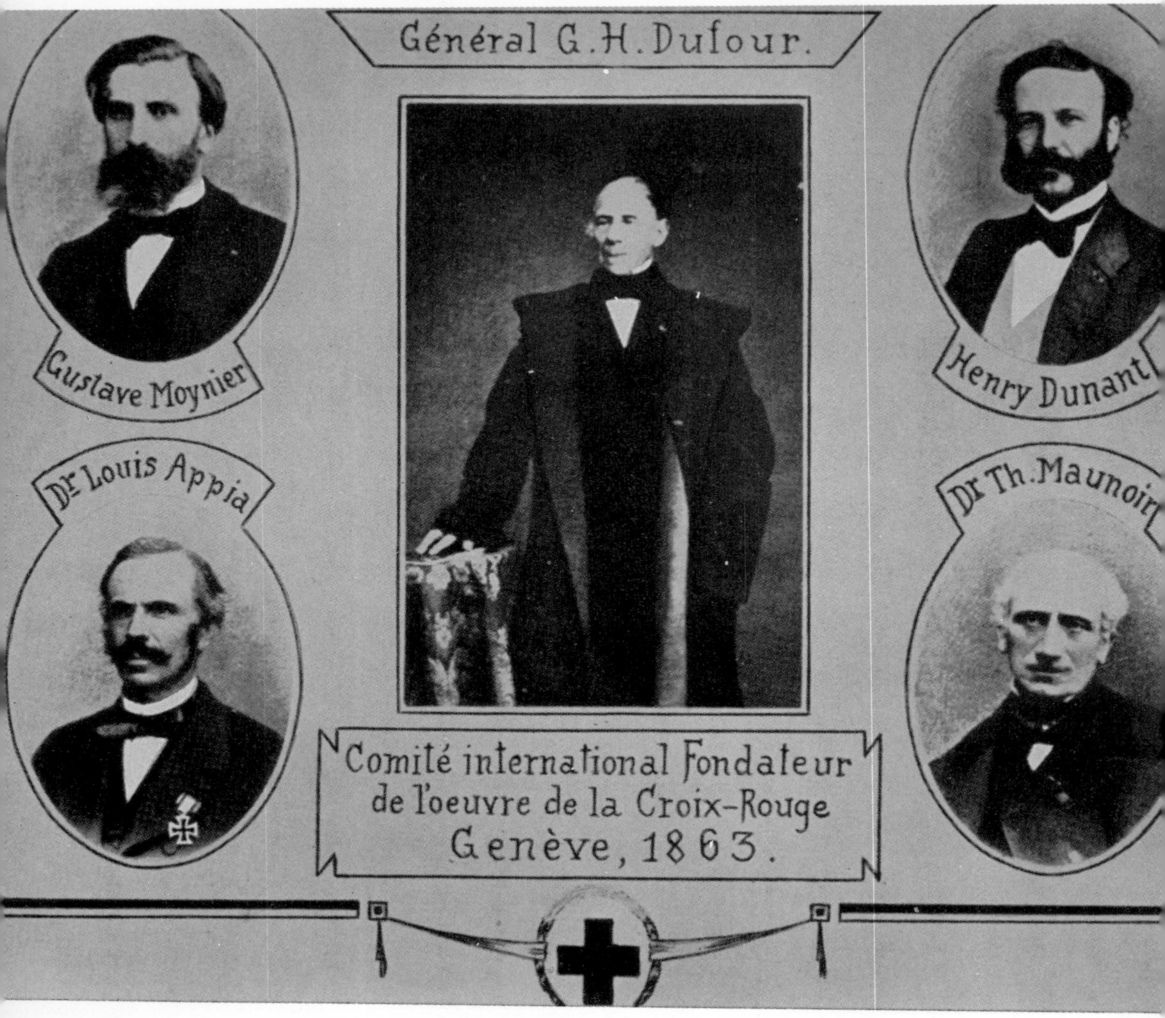

The Red Cross. In 1863 this Committee of Five laid the groundwork for the signing of the Geneva Convention.

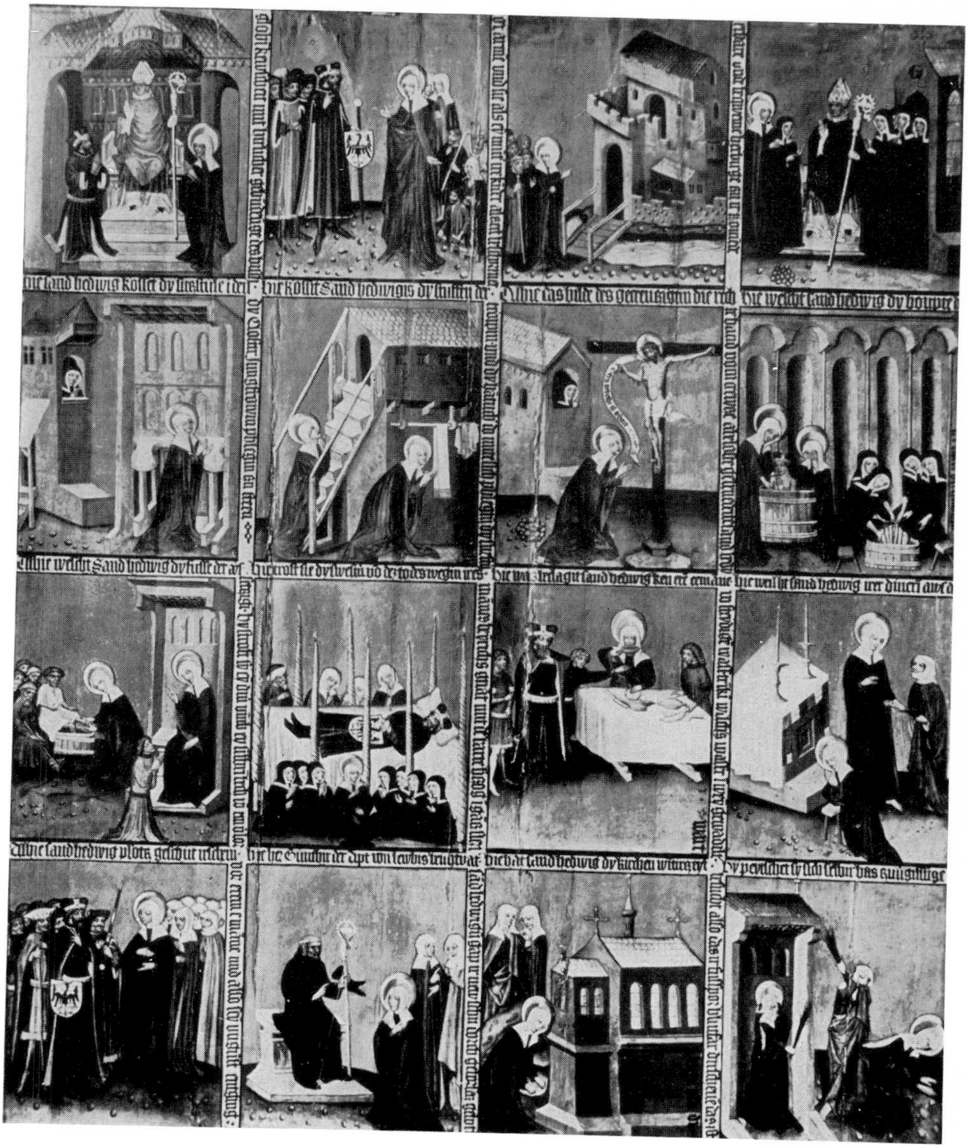

The "Hedwig panel"—scenes from the life of St. Hedwig, showing her ministry to the needy of her land. By an anonymous Silesian artist.

Historisches Bildarchiv Handke, Bad Berneck

POSTE LIRE 100 VATICANE
POSTE LIRE 15 VATICANE
DEUTSCHE DEMOKRATISCHE REPUBLIK
HELFER DER MENSCHHEIT
DEUTSCHE BUNDESPOST
20 DEUTSCHE
BUNDESPOST
HELFER DER MENSCHHEIT
DEUTSCHE BUNDESPOST
HELFER DER MENSCHHEIT
DEUTSCHE BUNDESPOST
DEUTSCHE BUNDESPOST
HELFER DER MENSCHHEIT
DEMOKRATISCHE
DEUTSCHE
REPUBLIK
DEUTSCHE BUNDESPOST
HELFER DER MENSCHHEIT
RHEINLAND-PFALZ
10 DEUTSCHE
BUNDESPOST
HELFER DER MENSCHHEIT
DEUTSCHE BUNDESPOST
HELFER DER MENSCHHEIT
DEUTSCHE BUNDESPOST
10 DEUTSCHE
BUNDESPOST
DEUTSCHE BUNDESPOST
HELFER DER MENSCHHEIT
GROSSDEUTSCHES REICH
Deutsches Reich
DEUTSCHE BUNDESPOST
UNITED STATES POSTAGE
DEUTSCHE DEMOKRATISCHE REPUBLIK
DEUTSCHE BUNDESPOST
KRIEGSGRÄBERFÜRSORGE
DEUTSCHE BUNDESPOST
ZEHN JAHRE VERTREIBUNG 1945 1955
DEUTSCHE BUNDESPOST
BUNDESPOST
DEUTSCHE
WOHLFAHRTS
MARKE
VOLKSDIENST
NEDERLAND
SAHARA ESPAÑOL
CORREOS
REPUBLIK ÖSTERREICH
BELGIQUE BELGIË
BELGIQUE BELGIË
BELGIQUE BELGIË
DEUTSCHE BUNDESPOST BERLIN
UNITED STATES POSTAGE
BELGIQUE
Kampf dem Krebs
Lutte contre le cancer
Lotta contro il cancro
1910-1960
HELVETIA 10
DEUTSCHE BUNDESPOST
KUNA
HRVATSKA
MAGYAR KIR POSTA
MAGYAR KIR POSTA
JUGOSLAVIJA
SUOMI
REPUBLIK
INDONESIA

David Zeisberger with his Delaware Indians. From an engraving by J. Sertain.

The story of mercy in postage stamps. The montage here is a selection of stamps from many nations presenting by picture or theme one chapter of the story. (Issuing countries in parentheses.)

Row 1: *St. Cyprian of Carthage, St. Laurence (Vatican); Hedwig of Silesia, Bishop Otto of Bamberg, J. A. Comenius, St. Vincent de Paul, J. F. Oberlin (Germany).*
Row 2: *Elizabeth Fry, Theodor Fliedner, Amalie Sieveking, Friedrich Fröbel, Adolf Kolping, Archbishop W. E. von Ketteler, Lorenz Werthmann (Germany).*
Row 3: *Dr. Carl Sonnenschein (Catholic pastor and leader in social work in Berlin from 1918 to 1929), F. W. Raiffeisen, Hermann Schulze-Delitzsch, Ignaz Semmelweis, Dr. Samuel Hahnemann (homeopathy), Robert Koch, Emil von Behring (Germany).*
Row 4: *Von Behring and Paul Ehrlich (Germany); Abraham Lincoln, the great emancipator (USA); Ernst Abbe; prisoner of war commemorative; War Graves Commission, refugee commemorative (Germany).*
Row 5: *Welfare stamps (Germany, Holland, Spain) sold at regular postal rates plus a surcharge which goes to welfare organizations and relief agencies.*
Row 6: *World Refugee Year, 1959–60 (Germany, Austria, Belgium); relief for victims of flood-damage in Berlin (Germany).*
Row 7: *Polio drive (USA); Red Cross blood-donor drive (Belgium); TB drive (Spain); cancer drive (Switzerland); Red Cross stamps (Germany, Slovakia).*
Row 8: *Red Cross stamps (Hungary, Yugoslavia, Finland, Indonesia).*

William Penn wants peace and friendship with the Indians. In the early 1680s he buys the land for his colony from the Indians, even though according to English law he is already the owner.

Historiches Bildarchiv Handke, Bad Berneck

alleviate the social and economic ills and to reduce the level of famine. Clothes for Indian children are made at the Weimar court. Danish and English families pay the cost of feeding Indian children attending mission schools.

In 1709, when Sweden is defeated by Russia in the Battle of Poltava, and thirty thousand men, women, and children end up in Siberian prison camps, Halle launches a large-scale relief campaign. Francke's writings had sparked a revival among the prisoners, which in turn had inspired a number of lonely and homesick Swedes to found, in Tobrusk, a school patterned on the Halle prototype and to ask Francke for advice and aid. The indefatigable Francke sets about raising money and gifts; and by working through his friends in government in Moscow he is able to see to it that the prisoners get their mail from home on a regular basis.

Prison work and prisoners' mail in the eighteenth century! Not only that, but care of emigrants as well. In 1709, fifteen thousand Germans from the Palatinate are suddenly hit by an attack of *wanderlust*. Almost in a panic they leave their homeland and stream across Holland to England. The precipitous arrival of fifteen thousand immigrants creates such a crisis that Queen Anne appeals to her subjects for help; they collect the equivalent of 55,000 talers (around 550,000 dollars). Francke, who is regularly in touch with the English, hears of this and starts a similar campaign in Germany. German Protestants living in London enlist in the cause. As a result of the interaction that develops, underprivileged London schoolboys find themselves sitting in Francke's classrooms in Halle while university students in England study his teaching methods.

Meanwhile there comes an appeal from another quarter. A group of religious exiles from Salzburg have been living temporarily on the generosity of fellow Germans who had spontaneously sent in donations from all over the country. But this source of help dries up all too soon, and so Francke and his associates move to assist them. The assistance is maintained long after the Salzburgers have resettled in East Prussia. Francke gets support for this venture both from England and from Russia.

Even the refugees who emigrate to America are not forgotten. Francke's friend Samuel Urlsperger intercedes for them, relays

As the Protestants were driven out of Salzburg, Jews are driven out of Vienna in 1670. A contemporary engraving.

Württemberg Landesbibliothek, Stuttgart

numerous gifts to them, and publishes a newspaper that becomes a link between them and their homeland.

In addition, there is a steady stream of refugees from Bohemia and Moravia, where many Protestants are forced to leave their homes. In Grosshennersdorf, Saxony, a regular reception center is set up as a haven for the exiles. Once again it is Francke who raises the money for this relief project; and, like all his other works, this one is carried on after his death in 1727. Halle, the work that began so modestly, has come to have a world outreach.

Count Zinzendorf and His "Brethren"

Count Nicolaus von Zinzendorf is brought up under Francke's tutelage in Halle. Here his special interest in a fellowship centered on the word of God is already evident. Zinzendorf and a few friends found the "Order of the Mustard Seed." He remains loyal all his life to the watchwords of the order: tolerance, loving one's neighbor, and keeping the faith.

As a law student in Wittenberg, Zinzendorf jumps into the middle of the intercollegiate feud between the sister universities of Wittenberg and Halle. He tries to reconcile the antagonists but, considered too impetuous by his own fellow students, is sent on a long trip to Paris and Holland to get him out of the way and keep him from doing mischief to the cause. During this trip he becomes convinced that the Christian must discern the best in all churches and avoid factionalism of every kind. He begins to realize that every man has weaknesses and shortcomings. He is not free of them himself, as we learn from many of his contemporaries.

Who knows whether Zinzendorf would ever have become the Zinzendorf we know, the man of faith and tolerance, the man who loved his neighbor, if he had not been given the right associates? He might have been caught forever in a vain mystical fervor. The fact is that he was given the right associates, and that a different future awaited him.

After finishing his studies at the university, Zinzendorf becomes a Councilor in Dresden. He also acquires an estate in Lusatia on the slopes of a hill or mountain that came to be called the Hutberg. It is the time of the Bohemian and Moravian expulsion. One day a plain-appearing man, a carpenter named Christian David, calls on Zinzendorf. An advance scout of the exiles, he has come to ask whether they might settle at the foot of the mountain. The count consents and gives no further thought to the matter.

The settlers are far from idle. They quickly fell trees on the mountain slope, grade the land, fit logs together, and before winter arrives they and their families are able to move into a number of trim little cabins.

On December 22, 1722, Zinzendorf chances to pass by the new settlement, and he is frankly astonished at what the men have accomplished in so short a time. He stops at one of the houses and finds there people who are brave and honorable, devout and strong in faith. As Zinzendorf chats with them, others come in and join the circle: simple folk, but all of the same character. Together they pray: the count and the refugee-farmers and craftsmen, and in prayer they find each other. Zinzendorf takes the settlement under his sponsorship and commits himself and the settlers to the watchful care of the Lord. Thus is born *Herrnhut,* the Lord's Watch.

This is not the place to discuss the free church aspects of the Moravian Brethren. Beyond all the differences and difficulties (due partly to the active hostility of the state church) a common Christian mission provides the basis for fellowship and unity. From the beginning the count has been filled with a concern for outreach, and soon the opportunity comes to lay on the hearts of his Moravian brethren a cause that will carry the seeds of Herrnhut to all the world.

The occasion does not seem epochal. While visiting at the court of the king of Denmark, Zinzendorf gets to know a baptized Negro servant named Anthony. Anthony tells him about the conditions on the island of St. Thomas in the West Indies. What Zinzendorf finds out about the life of the Negroes who have been transported there is so hair-raising that he is not able to keep silent. He takes Anthony with him to Herrnhut, and Anthony addresses the community. The people become thoroughly aroused. The call of God, whose will is the deliverance of the afflicted, is unmistakable. As a result, two members of the community, Leonard Dober and David Nitschmann, volunteer to sail to the remote island and carry the gospel to the slaves there. They are well aware of what they are undertaking. Preaching alone will not help. There must be fellowship in suffering. The two propose, therefore, to live as slaves among slaves. Thus begins the "Herrnhuter" Mission and with it a new chapter in the history of Christian love.

Eskimos and Indians

Christian David, the carpenter, also leaves Herrnhut. He travels to Holland, Livonia (now part of the USSR), Greenland, and the North American colony of Pennsylvania. When he is not preaching the gospel he is building houses. In Holland a church is established at Heerendyk; in Livonia the Brinkenhof settlement is born. David builds homes for the Eskimos in Greenland and for Indians in North America. Herrnhut missionaries are resolved to go to the world's forgotten tribes, where the gospel has not yet been preached. Zinzendorf got his global perspective from Francke; and like Francke, he also maintains close ties with the Danish court, which is very open to his work.

The king of Denmark also sponsors a mission to the Eskimos under Hans Egede, a Norwegian pastor who works on the Lofoten Islands. His wife Gertrud at first opposes the adventurous plan because of the children, but finally she agrees, and in 1721 they begin their work together in Greenland. Very much alone with his burden for the Eskimos, Egede is following the call he received through the reports of his brother-in-law, who works as a whaler in the northern seas. Ten years later, when a new king recalls all Europeans from Greenland on the grounds that the mission has succeeded poorly, Egede and his family stay on. He cannot abandon the work and the people. However, he does send six young Eskimos to Copenhagen along with the returnees; they are to be trained as evangelists.

The good intentions miscarry dreadfully; five of the boys die in the alien environment and the sixth returns to Greenland with smallpox, which spreads rapidly. Nothing can check the epidemic. Those who are afflicted by it try to save themselves by fleeing, and as a result they carry the disease from settlement to settlement. The final toll is three thousand Eskimos. Egede is torn by doubt: should he persevere or give up? He gets his answer at the deathbeds of those entrusted to his care: he must stay. And so he stays, exhausting his strength in caring for the sick and dying. The task seems almost superhuman—his own wife dies of the strain—but Egede does not leave his post. His example of Christian love does more to open the hearts of the Eskimos to the gospel than any sermon.

When the epidemic subsides and a group of Herrnhuter brothers arrive as reinforcements, Egede is able to put the work into the hands of his son, who has grown up among the Eskimos, knows them better than his father, and understands how to reach their hearts. But for twenty more years Hans Egede keeps on working for the Eskimos—now in Copenhagen as a teacher in a Greenland training program. He teaches the Eskimo language to other missionaries who will go out to carry on the work.

Dark shadows fall across North America during the decades of conquest. Here Indians are sent into battle against Indians: the Algonquins (and French) on one side; the Iroquois on the other.

Like Egede among the Eskimos, the Herrnhuter missionary David Zeisberger works with the Indians of North America. Seldom has a Christian seen such extremes of guilt and grace, hate and love, so juxtaposed as Zeisberger did.

Zeisberger comes to America with his parents as a young boy, early enough to see the founding of the Moravian settlement at Bethlehem, Pennsylvania. He quickly picks up the language of the Indians around him and becomes familiar with their customs and folkways. He lives among them as one of them, and the Iroquois and Delaware tribes make him a full-fledged brother. He is given the Indian name of "Ganousseracherie."

Zeisberger is a dedicated Christian. He has only one goal: to lead his Indian brothers to the truth of the gospel and to help them in any way he can. He belongs to them as no other white man ever has; he smokes the peace pipe with them and bears arms with them, he shares their hardships, their hunger, and their privations, knowing that these tribes are destined to be wiped out by the white man. For that very reason he sticks with them and suffers what they suffer.

The first beachhead of the Herrnhuter Indian mission is established at Gnadenhutten on the banks of the Mahoning. Here the Indians live in an atmosphere of real Christian community. Their days are spent in hunting and working the fields. They are taught to live for one another, to share with one another, to care for their sick, and to make regular provision for the future and for any emergencies it might bring.

In 1755 war breaks out between England and France. The mission tries to stay neutral, and for its pains it is accused by both sides of unfriendly behavior. The Indian Christians are similarly regarded, and in November Gnadenhutten is burned down. The great exodus now begins. On orders from the governor, the Indians lay down their arms and pack themselves into grossly inadequate barrack-quarters in Philadelphia. A year later they are allowed to resettle, but their number has been reduced to a pitiful eighty-three. This remnant finds no rest. Like hunted animals they scurry from place to place, Zeisberger and a few other missionaries with them. They build and rebuild new homes for themselves, hoping to be left in peace. In the space of four decades they settle in seventeen different places, rarely longer than one or two years, driven off each time by the ill will of some chief, the greed of the whites for land, or hate and misunderstanding. But their gospel is more important to them than life and liberty; they know that on this earth they have no continuing city. As pilgrims their real home is still ahead of them.

At the end of the 1770s Zeisberger is finally able to organize his flock into four communities: well-laid-out villages between the Ohio and Lake Erie. Broad stretches of land are plowed, large herds of cattle roam the fertile pasturelands. Zeisberger is also able to keep his charges away from the Indians' greatest temptation—alcohol—and thus order, cleanliness, and peace prevail in his camps.

In a felicitous move Zeisberger makes the Indians responsible for governing themselves. He is on hand as elder statesman whenever his counsel and guidance is needed, but the deciding voice in all matters is not his but that of the Indian Council. Things are now going so well, in fact, that Zeisberger is just beginning to envision a cloudless future when his dreams are shattered by the American Revolution. The Indian Christians want to stay out of all fighting, but a Huron chieftain in the pay of Christian England breaks into the settlements, burns down the houses, destroys the harvest, and drives the people off.

Once more they are homeless; once more the quest begins for bread and grain, pastureland and homesites—this time in the middle of a war. Once a band of Zeisberger's Delawares who are scouting around for provisions run into some American soldiers. The Indians are ordered to disarm. Suspecting nothing, they hand the white men what weapons they are carrying; and once they are defenseless the soldiers massacre them. Those who are not shot or stabbed are bludgeoned to death. And these Americans all call themselves Christians.

Not until eleven years after this enormity do the few remaining Indians, Zeisberger still at their head, find a new home on the shores of Lake Erie. In his journal Zeisberger writes of those nomadic years: "Where are we to find refuge? Oh for just a patch of earth, whither I could flee with my Indians; but the world is not big enough. We can hope for no protection from the whites, though they call themselves Christians; and we have no friends left among the heathen." These words might be written in many parts of the world today.

At the end of the war the American government gives the Moravian mission 12,000 acres of land in Ohio for its Indian converts. But not until fifteen years later is the mission able to move there. Then, on the site of once-thriving Indian villages that have become little more than overgrown ruins of walls, another settlement is built to plans that Zeisberger draws up. This settlement, his thirteenth and last, he calls Goshen. Here the Indians would be able to live out their days in peace. But even Zeisberger cannot arrest their decline as a people.

At the age of eighty-seven Zeisberger, now blind and deaf, preaches his last sermon to his red brothers. He has to summon them to repentance, for they have now yielded, after all, to the

The Country wee now call Virginia beginneth at Cape Henry distant
from Roanoack 60 miles, where was Sr. Walter Raleigh's plantation:
and because the people differ very little from them of Powhatan in any
thing, I have inserted those figures in this place because of the conveniency.
daughter Pokahontas beggs his life
and how he subiected 39 of their kings. reade ÿ history.

In the fierce struggle between the white man and the red man, mercy is not infrequently shown by the Indians. This 1624 engraving shows Pocahontas, the Indian princess, whom tradition credits with saving the life of John Smith.

lure of alcohol. He says to them: "A youth was Ganousseracherie when he became a friend of the red man. Sixty summers have since passed, and his hair is grown white. Gladly he recalls the days when he walked with his red brothers across the prairie and shared their joy and sorrow. Now that he is old, he is pained. May Goshen become again a place where the Indian shuns the firewater which, together with the white man's greed for land, has caused his undoing." Zeisberger dies in 1808. For a generation thereafter, Goshen remains a haven for the Christian Indians; then the community dies out.

Meanwhile, the oppression of another race has begun. Once more it is those who call themselves Christians who sin against their brothers before God, human beings of a different color. And once more there are Christians who move to redress the wrong-doing of the white man. But before we follow the path of reconciliation taken in America by the white man John Woolman, we must pause for a look at England, where a Christian community is formed whose members commit themselves to live, as Count Zinzendorf and the Herrnhuter Brethren tried to do, in tolerance and Christian love toward their neighbors.

George Fox and the Quakers

This time God's man is not a count but a simple shoemaker. George Fox is born in England in 1624, the son of a weaver. In early youth he is apprenticed to a shoemaker. As a result of a revelation he experiences one day, the young Fox is led to a search for spirituality that takes him outside the established church. This in turn leads to a fight for freedom of belief and of conscience; for in seventeenth-century England the status of these freedoms is precarious: the Puritans, leaving their homeland over precisely this issue, sailed for America and religious liberty not very long before.

Fox begins to travel and to preach, touring England and the Continent and finally landing in North America. An evangelist he is, but not a religious ecstatic. His thinking is clear and temperate, his words trenchant and persuasive. Before long he has a group of followers, and the group acquires the odd nickname of "quakers," reputedly because of Fox's admonition to a judge to tremble at the word of the Lord—or because of the group's reputation for trembling at their religious meetings. In time, what originated as a mocking epithet becomes an elegant way of referring to the Society of Friends, as they call themselves.

The Quakers' first and foremost concern is to aid the poor and the oppressed. Undeterred by prison sentences of several years, Fox and his followers continue to speak out for freedom of religion and conscience. They never forcibly resist any punitive action against them, and they suffer banishment, maltreatment, whipping and other cruel punishments, prison, even hanging and beheading. Not even their children are safe from these latter-day inquisitors.

At his estate at Swarthmore in the English Lake District, Fox draws up a simple set of bylaws for the Society. The most important provision is the assistance to be rendered the poor, the sick, and the imprisoned. Before his death in 1691, Fox lives to see the institution (by William III) of the Toleration Act of 1689, which restores to the English people their former rights and grants a large measure of freedom to religious dissenters.

At Fox's side during these years of active crusading and passive resistance is his wife Margaret, who not only shares the heavy load of his many responsibilities but also launches projects of her own. She mobilizes the women of the Society and also revolutionizes their status in the church: instead of being spiritually subordinate to the man, the Quaker woman stands on equal terms with him. Women's circles are started and a large fund for a variety of benevolent programs is established. The field of opportunity for such programs is great, and it begins right at home; not only are there the persecuted and imprisoned Friends to look after, but also a large number of widows and orphans, whose husbands and fathers have sacrificed their lives for the faith. The sacrificial spirit of the Quakers is illustrated by a written petition in which 164 Quakers volunteer to go to prison in order that other prisoners may regain their freedom. Their spirit is reminiscent of the early Christians.

It is astonishing to note how far ahead of their time the Friends are in their social action programs. In 1601 Queen Elizabeth instituted the Poor Laws. Welfare funds were to be raised by the parishes by means of local levies. There being no overall government supervision, the system broke down wherever the local parish was unwilling or unable to raise the money. The Quakers learn from such past mistakes. They take the Puritan principles of Christian conduct and apply them to their social welfare activities, maintaining throughout their levelheadedness and prudence.

They begin by distributing food to the poor after their service or "meeting," thus taking a leaf from Scripture. This custom evolves into a welfare program which grows larger from year to year and which, because it is well organized and so designed as to deal with existing conditions, becomes genuinely effective. The medieval practice of almsgiving is frowned on (the Quakers believe that it would teach the recipients the wrong lesson), nor are any debts assumed. But the Friends do include in their assistance program the payment of rents, heating bills, doctors' bills, and the costs of medicine. More important, however, is the effort to help the poor to get a new start in life. Thus we read of scholarships, loans, and the founding of new businesses. The Friends become the most active spokesmen for fire insurance when emergency relief work following the Great Fire of London in 1666 takes a heavy toll of their resources.

The domestic concern of the Friends is shown by their dowry provisions; youth education and vocational training attest their progressive thinking. They see education as the best means of doing something about backward social conditions. Here is a problem the whole world faces today in the developing nations; the Friends saw it plainly three hundred years ago, displaying a grasp of its ramifications that has yet to be duplicated today.

It goes without saying that people who are jailed as regularly as were the seventeenth-century Friends will be particularly open to the needs of prisoners. Fox and the Friends work steadfastly for the improvement of the wretched prison conditions of the day. It is no happenstance that, more than a century later, the champion of prison reform turns out to be a Quaker woman: Elizabeth Fry.

In 1662 the Friends begin acting as "middlemen" in finding and providing jobs. At the Meetinghouse they give out flax for spinning or material for netmaking, collect the finished work, pay well for it, and then pass it on to the mills and fisheries. They try especially hard to find good jobs for maids—who, incidentally, can now get health insurance and pension provisions.

Also noteworthy in this connection is the work of the economist John Bellers, a Quaker who lives during this same period and whom Karl Marx later cites several times in his writings. Bellers wants to bring jobs and the jobless together, but not by way of the workhouse, the penitentiary, or the work farm. He has in mind a "College of Industry," a kind of work-study college on a cooperative basis. In accordance with the theory of surplus value, the work of two-thirds of the participants would produce enough to provide for the subsistence of the entire group, so that the overproduction of the other third would finance the operation of the college and leave enough over to start a pension fund. The college would include all the essential occupations. While the plan unfortunately failed to materialize for lack of sufficient backing, its intellectual impact was strong, particularly upon the English social reformer Robert Owen.

But the outstanding social achievement of the early Quakers is unquestionably the American colony of Pennsylvania—"Penn's woods"—with its consistent application of the idea of state tolerance. Penn's legacy on his father's side includes a large claim against the crown. Considering it unlikely that it will be redeemed in cash, Penn successfully petitions for payment in the form of a land grant in America. Although he is now the legal owner so far as England is concerned, Penn buys the land again from the Indians rather than simply taking it away from them. He and the Indians conclude a number of treaties, the most famous of which was described by Voltaire as "the only treaty not sworn to and never broken." A court of arbitration, made up of an equal number of whites and Indians, is appointed to settle any disputes in the new colony. Pennsylvania is almost as large as England itself, yet there are no major disorders for seventy years, even though more than ten of the Indian tribes living in it are known for their savagery. Liquor is banned and stays banned. There are no trade monopolies. Penn goes so far as to learn the language and customs of the Indians, living among them as Zeisberger was to do later. The capital city is given a name meaning "brotherly love," Philadelphia. For the first time a state constitution is established on the principles of liberty, equality, and fraternity. Its message is: freedom without obedience is anarchy; obedience without freedom is slavery.

Initially the state of Pennsylvania refuses to fortify its borders and, in fact, renounces all use of force. It also grants full religious tolerance to its citizens, and it recognizes no distinctions of race. This and much else provides a foundation for the future Constitution of the United States, which is drafted in 1787.

The Christian settlers of Pennsylvania not only treat the Indians with humanity and brotherly love; they also treat Negro slaves as human beings rather than chattel. Hence it is not surprising to find that the crusade against slavery originates in this state. Once again we find Quakers taking the lead.

For a long time it was thought that the evil of slavery had been eradicated. While slaveholding was taken for granted in antiquity, during the Middle Ages one finds very little trace of it. Since the slave is no longer a significant economic factor anyway, the Christian trader can conveniently remind himself that slavery is incompatible with loving one's neighbor. But with the discovery of a new continent, the slave trade is suddenly revived.

The conquerors of the New World, who did not hesitate to decimate the Indian population, also find a pious pretext for one of the most infamous operations of the entire business: the slave market in the West Indies. Bartolomé de las Casas puts forward the "humane" plan of "importing" Africans to the West Indies because the Indians cannot stand the tropical climate of the islands. He secures the approval of Emperor Charles V by pointing out that the Negroes should be evangelized and that the only means of their salvation lay in slavery, a position he repudiated only some time later.

King Louis XII of France allows himself to be similarly persuaded. England's great Queen Elizabeth accepts the sea captains' promises that the Negroes would not be abducted against their will, and on the strength of these promises she authorizes the "slave trade," as the new form of bestiality is openly called.

Thus develops a triangular system of commerce that yields rich profits and lulls the consciences of the investors to sleep. The sea captains carry European goods (mainly liquor) to Africa, exchange them for slaves, transport the slaves to the colonies, and take on a profitable load of sugar for the voyage home. Writers of the time call this traffic the foundation and basis of all trade and commerce. No nation, however Christian, stays out of the manhunt, but England gets a corner on the market by securing, as spoils of the War of the Spanish Succession, the exclusive license

A cartoon from the "Fliegende Blätter," 1848. The quotation in the caption states that shipowners are vying with each other to make the emigrants as comfortable as possible on their voyage. The sketch shows the emigrants being stuffed into barrels and rolled off.

for importing slaves into the Spanish colonies. The whole shameful business is rationalized by pointing to the economic boost it gives the colonies and the domestic port cities.

If, therefore, England's guilt is especially great, it is also in England and its North American colonies that the first steps are taken toward abolition. The abolition movement begins in the Quaker state, Pennsylvania, where in 1683 the first German emigrant groups arrive from Krefeld. Thirteen Mennonite families have risked the voyage to the faraway land of liberty in order to escape religious oppression at home. In some ways these Mennonites are more consistent than the Quakers. Both refuse to bear arms; but while slaveholding is still practiced among the Quakers, the Mennonites categorically reject it.

The German immigrants, inspired perhaps by their own newfound freedom, are among the first to protest. They are joined by other Mennonites or friends of Mennonites, such as the first mayor of the emigre settlement of Germantown, Francis Daniel Pastorius, as well as several Quakers. A public protest against slavery, brought before the Friends' Meeting at Germantown on February 18, 1688, says in part:

> We hear that ye most part of such Negers are brought heither against their will & consent; and that many of them are stollen. Now, tho' they are black, we cannot conceive there is more liberty to have them slaves, as it is to have other white ones. There is a saying, that we shall doe to all men, licke as we will be done our selves; making no difference of what generation, descent or Colour they are. And those who steal or robb men, and those who buy or purchase them, are they not all alike? Here is liberty of Conscience, wch is right & reasonable; here ought to be lickewise liberty of ye body, except of evildoers, wch is an other case. . . . And we, who know that men must not comitt adultery, some doe comitt adultery in others, separating wifes from their housbands and giving them to others; and some sell the children of those poor Creatures to other men.

The sensitivity with which the conscience of these Protestants registers the injustice of slavery is clearly shown here. The proclamation continues with these almost prophetic words:

> If once these slaves, (:wch they say are so wicked and stubbern men:) should joint themselves, fight for their freedom and handel their masters & mastrisses as they did handel them before; will these Masters and mastrisses tacke the sword at hand & warr against these poor slaves, licke we are able to belive, some will not refuse to doe? Or have these Negers not as much right to fight for their freedom, as you have to keep them slaves?

The governing officials of Pennsylvania are all Quakers. Despite their willingness to listen, and despite the clarity of the protest, no act of true emancipation follows. But now the consciences of men have been pricked, and the issue will not die.

From this point on, more and more voices are raised in protest. Benjamin Lay, a little hunchback who lives in the most primitive circumstances in order to avoid profiting unjustly from the oppression of the innocent, sees plainly that men's minds must be transformed if slavery is to be recognized as the injustice that it is.

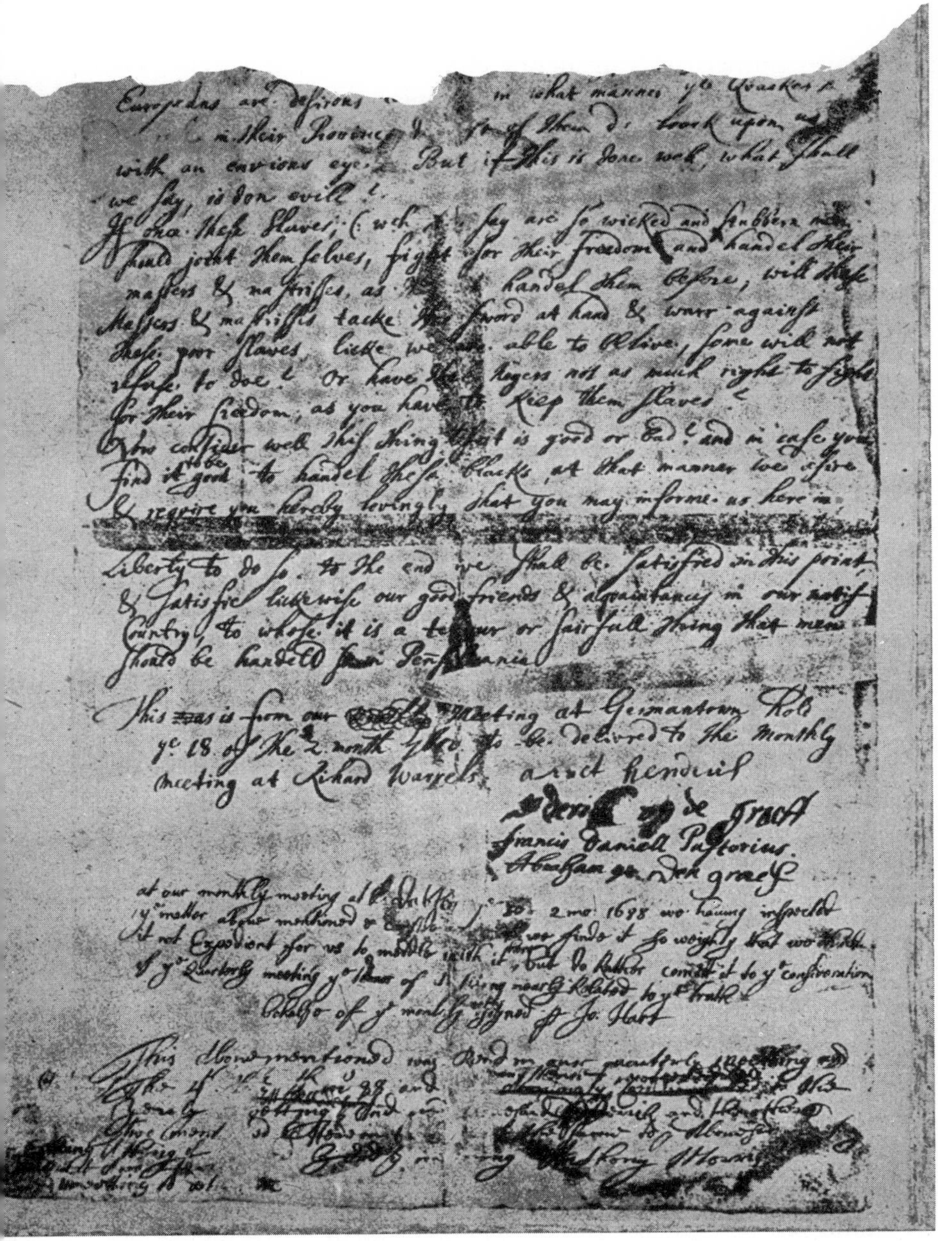

Europeans are desirous [illegible] in what manner ye Quakers [illegible]
[illegible] in their Province; & [illegible] of them doe looke upon us
with an envious eye. But if this is done well, what shall
we say is don evill?
If once these slaves, (wch they say are so wicked and stubborn men)
should joint themselves, fight for their freedom and handel their
masters & mastrisses, as they did handel them before; will these
masters & mastrisses tacke the sword at hand & warr against
these poor slaves, licke we are able to believe, some will not
refuse to doe? Or have these negers not as much right to fight
for their freedom, as you have to keep them slaves?
Now consider well this thing, if it is good or bad? and in case you
find it to be good to handel these blacks at that manner, we desire
& require you hereby lovingly, that you may informe us herein
[illegible]
Liberty to do so, to the end we shall be satisfied in this point,
& satisfie likewise our good friends & acquaintances in our natif
Country, to whose it is a terrour or fairfull thing that men
should be handeld so in Pensilvania.

This is from our [illegible] meeting at Germantown hold
ye 18 of the 2 month 1688 to be delivered to the monthly
meeting at Richard Warrels.

gerret hendericks
derick up de graeff
Francis daniell Pastorius
Abraham up Den graef

February 18, 1688: Francis Daniel Pastorius signs the protest against slavery.

Lay plants himself in front of the churches after the service, vividly describes to the departing worshippers the sufferings of the slaves, and pronounces the slaveholders guilty of their blood.

John Woolman shows a similar concern when in 1758 he begins his own crusade. The New Jersey tailor is convinced to a degree equaled by scarcely any of his contemporaries that goodness must survive in the world if the world itself is to survive. He not only fights against the gross injustices of slavery; he goes so far as to maintain:

> Oppression in the extreme appears terrible: but oppression in more refined appearances, remains to be Oppression; and where the smallest degree of it is cherished it grows stronger and more extensive.

Woolman decides to go from farm to farm, speaking to the conscience of the people. Perhaps his particular concern on such tours is to begin by singling out those lesser evils. He appears to have little regard for grandiose petitions or thundering tirades. He knows the power of the heart that communicates itself in familiar, personal exchanges; and through such exchanges he is able to carry on his crusade against slavery. Nor does he hesitate to go directly to England to fight for his cause when he finds that there are adamant defenders of slavery not only on the sprawling farms and plantations of America but also in the land of his fathers. It is on one such trip back to the mother country that he dies.

But not without finding successors. A Pennsylvania Quaker makes a start by unconditionally freeing his slaves. Elisha Tyson is instrumental in the freeing of two thousand slaves and establishes in Baltimore the first African church. More and more people, especially Quakers, are minded to give the slaves their freedom. In 1780 the necessary legal groundwork for emancipation is laid, but the struggle is not yet over. Several neighboring colonies are grimly determined to hold onto their slaveholding rights; slavery is enormously profitable. The Quakers respond by organizing the Underground Railroad to aid runaway slaves on their way north. Its unofficial "President" is Levi Coffin, who is instrumental in freeing some 3,500 slaves. An underground "train" announces its arrival by a light tapping at the door. The fugitives are noiselessly admitted, fed, and concealed in a variety of imaginative ways.

One day an Underground Railroad conductor named Thomas Garrett is taken to court by angry slaveholders and sentenced to pay damages. Although the fines will leave him a ruined man, he pays them without resistance like a good Quaker. But tradition tells us that before leaving court Garrett has the last word.

> Judge, thou has not left me a dollar, but I wish to say to thee, and to all in this court-room, that if any one knows of a fugitive who wants a shelter and a friend, send him to Thomas Garrett and he will befriend him.

None of the runaways Garrett befriends is ever recaptured.

Clarkson and Wilberforce in England

The Quakers in America differ with each other initially on the slavery issue, but in 1761 the Quakers in England adopt an unambiguous stance. All Friends are required to refrain from trafficking in slaves, and offenders are summarily expelled from the Society. The English Friends are supported in this by John Wesley's group, the Methodists, who know only too well the evils of slavery in America. It may also be that the ideas of the Enlightenment are teaching the man of these times a loathing for the degradation of his fellowman. The public is learning more and more about the callous inhumanity of the slave trade. London's newspapers carry announcements of slave auctions: a Negro mother may be offered for sale with or without child. It is commonplace for the well-traveled English gentleman to return home with a slave or two for his household. Not infrequently these pathetic creatures are so mistreated that they run away to seek the aid of some kind person.

One such kindly benefactor is Granville Sharp, a frontline fighter against slavery. He intercedes repeatedly on behalf of runaway slaves, even defending them in court, though he is not a lawyer. Slaveholding is still officially sanctioned in England, however, and if there are going to be any thoroughgoing reforms, they will have to come from Parliament. But Parliament isn't interested. On one occasion a Quaker who submits a reform proposal is not even admitted to the debate.

In 1785 an English youth named Thomas Clarkson who is studying at Cambridge on a scholarship reads the announcement of a Latin essay contest. The subject, proposed by the vice-chancellor of the university, is *"Anne liceat invitos in servitutem dare?"*—Is it right to make men slaves against their will? Ringing in Clarkson's ears are the words of a minister who, two years before, branded slavery as a national disgrace. There is no doubt how the question must be answered. Clarkson immediately begins collecting material, and he is stunned at the atrocities he uncovers. The project becomes an ordeal, for the facts confronting him in historical and contemporary sources are so dreadful that he can scarcely continue. He manages somehow to finish the essay, which becomes a scathing attack. Clarkson is awarded the prize. People come to hear the public reading, they listen, and then they disperse again. In terms of action elicited, the impact is nil. But Clarkson has found his calling. He has experienced something that will not let him go.

The work Clarkson has cut out for himself is too big for one man, and Clarkson knows it. Thus he is grateful when some Quakers put him in touch with Granville Sharp. Already in possession of a rich store of material, Sharp has just added to his collection the records of the appalling "Liverpool case": A sea captain had dumped 130 sick Negroes into the middle of the ocean in order to save the rest of his cargo of slaves and—above all—to collect insurance on the loss. The captain was tried in Liverpool—not for mass murder but for insurance fraud. Sharp took notes on the entire court proceedings and sent a copy of them, along with a note of protest, to high government officials. They never answered.

Clarkson also hears of Reverend James Ramsay, who has given an eyewitness report of the brutal treatment of the slaves on the plantations of the West Indies. By this time Clarkson sees that there are enough men with enough courage to speak out. The next thing is to unite these voices into a chorus of protest. A flurry of letters, personal calls, reports, and consultations is the result; Clarkson puts in sixteen hours a day at the task. He also

African slaves being marched toward their destination in 1880. The slave trade was finally abolished in Brazil in 1888; in Ethiopia, 1923; in Nepal, 1924; in southern China, 1927. The brutal methods of some economic systems, however, which treat men as merchandise are not yet a thing of the past. Moreover, there are still, in fact if not in name, two million serfs in the world.

tries to keep in touch with things firsthand: one day he visits a slave ship and verifies with his own eyes that human beings are being stowed on board like freight. So that the maximum number of slaves can be transported on each voyage, they are precisely and efficiently "packed" side by side, sitting or lying, and chained in pairs. Unable to move for long periods of time, even for weeks, they endure the voyage itself as an unspeakable kind of torture.

Clarkson is instrumental in enlisting William Wilberforce, a member of Parliament, in the cause; and in Wilberforce the abolition movement finds its champion—the man who, after a twenty-year siege, would bring about the collapse of formidable Parliamentary opposition. But it turns out to be an uphill fight all the way. The efforts of Wilberforce, Clarkson, and other progressives are steadily opposed by men who are making a very good living from the slave trade: shipowners, sea captains, planters, traders, and an assortment of demimonde figures, including the proprietors of waterfront dives who act as contact men for slave ship captains looking for crewmen.

In short, it is a regular lobby, whose connections reach to the top levels of government, since a number of members of Parliament and high officials have their involvements in the slave trade. Wilberforce sees clearly that he must advance on his objective one step at a time. He therefore persuades his friends that the first attack should be directed only against the African slave trade as such; the fight for general abolition would come later.

Before he can introduce his motion in Parliament, he suffers a physical collapse that nearly takes his life. The strain has proven too much. But his friend, Prime Minister William Pitt, who has promised to stand in for him, puts the issue on the agenda for the next session. During the course of the prediscussions, however, one of the other members introduces a bill of his own. The description he gives of the conditions prevailing on a slave ship he personally inspected supports Wilberforce's position, but he proposes that for the time being the slave trade merely be *regulated.* The captains should no longer be allowed to pack their human cargo any way they please; it must be done according to standards. The number of slaves should be regulated by the tonnage the ship is permitted to carry: a maximum of five slaves to every three tons.

No one recognizes the enormity of such a proposal. It is tantamount to legalizing a system of abduction and murder. But the bill passes nonetheless. Feeble though it is, it arouses the ire of the shipowners and planters and their champions, who prophesy the doom of colonial trade.

Contrary to all medical expectations, Wilberforce recovers. It is as if his good health is specifically restored to him for the years of parliamentary struggle ahead. On May 12, 1789, he delivers his first speech in the House of Commons against the slave trade. It is an unsparing attack, yet at the same time it contains an overture toward reconciliation: The guilt of the slave trade is the nation's guilt, says Wilberforce; abolition is the means of active repentance. It is a magnificent speech and its logic is compelling, but those with a vested interest in the slave trade succeed in delaying a vote. The anticlimactic outcome, weeks later, is a renewal of the previous regulations and nothing more.

Near despair, Clarkson goes to Paris to rally support for the abolitionist cause, but his mission fails. He then begins compiling more evidence, while Wilberforce plans his next parliamentary moves.

The debates on the slave trade read like scenes in a tense drama. On the one hand, they attest the humanity and compassion of the champions of abolition; on the other, they are a shocking indictment of human failure and hardheartedness. In the debates of April 18 and 19, 1791, Wilberforce, who up to this point has refrained from going into specifics, now describes the atrocities in detail; but in the end his opponent, Colonel Banastre Tarleton, who represents Liverpool and the commerce it has grown rich on, wins the majority to his side. Tarleton issues an incredible piece of advice: Do not, in these enlightened times—he says—allow a mistaken philanthropy to be turned into a false pretext for dangerous attacks upon property and character.

This setback has one positive result. Public opinion in favor of abolition gains much ground. The parliamentary debates have awakened the conscience of many people. A boycott of "slave-grown sugar" develops almost spontaneously, and Clarkson succeeds in fanning the flames of protest to a blaze that spreads all over England.

The debates also accomplish something else. Wilberforce secures parliamentary approval for the "Sierra Leone Company," one of whose missions would be the transportation to Sierra Leone of Negroes who had fought on the side of the British during the American Revolution and who had subsequently been deposited in various places: a thousand of them, for example, on Nova Scotia. With the financial backing of the new company, Clarkson's brother John, a young naval officer, transports the first shipload of Negroes to their newly founded settlement of Freetown.

In 1792 Wilberforce returns to the attack in the House of Commons, this time reinforced by 517 public petitions. The conscience of Parliament seems now to be aroused, but the proslavery bloc throws all its resources into a counterattack. New plans, new regulatory measures are proposed. Finally at the end of an all-night debate, an immediate ban is rejected and an "amended" (actually mutilated) motion calling for the "gradual" abolition of the slave trade is passed. In the House of Lords, however, action is again delayed by lengthy hearings. Clarkson has been worn down by the war of attrition, but Wilberforce hangs on with British tenacity, introducing motions in the House of Commons almost every year; and in 1796 he succeeds in securing a majority on the first two readings of his bill. On the third reading, with victory almost within reach, the bill is narrowly defeated. A number of legislators who favor abolition, and who might have tipped the scales the other way, skip the ballotting in order to attend a much-touted opera premiere.

Victory finally comes in 1807 when, as a result of Wilberforce's efforts, both houses vote overwhelmingly to abolish England's share in the African slave trade. The outcome is almost a surprise. Denounced and maligned for twenty years while he kept up the attack, Wilberforce becomes overnight a national hero. Has reason triumphed after all? Has Parliament recovered its humanity and compassion?

Unfortunately, the real reason for the change is not as noble as all that: The slave trade has simply lost its commercial attractiveness; the politicians and merchants are instead preoccupied with an emerging industrialism. But this does not diminish the achievement of those men whose moral convictions and Christian faith motivated them to commit their lives to the battle for humanity.

The abolition of the slave trade in England does not mean the end of slavery in the world, of course. While the same year—1807—sees the United States join England in prohibiting the slave traffic, there are still plenty of other nations that accord this squalid commerce the protection of their flag. Slave trading is a world problem; and after 1807, English foreign policy begins to deal with its international aspects. British warships patrol the African coast and seize all vessels transporting slaves. In 1813 and 1814 laws banning the slave trade are passed in Holland and in the nations of South America and Scandinavia; and beginning in

UNCLE TOM'S CABIN;

OR,

LIFE AMONG THE LOWLY.

BY

HARRIET BEECHER STOWE.

VOL I

ONE HUNDREDTH THOUSAND.

BOSTON.
JOHN. P. JEWETT & COMPANY
CLEVELAND, OHIO:
JEWETT, PROCTOR & WORTHINGTON.
1852.

In her famous novel, Harriet Beecher Stowe describes in dramatic fashion the plight of the Negro slaves. Even after the battle against slavery had been won, her book continues to attract a large audience. Here, the title page of the first edition.

1823 Clarkson, Wilberforce, and Thomas Fowell Buxton lead a parliamentary campaign to abolish slavery altogether.

Stopping the traffic in slaves, however, does not free the hundreds of thousands already enslaved. In 1833 a newly elected English Parliament votes to abolish slavery and provides for the emancipation of the slaves in all crown colonies, upon the payment of twenty million pounds sterling as compensation to the colonial planters for any injuries thereby sustained. A merciful providence allows Wilberforce to see the victory; he dies just a few days after passage of the bill is assured.

For all this, the slave trade is never completely stopped. What was open commerce becomes a smuggling operation that is extremely difficult if not impossible to trace. As recently as the middle of the last century, an estimated 120,000 nonwhites were being abducted into slavery *annually*. By contrast, over a thirty-five-year period, only 100,000 slaves were discovered and rescued from the hands of the smugglers who kidnapped them. The dismal truth is that even in our own time slavery is not dead. To this day there are slaves and slave traders in the Arab countries, despite the efforts of Interpol, the United Nations, and UNESCO. We know this. We also know that slavery is an international problem which, like all great human problems, can only be solved on an international basis. But the path leading to this perception has been a long and difficult one. At its beginning stood a small band of Mennonites and Quakers.

7. Doctors and Teachers

The Beginnings of Modern Education

A popular cause in the last years of the eighteenth century is physical and spiritual emancipation. Besides the crusade against the literal bondage of slavery and the slave trade, there are various efforts to emancipate man from the less tangible bondage of traditional social forms and conventions. The stage for the new era is set by the Age of Discovery, the Renaissance, and the Reformation. The individual is distinguished from the mass; intellectual freedom is cultivated. Among the political and military consequences of this turn of events are the American and French Revolutions. They lead by way of bloodshed and violence to the legal securing of the inalienable rights of man.

The new global perspective—initially suffused with an extravagant global mystique—ushers in an age of education that is without historical precedent, the great advances and achievements of the Greeks and Romans and other ancient cultures notwithstanding. Nowhere are the efforts to liberate man from poverty of thought and narrowness of spirit more evident than in the field of education. A radical change is in the making.

The instinct of primitive peoples is typically to use education as a means by which the younger generation is induced to adapt itself to the status quo. There is no thought of *reform*.

In the Middle Ages we find three very different kinds of educational programs; and, like the times, they are heavily influenced by the church and the social structure: there are the parochial schools, the aristocratic schools, and the training schools run by the guilds. Different as these three are, they have one thing in common: the ossification of tradition. The man of the age believes in preserving tradition. But the result is that the horizons and methods of education are perceptibly narrowed. Bound by the social caste system in which he must live, medieval man has little individual freedom.

But many men and many events are setting the stage for a new era. Luther's accomplishments in education are just as vital here as the Jesuit academic program instituted by Ignatius of Loyola. The work of John Amos Comenius has more than passing significance, the influence of Jean Jacques Rousseau is still felt in our own century, and August Hermann Francke develops an educational curriculum that combines heavenly goals with a practical caring for others: the neighbors across the seas as well as the neighbor next door.

But nowhere is the application of love, idealism, and reason more conspicuous than in the life and work of Johann Heinrich Pestalozzi (1746–1827), the Poor Man's Fool of Neuhof and the Orphan's Father of Stans. By borrowing from a bank in Zurich, his native city, young Pestalozzi manages to acquire an estate near the village of Birr, Switzerland. He has great plans for it, and is sure of being able to repay the money in a few years; but as time goes on, the master of "Neuhof" looks more and more like a ne'er-do-well farmer, and finally the bank calls in the loan. Was Pestalozzi too much of a dreamer to face the realities of hard work? He planned to educate his own son in the freedom of nature taught by Rousseau, and he actually gets as far as a few experiments along these lines. But soon he sees that he must part company with the great Frenchman, whose thought is stirring the minds of Europe. Freedom in itself is not enough. Seeing one side of truth is not enough either. Pestalozzi sees that he must correlate his pedagogical experiments: freedom *and* obedience are the true pillars of education. Pestalozzi is a child of the Enlightenment, but he does not forsake the Christian faith.

Not even when he finds himself without money, without credit, and without any idea what to do next. In this hour of humiliation it occurs to him that he has more to contribute to the world than the fluctuating fortunes of a farmer. In view of his circumstances, the course he then embarks on is incredible. He begins taking in abandoned children to live on his mortgaged estate. He wants to give them the kind of rearing that will restore them, as it were, to the human community. He won't be saved by money, but by the things he does to save others. Virtually obsessed with his vision, he plunges into his new work. Not only is he the children's teacher; he is also their father and friend. He lives with them as only one who fervently loves them could do. Part of his school program is practical work: harvesting, spinning, housekeeping. Pestalozzi never overtaxes the strength of his charges; he aims to develop their strength and to reinstill courage and faith in hearts made timid and fearful by force of circumstance. He is positive that the love he gives to the children will not go unrequited.

Pestalozzi wants Neuhof to be an object-lesson. He makes mistakes, both in educational theory and practice. He faces up to the mistakes and keeps pushing on. He is misunderstood and ridiculed, and he is defenseless against the abuse of angry parents. He is, in fact, that poor beggar who is all heart and nothing else, the Poor Man's Fool of Neuhof, not worth paying attention to. Neuhof is still not paying its way. The enterprise continues to teeter on the brink of financial ruin. In 1780 it collapses.

But Pestalozzi now knows where he is going. He has found his real mission, and from this point on he never wavers. Turning to writing, he spends the next twenty years setting forth the principles of an education that will safeguard the integrity of the home and develop the mental resources of the child. All this is composed against a background of social and political upheaval culminating in the French Revolution. Pestalozzi is probably a social revolutionary himself at this stage, but he is never a man of violence. He cannot help thinking revolutionary thoughts when he looks at the miserable conditions around him, for he cannot keep silent in the face of injustice. Although not wholly free from inconsistency himself, he is able to perceive and expose the inconsistencies in the violent movements of the age. When he decides to enter the service of the Helvetian Republic, which is under the thumb of Napoleon, his purpose is at least partly to be able to curb the evil effects of such inconsistencies. He also feels the urge to get away from writing and back into teaching. The Minister of Education,

P. A. Stapfer, is willing to promote his career, but when he offers Pestalozzi the principalship of a teacher training college, Pestalozzi turns it down. He has, after all, little solid teaching experience himself.

Meanwhile, disaster strikes the half-canton of Nidwalden. Its abortive attempt to oppose the new political order and retain its autonomy is crushed by Napoleon's troops in the battle of Stans. Men, women, and children fight and die in the insurrection. Many of the survivors are left homeless. This state of affairs goes on for two months before the government makes up its mind to do something. Pestalozzi is commissioned to open an institution for homeless children in Stans, in the annex of a convent. In December 1798 he goes to Stans to supervise the necessary renovation. The carpenters are kept busy. By the middle of January 1799, even before the tools have been cleared away and schoolbooks have been procured, the first children move into their rooms. Two weeks later, with everything still in the disarray of renovation, there are forty-five children living in the house. Soon there are eighty. Pestalozzi is carrying the full load of the enterprise on his shoulders; the only assistant he permits is a housekeeper. He is determined to see the venture through alone and to teach these brutalized, traumatized children how to smile again. Without aid, himself assuming the role of supervisor, paymaster, houseboy, and maid, Pestalozzi commits himself wholly to his new charges, still branded by the terrors of war, totally neglected, dirty, scabies-infected, vermin-ridden, some cowering with fear, others obstinate and unmanageable.

To these children, too, Pestalozzi becomes a father. Every victory over filth, scabies, obstinacy, and rejection gives him more confidence. Within a few weeks' time, the convent in Stans has become a different place. The "father," who doubles as maid, has also become the schoolmaster. He teaches eighty children at a time, sings with them, prays for them, drills them in reading, writing, and arithmetic—all the while meticulously considering each of his educational innovations without losing sight of the whole. It is an almost insuperable task, and it takes every ounce of dedication Pestalozzi has, day and night.

His work begins to bear fruit, although the outward signs are small: the grin of a youngster formerly too embittered to smile, or

Yverdon Castle, location of one of Pestalozzi's schools.

Rösel/Hegi engraving in the Zentralbibliothek, Zurich

the handclasp of a child who has lost his fear. There are even greater fruits, for Pestalozzi has helped his children personally to experience something of goodness. In April 1799 the nearby town of Altdorf is destroyed by fire, and as he is discussing the calamity with his charges they beg him to take in some of the homeless children, even if they themselves have less food and more work as a result. Some of the scenes in Pestalozzi's best-known book, *Leonard and Gertrude,* may strike us as maudlin, but they became reality in Stans, where one unfortunate would weep over the kindness and gratitude of another.

After less than half a year, Pestalozzi has run aground once more. War has turned the school into a military hospital; and Pestalozzi, exhausted and sick, is unable to return to it when the soldiers have finally withdrawn. He is hooted and jeered. His contemporaries do not realize that his ideas have created an utterly new breed of teacher; not a skilled workman whose specialty happens to be education, but a human being who gives himself to the child he is responsible for educating.

His ideas are a living monument to Pestalozzi: the man who in his time was apparently only a loser and a failure, a bumbling, unkempt old man. The experimental schools in Burgdorf, Münchenbuchsee, and Yverdon produce more trials and misunderstandings than successes. Yet he triumphs precisely in his failures. He becomes the founder of the modern elementary school, the "educator of mankind," as his epitaph records.

When Pestalozzi dies in 1827, it has long become obvious that education cannot ignore his methods and still survive. In meeting educational difficulties and everyday problems, Pestalozzi used to rub colleagues, children, and parents the wrong way; often he was even at odds with himself. But these frictions and tensions were the crucible out of which he forged the very substance of modern education. And although we might mention others who explored similar avenues, none of them managed to do what Pestalozzi consumed his life in accomplishing; out of his Christian faith and social concern he was able to proclaim a quality of humanness attainable through proper education.

Help for the Deaf-Mutes and the Blind

It is not only the materially poor who are the have-nots. There is the more extreme poverty of all those who are prevented from living a full life by disease and physical disability. For hundreds and thousands of years, much has been done for the sick and the invalid; the care of those unable to care for themselves has long led the list of works of mercy. There are two groups of disabled people, however, for whom little could be done: the deaf-mutes and the blind, the very people Jesus Christ had particular compassion on.

To be sure, we have heard of Thalassius, the seventh-century monk who gathers blind beggars around him, teaches them, and supplies their wants; and we know that France's sainted King Louis IX founded an institution in Paris housing three hundred blind beggars; but these efforts do not go far enough. Really helping a blind man means training him to help himself. Those beggars in Paris got nothing more than a place to stay; for everything else they were still dependent on begging. There was simply nothing else they could do; they were unemployable.

The deaf-mutes are rather better off. In the late sixteenth and early seventeenth centuries two Spaniards, Pedro de Ponce and Juan Pablo Bonet, make a start at training deaf-mutes; and in Holland Johann Amman develops a method of teaching them to speak. In 1778 Samuel Heinicke founds an institute for deaf-mutes in Leipzig that represents a milestone in their training. It is a process of trial and error, but the new methods lead to the training for the deaf as we know it today. Deaf-mutes are taught to communicate.

Similarly it is not until recent times—the end of the eighteenth century—that help becomes available for the blind. The breakthrough is due to the work of a Parisian named Valentin Haüy.

One day the twenty-six-year-old Haüy is shocked when he witnesses a publicity stunt staged by the proprietor of a Paris tavern. The attraction is a blind men's band, and it packs the house for weeks. The customers like a good laugh, and the owner thinks a blind band is simply hilarious. The musicians sit there, wearing cardboard glasses without lenses, scores upside down on their stands, their conductor wearing a pair of oversized donkey's ears. Misery is cheaply had; the musicians get a couple of sous, and the proprietor fills his cash register with bills and silver. Respectable citizens tolerate this grotesque show without protest. Häuy is utterly revolted. *"Je les ferai lire!"* he cries. "I will teach them to read!" Fourteen years later the whole world knows him as the brilliant, dynamic founder of the first school for the blind.

The road is long, and the obstacles are many; but Haüy gets much support, inspiration, and encouragement along the way, a large part of which comes from Abbé Charles Michel de l'Épée, a deaf-mute instructor. This abbé, who once happened to have been assigned the task of instructing two deaf-mute girls, had developed a sign language. Indeed, with the help of a highly gifted pupil, he had so developed it that even a person deaf and dumb from birth could learn to formulate and speak his own thoughts. The advice of Abbé de l'Épée is priceless.

In 1783 Haüy meets a blind pianist, a woman who has learned to read music by means of pins stuck in a cushion. She also uses the pin method to read maps, and she even has a case of type with which she prints her own letters. One of her correspondents is a blind man in Mannheim, Germany, who taught her how to print. The disadvantage, of course, is that both must have their letters read to them.

Haüy is picking up many ideas from various quarters. He sees the general course he must follow, but doesn't know precisely how to get started. The real problem is still unsolved.

One day he meets a seventeen-year-old beggar named François Lesueur, who is blind from infancy. Upon being urged by Haüy, the beggar agrees to take training, on condition he is paid for his time. Haüy accepts the condition, for he sees that François is a gifted boy. But it is questionable whether Haüy's efforts would have succeeded except for a happy accident. François, who likes things neat and in order, is cleaning out his tutor's desk one day when his hand brushes against an old printed card, so heavily printed, in fact, that the type has made indentations. François finds that he can decipher a few of the letters by tracing them with his finger, and he proudly gives his teacher a demonstration of his new skill. Haüy holds his breath. He now knows what he is looking for. *Raised* printing will be the signposts guiding the blind to literacy.

Soon afterwards Haüy is given charge of twelve blind children by the "Philanthropic Society," whose president is also the Paris chief of police and a genuinely civic-minded man. These blind children receive their support from the Society, and with its assistance Haüy is able to open the first school for the blind in 1784. France is on the verge of the uprising which would try to achieve the ideals of liberty, equality, and fraternity by way of a bloodbath, destroying in order to create. But Haüy's school emerges from the French Revolution unscathed.

When the political storm has spent itself, Haüy receives generous aid from many quarters. He takes a trip around Europe and, in Berlin and St. Petersburg (Leningrad), he founds schools for the blind modeled on the Paris prototype. When he dies in 1822, his work is solidly established and continues to bear fruit. Claude

Montal, who is educated in the Paris school, later develops a system of teaching the blind how to tune pianos. Seven years after Haüy's death, Louis Braille invents the alphabet of raised dots which bears his name and which is in common use everywhere today. Still another graduate is Maurice la Sizeranne, who, decades later, founds an association dedicated to the care of blind children unable to attend regular schools.

Schools for the Mentally Deficient

About the same time that Braille is working on his raised dots, the world's first institution for the mentally deficient is founded in Salzburg, Austria. Until well into the eighteenth century, "idiots" and "madmen" are put in "madhouses" and treated like criminals. But in the second half of the century of Enlightenment, an increasing number of physicians begin to see "madness" as mental illness. It is due to their efforts that the virtual prisons housing the mentally ill are gradually replaced by institutions of healing, the first one—the Goggenmoos institution in Salzburg—being followed by others in Württemberg and Paris. In 1840 the Abendberg hospice in Zurich is founded by Dr. J. Guggenbühl, who with other physicians and teachers of the age believes that the incidence of cretinism—one form of mental deficiency—is limited mainly to valleys, and that pure mountain air is an essential condition for any healing. Guggenbühl's hospice is located on a mountain, as is the Mariaberg asylum, the latter situated in the highest part of the Schwäbische Alb. Here a student of Guggenbühl's, Dr. Jakob Heinrich Helferich, brands as error the notion that mental deficiency can be cured by medical treatment. He maintains that "these unfortunates can only be helped by giving them the care and treatment available through education and training in the broadest sense of the terms. It was a delusion to think that their treatment was first and foremost a medical treatment. Except for regulating diet and seeing to such things as fresh air, and washing and bathing to ensure cleanliness—which are prescribed in physical training anyway—I do not know at all what positive benefits these children might gain from the current medical thought relating to our task, since medical treatment, apart from cod-liver oil and rubdowns, is unknown."

Thus the mentally deficient need remedial education and training; and there are no institutions in which cooperation between doctors and teachers will come to be so close as in the institutions for the retarded. Later scientific advances will also point the way to medical treatment in this field. In fact, the nineteenth century sees discoveries of major importance in all fields of scientific endeavor; and doctors contribute to human welfare and progress in a much more comprehensive way than in the past.

Before following this later progress, however, we must pause for a look at what has gone before.

The Heirs of Hippocrates

As long as men have lived on earth, they have studied the arts of healing. The physician is as old as man himself. The ancient myths are full of accounts of wondrous healings and great doctors. The first doctor to emerge clearly from the shadowy outlines of mythology is Hippocrates; for although we know little or nothing of his life (c. 460–c. 370 B.C.), many of his writings have been preserved. To this day he is known as the father of medicine.

At first, practicing medicine means supplementing and channeling the natural forces of health and healing. Thus the primary treatment is dietetic: regulating living and eating habits. This insight is the great contribution of Hippocrates, and for it he is still honored today. Only very gradually does the emphasis shift from nutrition to medication; and only when both of these methods have failed does the physician resort to hot irons and the knife. For hundreds and thousands of years, the medicine men of primitive peoples try to heal the sick by relying wholly on folklore—magic and incantation; the physicians of Greece, on the other hand, observe and analyze nature—man, animals, and plants—and try to be objective and precise in their methods. Some of these ancient Greeks call to mind the health reformers of our day. In the fourth century before Christ, for example, the Greek physician Diocles of Carystus writes a book describing hygiene as the basis of public health. He pictures the ideal type, the integrated man, healthy in body and soul. For Diocles, hygiene means the regular care of the whole man.

During the reign of Alexander the Great, there is a lively exchange of medical knowledge and experience among the nations of the empire, and it is the healing arts of the Egyptians that prove the most fruitful and influential. But gradually a variety of false notions creeps in. Not infrequently, the medical schools submerge their students in theory, prompting Heraclides of Tarent to remind his colleagues that sickness is cured by more concrete means than rhetoric. By the first century before Christ, the Roman Empire is flooded with Greek physicians, but many of them are nothing more than quacks who are justifiably mistrusted. It falls to the great Asclepiades to acquaint the Romans with the rudiments of the ancient Greek medical arts, which he sets forth in the clarity and simplicity native to the Roman mode of thought.

During the first few centuries after Christ, there is no progress at all. In fact, European Christians take a dim view of science. There is no forward movement anywhere, nor is there any attempt to preserve the insights of the past. Instead, men frequently revert to the sphere of the occult, the esoteric, and the magical, attributing more power to amulets and votive offerings than to keeping fit or using natural remedies to get well.

The Orient and the world of Islam are on the threshold of their golden age of medicine. Rhazes (c. 865–c. 923) studies smallpox and measles and reports his findings in detail. Some time later, Avicienna, a Persian physician born in 980, writes "The Canon of Medicine," which reaches the West via the crusades and remains a standard work for centuries. One man is greatly instrumental in the spread of these insights throughout the Christian Occident: Constantine the African (c. 1020–1087), who studies the Oriental wisdom literature on the long trips he takes, subsequently withdrawing to the quiet of the monastery on Monte Cassino, where he sets down what he has learned and translates numerous medical treatises of the Orient. Eventually the monasteries add these writings to their libraries, where they are studied by generations of doctors.

In the age of the Reformation, two names stand out. In Italy there is Girolamo Fracastoro; and in Germany, Theophrastus Bombastus von Hohenheim, known as Paracelsus.

The details in this woodcut, taken from Paracelsus's book on the treatment of wounds, speak for themselves: amputations performed without anesthetics, operations performed with what look like instruments of torture.

Fracastoro takes up the study of syphilis (the name comes from a poem by him), which by the end of the fifteenth century is prevalent in many regions, including Europe. It is not as deadly as the plague, nor is it incurable, as leprosy was in those days, but it is awful enough. By studying it, Fracastoro infers that communicable diseases are transmitted from person to person by an infection-carrier: sometimes through direct contact, sometimes by air. Fracastoro knows nothing of microbes, which will be hunted three centuries later by Pasteur, Koch, and others; but his conclusions are basically correct, and they lay the groundwork for those later discoveries.

Paracelsus is the cosmopolitan physician, at home all over Europe. He undertakes a reform of medical science. This is not done without intrigue and bitter controversy, but the name of Paracelsus is linked with the revolutionizing of the discipline. Another major figure is Ambroise Paré, the great Parisian surgeon and physician in the cause of mercy, who once sneaks into Paris during a state of siege in order to aid the wounded. Many names follow: those of Englishmen, Italians, Frenchmen, and Germans, better known to scientists than to laymen. They all help to prepare for the war of doctors and scientists against pestilence and epidemic, until at the turn of the nineteenth century one man decides the outcome. His name is Edward Jenner.

Jenner's Serum against Smallpox

Rhazes the Persian and his treatise on smallpox are now ancient history; yet there is still no remedy for this dire infection that is devastating Europe and other parts of the world. It is reported that in Germany alone smallpox is taking the lives of 30,000 people a year. Countless others who recuperate find their faces permanently scarred by the disease. The pockmarked faces that one sees today chiefly in the Orient were once common everywhere.

But the doctors are no longer wholly in the dark. Experience has shown that people who have survived an attack of smallpox will not get it again. And since the epidemics vary in severity, some people deliberately expose themselves during a light siege so that they will be protected against a heavy one. Thus in India, babies are wrapped in the clothes of smallpox victims; and in China, people crush smallpox scabs to a powder and inhale them through a tube into the nose. When it is discovered that the pus produced by smallpox loses some of its virulence in the process of drying, the substance is "injected" into healthy persons by means of pinpricking: not a very far cry from vaccination. The method is used in central Asia, but not in Europe. In Africa, slaveholders "vaccinate" their slaves in similar fashion as a safeguard against "property" loss. In Turkey as well, it is customary to vaccinate especially well-formed Caucasian slave-girls during childhood. A vaccinated slave has a higher market value, and she is a good drawing card for business. When an Englishwoman learns of this method in Constantinople (now Istanbul), she has her own children "vaccinated" by a Greek doctor and recommends the idea at home; and from 1722 on, this kind of immunization is practiced in England. There are even regular vaccination centers operated by "specialists." In 1749 the method spreads to the Continent and saves many lives there.

But smallpox remains a menace; its incidence does not decline appreciably, probably because the vaccination method is still not in general use. Then too, fighting infection with infection is not without risk, especially as the vaccine used may transmit other diseases besides smallpox, diseases such as syphilis for example. Thus vaccination of any kind is still widely suspect.

Then in 1796 Edward Jenner discovers a usable vaccine. Jenner is an English surgeon in Berkeley, Gloucestershire, where he was born and to which he returns in 1773. During his years of practice he has learned the habit of careful observation, and he enjoys scientific research. One thing he observes is that the cows in the area sometimes contract a disease that reminds him of smallpox. The external symptoms are pustules on the udders. Jenner also notices that the milkers often break out with very similar pustules on their hands, suggesting that they had contracted the infection during milking. But the disease seems to be harmless. People say that anyone who has ever had the "cowpox" will never get smallpox, and Jenner discovers they are right. When he is called on to vaccinate the families and servants of the gentlemen-farmers of the area, he finds again and again that in some cases there is no reaction; the vaccine doesn't "take." And whenever Jenner makes inquiries in such cases, he finds out that the person has had the "cowpox," often more than fifteen years before.

Jenner has found the ideal vaccine, for it is completely safe. But since he is too much of a prober to jump to conclusions, he goes on recording his observations for years. On May 14, 1796, he ventures his first experiment, draining the pustule on the skin of a milkmaid who has the cowpox and using it to vaccinate an eight-year-old boy named James Philipps. As expected, the boy comes down with a light case of cowpox and quickly recovers. Six weeks later he is given a smallpox vaccine and shows no reaction. The test is repeated a few months later and the results are the same. Jenner has eliminated all doubt: cowpox makes people immune to smallpox.

For three years he has to contend with the shortsightedness of others, but in 1800 he wins his case. Vaccination proves its effectiveness during a smallpox epidemic in Vienna. Soon the practice is widely adopted in many countries; and fifty years later smallpox has vanished from most of the civilized world.

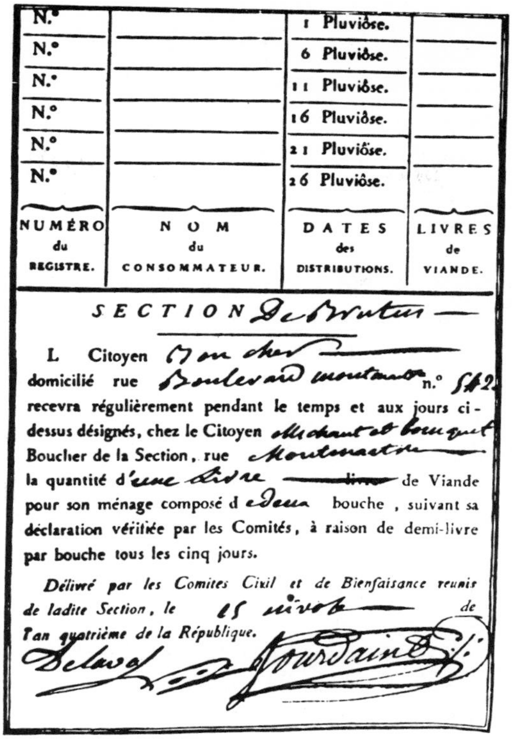

NUMÉRO du REGISTRE.	NOM du CONSOMMATEUR.	DATES des DISTRIBUTIONS.	LIVRES de VIANDE.
N.°		1 Pluviôse.	
N.°		6 Pluviôse.	
N.°		11 Pluviôse.	
N.°		16 Pluviôse.	
N.°		21 Pluviôse.	
N.°		26 Pluviôse.	

SECTION de Brutus

L Citoyen Boucher
domicilié rue Boulevard montmartre n.° 542
recevra régulièrement pendant le temps et aux jours ci-dessus désignés, chez le Citoyen Michaut et Bouquet
Boucher de la Section, rue Montmartre
la quantité d'une livre ~~livre~~ de Viande pour son ménage composé de deux bouche, suivant sa déclaration vérifiée par les Comités, à raison de demi-livre par bouche tous les cinq jours.

Délivré par les Comites Civil et de Bienfaisance reunis de ladite Section, le 15 nivôse de l'an quatrième de la République.

Delavol Jourdain

When the liberating influence of the French Revolution is counteracted by a bloody reign of terror and bitter want, meat is temporarily rationed in Paris in order to check an acute food shortage. Here one of the ration cards.

The record of medical science in these years shows a jagged line of peaks and troughs, but the general trend is upward. Jenner believes his vaccinations are potent enough to last a lifetime. As it turns out, they aren't. But now that the remedy is known, refining the technique is relatively easy. The doctors begin vaccinating at regular intervals, and this proves to be the answer.

Other doctors are striking out in other directions. There is, for example, that quiet contemporary of Jenner's, Johann Heinrich Jung-Stilling, a native of the Sieg River area of North Germany; well known both as a physician and a man of piety, he too is a "man for others." He masters the technique of operating for glaucoma, saves some two thousand people from going partially or totally blind. In most cases he accepts no fee.

In the age of the French Revolution, among the distinguished French doctors who develop new medical techniques is Philippe Pinel, director of a hospital and author of a highly regarded book on insanity. He is constantly probing for ways to alleviate the plight of the insane; in fact his major contribution is in the field of psychiatry. He is led in this direction by a personal experience. A friend of his becomes deranged, flees, wanders about in the wood far from human society, and is torn to pieces by wolves. The fate of this friend sets Dr. Pinel's course. In 1792 he becomes chief physician of the Bicêtre institution in Paris, which includes a women's ward for the insane. Pinel knows what he is getting into, for a pamphlet published in 1788 has exposed some ghastly facts about the Bicêtre. The conditions he finds there are without parallel: the patients lie in chains like wild animals; they have no physician, not one; there is no isolation or classification system, new arrivals being indiscriminately thrown into the arena.

The French Revolution brings a kind of liberation for these unfortunates too. Being human, the patients have rights like other people, one of which is the right to aid. They are now treated as sick people, for they are sick and in need of a doctor's care. After years of persistence, Pinel succeeds in having the virtual prisons for the insane turned into mental hospitals.

Semmelweis's Fight for Mothers

Jenner, Pinel, and their colleagues live at the beginning of this "century of medicine." At the end of it appear the names of the heroic fighters against infectious disease: the "microbe hunters" and the discoverers of new drugs and medicines. About midcentury there emerges in Vienna—the laboratory of distinguished professors of medicine—an obscure and probably erratic little Hungarian doctor. He is assistant to a division head in the Vienna General Hospital's Obstetrical Clinic, which serves women from the lower classes primarily. The assistant's name is Ignaz Philipp Semmelweis.

Vienna's dazzling reputation as a center of medical learning blinds no one to the disasters that take place in the Obstetrical Clinic every day. Children are delivered, but many of the mothers die. What is at this time known as childbed fever (puerperal infection) is the nightmare of all expectant mothers. No one knows its real cause, and everyone has a different theory. Especially puzzling are the contrasting mortality rates in the two divisions of the clinic. In the First Division, where medical students are taught, the mortality rate often reaches thirty percent. In the Second Division, where midwives are trained, the rate is much lower. Remarkable theories are advanced to account for these facts: "cosmic," "telluric," "hygrometric" forces are involved, according to some observers. No, say others, the women examined by the students feel their modesty violated and are thus rendered more susceptible to the fever. Yet another faction hits upon the idea of excluding all foreign students from the clinic; it is suggested that they are not gentle enough with the mothers.

All this merely points up the basic uncertainty of the experts; they are baffled. Many doctors who realize this ultimately resign themselves to the way things are. Perhaps a contributing factor to their resignation is the social caste of the patients: for the most part they are poor, or young and unwed, or victims of rape. Their offenses against morality—thus the doctors may have concluded—must now be paid for with the risk of their lives.

Semmelweis is appalled. To be sure, he is no distinguished medical expert, and he himself often appears to be pursuing a will-o'-the-wisp. But he sees what others have lost sight of: mothers, who by rights should be happy at the prospect of new life, are caught in the grip of mortal fear. What he especially notices is that these mothers-to-be fear not only death but, as a result, the doctor as well; they would rather not be delivered by him, for the doctor and his treatment bring death.

Semmelweis begins his fight. It is a fight to uncover the cause of the disease and a fight against the apathy, stupidity, and malice of his professional colleagues and of the authorities. Semmelweis wouldn't have been able to finish what he started had it not been for an incident that was for him an augury. Jakob Kolletschka, a doctor-friend of his, dies of an infection after being cut by a student's scalpel. They had been dissecting the corpse of a woman who had died of puerperal fever.

The scales fall from the eyes of the young assistant. The scalpel has had the same effect on his friend as the hands of the examining doctors and students on the unfortunate mothers—for the students were being instructed in dissection as well as obstetrics, often on the same day. Thus the scalpel in the one case and the students in the other have carried "death-dealing cadaveric particles" to the living. Semmelweis doesn't try to delude himself; he calls himself a murderer. He now campaigns more fiercely than ever on behalf of the victims, although he can expect neither understanding nor support. He compels all obstetric students to wash their hands in a chlorine solution before examining maternity cases, even though it earns him the name of a hygiene fanatic.

A few doctors recognize that Semmelweis is right, but his colleagues in the clinic are obdurate. Semmelweis calls obstetricians who do not adhere to his rules of hygiene assassins, and this is too much for them to bear. For years he is the target of gratuitous recrimination. But he knows that protecting young mothers from being killed has become his vocation.

The mortality rates drop to almost nothing, proving that hygiene is the answer. But the full implications of his friend's infected wound elude Semmelweis. The prophylaxis is right, but the actual cause is not discovered until later. Semmelweis doesn't know that living organisms are involved in infection; he only knows how to prevent infection, and he fights fanatically to do so. Ultimately he sacrifices his life for the mothers whose cause he has championed. Near the end his mental state is such that he has to be committed to an insane asylum, where he dies in 1865 at the age of forty-seven. The cause of death is apparently a cut incurred during an operation. Semmelweis becomes a victim of the same disease that killed his friend Kolletschka.

The Microbe Hunters

Those minute organisms Semmelweis could not see are later called microbes. Once their track is found, doctors and scientists set about hunting them down, and among them are discovered the seeds of infection, including the pernicious bacteria responsible for the sweeping epidemics that have been the scourge of humanity throughout history. And every disease is caused by a different agent.

Of the scientists who devote their lives to this new challenge, none is so successful as a tanner's son named Louis Pasteur, born in 1822 in the Burgundy region of France. Pasteur wants to be a teacher, but his marked scientific aptitude lands him a job as an assistant in a chemical laboratory, and chemistry becomes his career. In Lille he is faced with a very practical chemical problem posed by a major industry of the area, the alcohol industry. The problem is to find a way to keep wine from going bad. Pasteur has deduced that the yeasts used in fermentation are actually tiny organisms. By experimenting he discovers that other tiny organisms cause the undesirable products in wine; they also cause milk to sour, butter to turn rancid, and meat to spoil. His task, then, is to find the right way to destroy these organisms; that will slow down the process of food and beverage spoilage. Pasteur discovers the way: perishables must be heated, for heat kills the microbes. The new method of preservation he thus discovers is still known as pasteurization.

But at the moment Pasteur is far more interested in something else: where do the bacteria come from? In winemaking the answer is clear—the yeasts that start the fermentation process are *added*. But what about the microbes that cause milk to turn? Belief in spontaneous generation is still widespread in Pasteur's day. The assumption is that bacteria and all other microorganisms somehow generate themselves when certain conditions are fulfilled. Sour milk, it is inferred, fulfills these conditions. In other words, the microbes don't cause sour milk; sour milk causes the microbes.

Pasteur sets things straight. By years of experimentation and research, he proves conclusively that there are millions and millions of microorganisms in the air, that millions of them are inhaled by human beings, and that millions of them are contained in foods and beverages. Many of them are harmless, but many others can make man dangerously and even fatally ill. These conclusions are the foundation of all subsequent research dealing with the prevention and retardation of disease.

When the silk manufacturing industry in southern France is brought to the verge of collapse by an infection that kills off the silkworms by the millions, Pasteur finds the agent and develops a way to combat it, thus saving one of France's economic mainstays. Pasteur is also on hand when an outbreak of chicken cholera threatens to ruin the French farmers. He discovers a vaccine that makes the chickens immune. Finally, it is Pasteur who discovers a vaccine for hydrophobia, saving numbers of people from a horrible death. His contributions to science benefit all mankind. He not only makes perishables less perishable; he discovers the means of arming man against infection and disease.

Thousands of doctors pick up where Pasteur leaves off. Aloys Pollender discovers the anthrax bacillus in the body of a dead animal; O. von Bollinger and C. O. Harz find that a fungus is the cause of actinomycosis; and Friedrich Fehleisen traces the cause of erysipelas. Shortly thereafter the diphtheria bacillus is discovered by Friedrich Löffler, the tetanus bacillus by Arthur Nicolaier, and one cause of pneumonia by Albert Fränkel. Toward the end of the nineteenth century Alexandre Yersin and Shibasaburo Kitasato find the infectious agent causing bubonic plague; and soon thereafter the causes of dysentery, sleeping sickness, and syphilis are identified. The names of other discoverers—Kruse, Shiga, Forde, Dutton, Bruce, Schaudinn—show that the war against microbes is truly international. But among the great number of explorers and discoverers whose quiet quest is the common good of humanity, two names are particularly illustrious: Robert Koch and Emil von Behring.

A small-town doctor, Koch distinguishes himself early in his career through his research on anthrax bacilli. Laboring under the most primitive conditions, he makes an important discovery: these bacteria form spores that can live for years, inside or outside an organism. When they enter the body of an animal through the nose or mouth, they grow to bacteria again and produce the disease. This discovery solves a host of what were previously medical mysteries. "Miasma," the pernicious "vapors" in the atmosphere—these are not some vague element, not a mysterious, unfathomable something; they are fungi, bacteria, or the spores of fungi and bacteria. In a treatise on the subject, Koch lays the scientific groundwork for the exhaustive study of these agents: the science we call bacteriology. He photographs and exhibits the disease-spreading microbes, he describes how to grow them in a culture for study purposes, and finally he shows how they can be killed.

By 1882, Koch is able to pursue his research under distinctly improved conditions as a special appointee in the Imperial Health office in Berlin. Only two years later, in the Institute of Hygiene at the University of Berlin, he tells a distinguished audience of doctors that he has discovered the cause of consumption, or what would later be known as tuberculosis. Infesting primarily urban areas, tuberculosis has come to be an international plague; there is little hope for anyone who catches it. Thus Koch's disclosure that the tiny, rodlike tubercle bacillus can be transmitted by breathing comes as a shock. The health authorities in Berlin immediately act upon the knowledge; and although Koch does not succeed in finding a usable counteragent, hospitals begin isolating their tuberculosis patients and thus save thousands of people from certain death.

Koch turns to new challenges. Cholera has spread from India to Egypt and is threatening Europe. So Koch sails to India to study it firsthand. In 1833 he discovers the comma-shaped agent that causes it. He undertakes a series of expeditions, investigating rinderpest (cattle plague) in South Africa; bubonic plague in India; sleeping sickness in Africa; and malaria in Java. In the war against the enemies of human and animal life, Robert Koch is among the staunchest fighters: one of those who extract the secrets from the deadly insurgents we call microbes.

The frontiers are pushed back still further by Dr. Emil von Behring. Experiments on the diphtheria bacillus have already shown that the malignant bacteria in the bodies of animals and human beings produce a kind of poison, a "toxin." Behring discovers that the body defends itself by producing a kind of counterpoison or "antitoxin." By performing experiments on the blood serum of infected animals, he succeeds in isolating these antitoxins; and after repeated tests he is able to show that when antitoxins are injected into the human body, they will prevent infection and cure disease for a certain length of time. This is how Emil von Behring tames diphtheria, the children's disease which up to that point killed almost all its victims. Diphtheria immediately loses its terrors, for the effectiveness of the serum treatment is amazingly consistent.

Not always does the discovery of cause and practicable cure follow in such rapid succession. It takes more than twenty years for doctors and the big drug companies to develop an effective weapon against sleeping sickness. The answer proves to be the famous "Bayer 505," known as Germanin. A practicable cure for leprosy has been available only for a short time, despite countless elaborate tests, and even though lepers are a special concern of Christian missions and their medical missionaries in Africa and Asia.

Three healing agents should be mentioned here. Their development shows the determination of medical sceince, even after the initial period of discovery, to aid the diseased body in every possible way in its fight for health. In 1909 the Jewish doctor Paul Ehrlich finds the cure for syphilis, which has terrorized Europe since the 1500s and has taken a large toll of human life. In 1921 two Canadian doctors, F. G. Banting and C. H. Best, isolate the protein hormone insulin, a remedy for diabetes; and seven years later a remarkable accident leads Sir Alexander Fleming of England to the discovery of penicillin, without which modern chemotherapy is practically unthinkable.

But relief for the sick is not limited to fighting the agents of disease. There is, for example, the invention of a Würzburg professor named Wilhelm Konrad Röntgen, whose "X-ray" machine enables doctors to locate internal diseases, injuries, and malformations. And there is the whole battery of physical and technological aids and facilities, from the hearing aid to the iron lung, which bring the sick new life and hope.

Progress is also being made in the field of surgery and orthopedics. For centuries surgeons have been prevented from making extensive operations by the terrible fact of pain. It is hard for us to imagine what unhappy patients had to endure in earlier days, when the doctor amputated a leg or treated a serious injury. This obstacle is not removed until the pain-killing drugs and local anesthetics are developed. And when the surgeon Joseph Lister discovers a chemical disinfectant, gangrene and wound infection are no longer a menace. The development of antiseptic methods clears the way for major medical and dental surgery.

This is not the place to record all the advances in the broad field of medicine. In recent decades especially, the whole range of medical and technological discoveries and developments in the many areas of specialization—surgery, gynecology, orthopedics, psychiatry, and so on—would fill libraries. But here is the crucial thing: each of these discoveries, however modest or specialized in application, means help for mankind, relief from pain, even deliverance from death. So the examples cited here may stand as representative of the contribution of medical science as a whole. Anyone surveying the "history of mercy" cannot overlook the doctors. Whether Nobel Prize winners or obscure country physicians, they all belong among the benefactors and helpers of mankind.

8. Development of the Christian Diaconate

A Sheriff's Inspection Tour

The world soon comes to know and honor the work of the great doctors, just as today the world is quick to adopt the latest medical discoveries. Meanwhile, many other ministries of Christian caring are going on, quietly and in relative obscurity, their full implications rarely grasped. Who ever stops today to consider the unspeakable suffering formerly endured by men and women in prison, and who knows the names of those who dedicated themselves to prison reform?

The first people to try to improve the hideous conditions in prisons were the Quakers; they had experienced those conditions firsthand. In time, John Wesley's efforts would also have results. But there is one man who, above all others, systematically and unremittingly works for prison reform: John Howard.

Howard is born in England about 1726. At the age of thirty, he takes a trip to Lisbon during the Seven Years' War. En route, his ship is seized and he is carried off to the casemates of a French fortress. Although he is soon released (on his own word, in exchange for a French officer imprisoned in England), he has been through and seen enough to be able to speak from bitter personal experience. Once back in England, he writes a detailed report on the mistreatment of naval prisoners of war by the French. The British admiralty thereupon commissions him to make efforts to negotiate the exchange of British prisoners.

But it is not until seventeen years after his own exchange, when he is already twice a widower, that Howard finds his real calling. For one year he is the high sheriff of Bedfordshire, and during his tenure he decides to inspect the county prisons.

No sheriff before him had ever taken his job so seriously. To go even as far as the prison walls was an act of bravery, and anyone who actually had to go through the gate clapped his handkerchief to his nose and mouth and kept it there. It is not only the fetid odor in the prisons; it is above all the "gaol fever" that is common in almost all of them, as it has been for centuries, taking the lives of thousands of prisoners. Understandably, the wardens and inspectors of such prisons live in mortal fear of contagion, which is why no sheriff ever set foot in the prisoners' cells.

John Howard changes that. Heedless of the risk to his life, he enters the prisons, goes from cell to cell, and talks to the inmates. What he sees is horrible. Sanitation and hygiene are unknown. Filth, vermin, and stench are everywhere. In the subterranean dungeons he sees decaying wrecks of human beings. In dormitory cells men, women, and children are packed together in miserably cramped quarters. Here children are born and old people waste away. Greed, depravity, hunger, despair, cruelty, and futility—that is the atmosphere in which the prisoners are languishing. It is a breeding ground for crime.

Howard immediately sets about improving conditions in the jails of the county. He provides for adequate diet, fresh air, cleanliness, and order. But he soon realizes that the squalor of the physical conditions is not the worst feature of prison life. The inmates suffer far more from general injustice and the mental and emotional ordeal they are put through. Many of them are debtors—who according to the practice of the day are kept in prison until their debts are paid. Sharing the same quarters are criminal suspects who are kept under arrest pending their trial and conviction or acquittal. Convicted criminals are never sentenced to jail; their punishment, which ranges from flogging to hanging, is carried out immediately.

Many of the jails are in private hands, which explains why the owners regard the prisoners as a welcome means of income. Because of the owners' lust for profit and their unscrupulousness, the prisoners often have barely enough to live on, from which must be deducted what the keepers and the veteran prisoners get from them by extortion.

Howard may be the first high official to penetrate this jungle of injustice, cruelty, and corruption; and he proceeds in a realistic, no-nonsense fashion to attack it. In the winter of 1773–74 he makes a trip around the country, inspecting over fifty of the horror chambers called "gaols." Scrupulously he takes notes on all the atrocities he finds. He discovers the power of statistics, and those he reports—the first to be used in the cause of mercy—become the appalling Exhibit A of his case. It has become clear to him that the treatment of criminals in the prisons is itself criminal, and he feels called to rub the noses of his contemporaries in it. From this point on, he never stops traveling and observing; he has begun what Edmund Burke calls his "circumnavigation of charity."

After touring England and Scotland, he visits the Continent, going as far as Russia. What he observes and writes down resembles something out of Dante's *Inferno*. At the same time, however, he begins to feel ashamed of his own country, for nowhere are conditions so monstrous as in England. In Holland, Switzerland, and to some extent in France he finds ideas for a comprehensive program of prison reform. But even where conditions are far better than those in England, the picture is still an awful one. Howard's appeal to his contemporaries—that whatever the prisoners have done, they are human beings and must be treated as human beings—becomes a kind of preamble to a new charter of human rights. The fullness of time has come, a time in which the man behind bars is granted the status of a human being. When man sees in the outcast his fellow human being, then and not until then does he begin to love his neighbor in deed; and this applies equally to the fight against slavery and to the care of the mentally ill. Even the man in death row is still a human being, hence still a neighbor.

Howard builds up his case in clear and logical fashion. Soon it is no longer possible to ignore him or his demands. One day this man, who has financed all his prison tours out of his own pocket, stands before the House of Commons and gives a full report. He is listened to, and he is acclaimed. The tribute of appreciation voted him by the House of Commons opens the eyes of the whole nation.

The first positive results are two new laws. One provides that the fees then required of prisoners before their discharge may be paid out of county funds. This hits directly at one of the gross injustices of the prison system, for up to this time even acquitted prisoners have had to go on serving time because they couldn't pay the fees on which the "gaoler" (an unsalaried official) and others depended. The second law provides that the prisons shall be whitewashed at least once a year. It also prescribes ventilation facilities, baths, and medical care. Howard has thus cleared the first hurdle in a long course, during which he will also take up the issue of sanitary conditions in workhouses and institutions of correction. And while he is not able to realize his detailed program for penal institutions—which would replace punishment with rehabilitation—he is able in his last years to embark on a new task. As before, he prepares for it by careful observation and study.

The new task is that of combating epidemics, especially the plague. He enters isolation wards in France and Italy, and he even sails from Turkey to Venice aboard a merchant ship on which plague is suspected, in order to pursue his firsthand observations in quarantine.

Finally he takes another trip through Russia. Having heard that an epidemic is spreading among the Russian troops on the Crimean peninsula, he heads for the area as fast as he can. There he finds conditions that defy description: grim, mismanaged hospitals where as many as forty men die a day. The authorities try to put off the unwelcome visitor by showing him a few model wards, but Howard is not deceived. He pushes past these to the filthiest, most neglected quarters, becoming the accusor of those who are thus sinning against their fellowman.

This proves to be Howard's last trip. He incurs an infection which takes his life in January 1790, and is buried abroad. The life of this man is overshadowed by great personal tragedy. His two wives died, and his only son went insane. But Howard never wearied. He had experienced conversion, and made his pact with the Almighty, as he said himself; and this was the key to his endurance.

The Miracle of Newgate

Twenty-three years after Howard's death, an English Quaker, the mother of eleven children, stands before the gates of London's largest prison: Newgate. Her name is Elizabeth Fry. She is carrying a package of old clothes, which she wants to give to the inmates herself. The letter of a clergyman who once saw the inside of Newgate and was horrified at the conditions there has moved Mrs. Fry to action. Even now, after all John Howard's work, after the passage of new laws, the prisons are still in a shameful state. Elizabeth Fry wants to do what she can to help.

The governor of the prison, who at first tries to keep Mrs. Fry out, is ultimately obliged to yield to her importunities. He himself only goes into the prison accompanied by a guard, so as to be safe from attacks by the prisoners. Mrs. Fry goes unescorted. What she finds is worse than anything she expected. Nauseating smells assail her nostrils, a bedlam of sounds hammers at her ears—sounds that surely cannot come from human beings. Drunken hags screeching, men cursing, young boys screaming; and in between the small laments of babies. Overcrowded conditions, filth, and squalor have become their normal life. Critically ill inmates lie on rotting straw or on the bare floor. The babies and young children, especially those born in the prison, are almost naked. The misery is indescribable.

During her first visit, Mrs. Fry is permitted only as far as the bars. The scenes that are enacted upon her entrance will stay with her forever. Hands outstretched in supplication or greed; women trying to pull each other away by the hair; men fighting for a place next to the iron bars: all of them hoping for a handout. When Mrs. Fry makes her second visit, she asks to be let into the prison yard. She is undeterred by the warning of the turnkey.

The gate closes behind her and she suddenly finds herself on the other side, in the middle of an arena of brutalized humanity. For a moment there is total silence. The visitor, dressed in the dun-colored habit of the Quaker woman, is standing among the prisoners. She speaks first to a child, rubbing her hand over his head, and then as a mother to mothers:

> You seem unhappy, you are in want of clothes. . . . Would you be pleased if someone were to come and relieve your misery?

Earlham Hall where Elizabeth Fry spends her childhood.

With that the ice is broken. A chair is brought, and Mrs. Fry sits among the women and listens to the outpouring of tormented hearts. She stays several hours. Before she leaves, she tells them Jesus' parable of the workers in the vineyard.

The miracle of Newgate begins. It requires neither new laws nor special action by the authorities. The conditions in the prison are transformed by the prisoners themselves, and anyone who is curious is allowed to come and see for himself. Newgate is now the talk of England. It draws reporters, civil servants, even observers from abroad; and they all see what is new. They walk across scrubbed floors and talk to people who are washed and decently clothed. What amazes the visitors most of all is the morale. There are no more drunkards, cursing is infrequent, and the wrangling has stopped. Women sit together, making clothes for their children. Mrs. Fry and the group of women volunteers she has enlisted have taught them how to sew. There are also reading and writing classes, and, most important, Bible classes for children and adults. A society for the aid of female prisoners is founded in London; many volunteers begin working with inmates, and also with newly discharged prisoners whose return to society is often so difficult. Here one sees the logical outworkings of what Howard began. If it is true that the prisoner should be treated as a human being, how much greater the imperative to come to the aid of those who have paid for their crimes!

Mrs. Fry, like Howard, makes an appearance before Parliament (a House of Commons committee) ; she is the first woman ever to do so. And like Howard, she makes an impression on the members, who officially commend her.

Soon it is established on the basis of solid experience that most of the prisoners of Newgate become law-abiding citizens after their discharge. Elizabeth's work bears rich fruit. But one thing concerns her greatly. It is still customary to punish severe offenses with banishment overseas. Even at Newgate, women and girls are transferred from their cells to "convict ships" and deported to New South Wales, Australia, where they must stay for the rest of their lives. Moreover, the conditions on these convict ships are no better than on the slave ships: the vessels are loaded to the weight limit with passengers, and the sanitary conditions are beyond description. Many of the convicts who are not already hopeless cases become so on the ships, for the prevailing atmosphere is one of corruption and vice.

Like so many of her countrymen, Mrs. Fry possesses a practical instinct for dealing with the matter at hand. She knows immediately what to do. Going aboard one of the convict ships, she finds women and children left to fend for themselves. Nothing is organized. She divides the passengers into groups of twelve and has each group select a monitor. Then she supplies them with needlework, so that they will have something to keep them occupied on the long voyage. The finished work—patchwork quilts and the like—can be sold on shore, thus giving them a start on the way to building a new life in exile. Mrs. Fry also sets up a school for the children on the convict ships. Bibles and prayerbooks are distributed. For the first time, a convict ship leaves port without the usual chaos on board, its passengers no longer bereft of hope. This ship has many successors.

Mrs. Fry's work attracts international notice. Soon letters are arriving from Scotland, Ireland, and the Continent, including Russia. Some of them are invitations from city or national prison administrators and authorities. And so she sets out on a tour, going from prison to prison and country to country. Her method differs from that of Howard: instead of translating the conditions into statistics, she tackles the problems on the spot.

A new phase of prison reform is emerging. What Howard began, Elizabeth Fry carries forward. "Punishment is not for revenge," she says, "but to lessen crime and reform the criminal." She calls for worship services and for a program of spiritual guidance, as well as the provision of useful occupations in the jails and on the convict ships. As one of her biographers puts it:

> She seems never to have lost sight of that noble maxim, "Charity to the soul is the soul of charity."

The Deaconesses of Kaiserswerth

All told, Mrs. Fry goes on five long trips, one of which takes her to Germany. There, as everywhere, she visits the prisons but she is also received in princes' palaces. One day she visits the city prison of Düsseldorf. The German pastor accompanying her is Theodor Fliedner, a native of nearby Kaiserswerth.

Pastor Fliedner has had some unusual experiences in his career. His tiny Kaiserswerth church, deciding it could no longer support a pastor, wanted to release him. But Fliedner goes off on a series of fund-raising trips, and these are so successful that he does not have to abandon his flock. During the trips, which take him as far as Holland and England, he also makes a point of seeing the works of love being performed wherever he goes. He inspects hospitals, orphanages, schools, and rescue-work centers. In Holland he is particularly impressed by the ministry of the diaconate. In England he visits the Newgate prison, and although he fails to meet Mrs. Fry, he does leave with some new ideas. He is deeply disturbed that less—indeed far too little—is being done for prisoners in his own country. Germany is now a confusion of pocket-principalities, and the state of their prisons is universally bad.

On October 9, 1825, Fliedner holds his first prison service in Düsseldorf. From this time on he conducts a regular, unsalaried ministry to prisoners and also tries to secure better treatment for them. In 1826 he founds the Prison Society of Rhineland-Westphalia, which is dedicated to a complete revamping of the prison system. In 1833 he takes in a newly discharged woman prisoner who has no home to go to, accommodating her in the tiny summer cottage on the parsonage property. This is the beginning of a real ministry to prisoners: the post-prison follow-up work. The work grows, and in 1840 it is organized into the Magdalen Foundation and the Magdalen Homes.

Fliedner does not stop merely with prison work. During his travels he has become acquainted with the Mennonite churches in Holland, which have preserved the office and the active role of the deaconess. He may also have gotten some ideas from Vincent de Paul's Daughters of Charity. In 1836, after discussions with like-minded friends, he drafts a charter for a "Protestant Society of Christian Nursing," under whose aegis deaconess-nurses would engage in hospital work. But even at this early point, Fliedner sees clearly that caring for the sick is not the only legitimate field of work for Protestant deaconesses; for according to a clause in this first charter, "The Society shall provide appropriate opportunities of service for those nurses who prove themselves especially capable in attending prisoners, directing preschools for small children, teaching in charity-supported schools, or in caring for the poor."

Fliedner is a man of action. He does not stop merely with drafting plans. On October 13, 1836, in cooperation with a local hospital, he opens the Deaconess House of Kaiserswerth. He begins without funds. The first material assets of the organization are furniture that has been hauled from dusty storage places and stage-prop rooms, or begged from other sources. A just-vacated house is rather bravely purchased on borrowed funds. Gradually the sick begin to come, and nurses begin to volunteer. Gertrud Reichardt, a physician's daughter from a little town named Ruhrort, becomes the first nurse. Fliedner's wife Friederike takes charge of the practical affairs of the institution.

Soon there is more and more work to be done, and the ministry grows. Other organizations appeal to the Fliedners for nurses. Kaiserswerth deaconesses take over the general hospital in Elberfeld, a Frankfurt relief center, and hospitals in Kreuznach and Saarbrücken. Others treat syphilitic women in the Berlin *Charité*, a public hospital, and still others work with the mentally ill in the Marsberg asylum.

In 1844 a pastor from what is known at the time as the Ravensberg region of Prussia, an area that is being swept by a powerful revival movement, calls for a deaconess to work in the rural parish of Jöllenbeck. And thus is born a new ministry in the Protestant church, that of the deaconess parish (social) worker. About the same time, the Kaiserswerth Training Institute for Schoolmistresses is founded. The preschool for small children, started a few years before (1836), has opened a new occupation to the deaconesses, just as Fliedner had foreseen and provided for in his charter. Friedrich Oberlin and Luise Scheppler have opened a day nursery in Steintal (Alsace), thus broadening the scope of the Pestalozzi-inspired educational movement. In 1837 Friedrich Fröbel opens a preschool, for which he coins the name "Kindergarten." The year after that, J. B .F. Marbeau, a social economist in Paris, founds the first *crèche* or nursery home; and training schools for kindergarten teachers naturally follow in the wake of these institutions.

Thus two missions begin to emerge from Fliedner's deaconess ministry. One embraces the care of the poor and the sick. The other is directed toward the education and instruction of the young, including both neglected children and those from good homes. To a great degree, the rapid spread of Fliedner's program is due not only to his compassion and his knowledgeability in all fields of charitable work, but also to his superior talents for organization and administration. It is not long before he gives up his pastorate to devote himself completely to the deaconess program. Many Macedonian calls reach him from abroad, and they take him as far as the United States, where in 1849, with four Kaiserswerth deaconesses, he founds the Pittsburgh "motherhouse." Two years later we find him in Jerusalem, where he establishes a Near Eastern branch of the work that is still in existence today. He is also instrumental in founding motherhouses in Dresden, Berlin, Utrecht, Copenhagen, Oslo, Stockholm, Bern, and many other major cities in Europe. Elizabeth Fry also takes some new ideas back to England as a result of her meeting with Fliedner in Düsseldorf.

The pastor and his deaconesses never ask whether the area to which they are called is Lutheran or Reformed. The diaconate movement, as revived in Kaiserswerth, is interdenominational.

The numerous motherhouses founded in subsequent decades in cooperation with various Protestant churches and fellowships often differ markedly from each other, but they are all engaged in the same works of love. Several of the institutions become especially well known: for example, the Neuendettelsau homes near Nuremberg, founded in 1854 in a small rural community by Wilhelm Löhe, a Lutheran pastor; and the "Sisters of Peace," founded by Eva von Tiele-Winckler (1866–1930), a member of the Upper Silesian nobility, who receives her inspiration and training while staying with the deaconesses at Bodelschwingh's Bethel Community. Today, the Kaiserswerth Association of German Deaconess Houses alone comprises 105 motherhouses and about 35,000 deaconesses.

Fliedner himself watched over his work with untiring vigilance, taking special care to see that its channels remained unblocked. Of frail health, he was greatly sustained during his life and remained active until the end of it. Shortly before his death, when the Prussians and Austrians were fighting the Danes in 1864, he sent a number of Kaiserswerth deaconesses to work in the field hospitals. They were a kind of advance contingent of the Red Cross, which first proved itself in this same war.

Fliedner is numbered among the great trailblazers of the German "Inner Mission," as the work of the Protestant diaconate has been known since Wichern's time. But we cannot speak of Johann Hinrich Wichern and his call to organize the Inner Mission without recalling the other forerunners. In the Protestant sector, the new ministry of active Christian love begins with Francke and Zinzendorf. But we must also mention another man who, seven years after Zinzendorf's death, is named pastor of an out-of-the-way parish called Steintal in Alsace. The man is Johann Friedrich Oberlin.

Oberlin's Flock in Steintal

In the valley of Steintal are five struggling villages, apparently forgotten by the rest of the world. There is hardly a passable road leading to the three little chapels, the scattered farms, or the little homes. The people here are poor and ill-fed. They are Huguenots, who since the Peace of Westphalia have been allowed to practice their Protestant faith here, but who lack the basic essentials of life. Their strength is gradually ebbing. They are no longer equal to the struggle.

Their new pastor, however, is not only a man of burning love and strong faith; he is also eminently practical, and he has prepared himself for a challenge of this kind by some extracurricular study. He knows first aid and the rudiments of medical care, and he knows something about natural science. This knowledge will benefit both the farmers and their land.

But first he needs roads. If people are going to live together in a community, the roads must be in shape. And since they aren't in shape, they must be fixed up. Oberlin goes to work on them himself, but not many people join him at first. Not until he gets more tools from Strasbourg are the dispirited people more inclined to help. Soon he is able to have several work-squads busy at the same time. He drafts the plans himself, has boulders blasted, and gets a bridge built across the Breusch river. The bridge facilitates travel to and from Strasbourg, and Oberlin names it the Bridge Love Built.

After the road-building project, Oberlin immediately addresses himself to the problem of food shortage. Swamps are drained, arid fields are irrigated, torrential creeks are dammed, and precipitous and rocky slopes are graded. Oberlin studies the conditions necessary for growing agricultural staples and he actually puts his scientific knowledge to work. He procures clover seed, grain, and planting potatoes to improve the crop yield; and he manages to grow fruit trees in what up to this time had been a rather unproductive valley. Eventually he succeeds in cultivating new varieties of fruit that grow well in the infertile soil. And since the whole project is everyone's concern, young and old, the children are required to plant two fruit trees before confirmation. The livestock situation isn't good either; so Oberlin buys first-class breeding stock. Since many of the farmers are in debt, Oberlin sets up a loan fund. They need and get better farm implements; and one day Oberlin begins printing a kind of community paper on his own press. This means that the people living in the remotest cabin will be informed about community needs and community aid; it also means that the word of God reaches every person in Steintal.

"Papa" Oberlin (as he comes to be known) has one great concern: the preaching of God's Word. Better roads, fertile fields, healthy livestock, fruitful orchards, are useful to him only in helping people to live as children of God. There are two things he keeps constantly in mind: the general welfare and the individual. Spiritual care and social concern begin with the youngest members of the community. Oberlin's wife Salome and his faithful associate Luise Scheppler introduce knitting to the valley by holding training sessions for the children. This is only one of their many projects.

By the time Oberlin dies, the once cheerless valley of Steintal has become both a prospering settlement and an active Christian community. His achievements not only place him among the fathers of the Inner Mission, but also, and with equal justice, among the precursors of a new social order.

About the turn of the nineteenth century there is a Silesian baron named Hans von Kottwitz who lives in the Oder valley. At the court of Frederick the Great, the baron is very much a part of the social whirl of his peers, fond of worldly, amoral pleasures. He toys with the idea of emigrating to America and, in fact, is halfway there when he is persuaded to return.

After much turmoil of soul, the baron becomes a Christian. He gets acquainted with the Herrnhuter Brethren and he begins to view the need of his people as his own need. Thus he finds his calling: as a Christian he is going to help those who need his help.

When he finds out about the plight of the mountaineer-weavers, he acts immediately to provide work for the willing and able, and food for the hungry. Mills are built on his orders, and when they are finished he not only supplies the materials but pays well for the products. When it comes to marketing these products, however, he meets with a series of reverses. The venture is soon deep in the red. The baron invests more and more of his assets until his whole estate is in jeopardy. But he doesn't give up. Finally he succeeds in finding the manpower and the necessary support for his project, and is able to check the decline of the weaving craft in his time.

Later von Kottwitz goes to Berlin, which in 1806 is threatened with an acute food shortage. Again he is on hand to help. On the

Alexanderplatz in what is now East Berlin he finds and secures the use of a vacant army barracks dubbed the Oxhead. He lives there, serving the poor and unfortunate, instructing and providing for children and supplying food and jobs for adults. It is his life of meekness and humility to which the philosopher J. G. Fichte pays tribute, and which makes the young Johann Wichern stop to examine his own life.

The baron continues to operate the Oxhead after the food crisis is over, contributing some ten thousand talers a year out of his own pocket. After thirteen years, the city of Berlin takes over the "bankrupt private factory and welfare institution," but von Kottwitz remains in charge of its operations until his death.

Finally we would do well to mention Johannes Daniel Falk, whose theological studies at Halle are financed by the city council in his home town of Danzig. One of the councillors says to him in parting, "You remain our debtor, Johannes. If poor children should ever knock on your door, just imagine it is we, the old councillors of Danzig, and don't turn them away."

Falk remembers. After a short time at Halle, he switches his interests to literature and transfers to Weimar, where he establishes a reputation as a writer. But soon he comes to see that the kind of writing he is doing is a "very tawdry affair," and that he cannot make much of a contribution that way. About the same time he unexpectedly meets his first big test in life. French troops march into Weimar, and many inhabitants take headlong flight. But Falk courageously stays on, opposing the looting soldiers and arranging for food rations for those who have remained in the city. He also secures first aid supplies for the wounded and, ultimately, works as an interpreter for the French. This position makes it possible for him to soften some of the harsher features of the occupation army's sanctions. Later, Falk is again called upon to intervene in a similar situation. In 1812, when Spanish troops under French command devastate the area, he is commissioned by the Weimar government to undertake relief measures; and in so doing he risks his life more than once.

A year later death takes four of Falk's children, and he suffers a total collapse, longing that he too may die. But when he emerges from the period of despair he accepts his life as a new gift from the hand of God and dedicates himself to helping children who have lost their parents. Aided by his Society of Friends in Need, he is soon able to found an orphanage for a hundred children. The Lutherhof, as it is called, suffers many setbacks, but Falk is always able to keep it from going under; and when its financial resources are gravely threatened during the famine of 1816, Falk's wife gives her entire inheritance to preserve her husband's work.

Falk's educational methods break with the stern discipline of earlier institutions. "We forge our chains from within," he says, "and scorn those laid on us from without." He turns no one away, and it is certainly not the memory of the Danzig city councillors alone that motivates him. His whole life is characterized by faith; his deepest desire is to help everyone in need. "If only I could provide," he writes, "for all the destitute children wandering along the Rhine, the Elbe, and the Danube, often starving in body and soul." He has long since relinquished his old dreams of literary fame. He is a servant of the "least of these," and of the lowliest.

The more one leafs through the old histories, the harder it becomes to survey the whole panorama of mercy. Baron von Kottwitz's "Oxhead" does not stand alone, any more than the ministry of the deaconess-nurses of Kaiserswerth or Falk's school in the "Lutherhof" in Weimar. A poorhouse in Augsburg called the "Klauckehaus" (founded by one Beckle and backed by a philanthropist named Barth) dates from 1702. In Hanover during the famine of 1772–73, Mayor W. A. Alemann establishes a kind of soup kitchen for the poor. The Hanseatic city of Hamburg lays special stress on good works. As far back as Reformation times Hamburg has had a city-wide poor relief program, including a common chest. In 1526, a group of Hamburg citizens state that the reasons for the founding of this fund are laid down in the "divine Word," which teaches that men are "obligated to share the burdens of their neighbors in Christian love." Later an orphanage is founded in Hamburg. Its children are especially urged to pray for those who give food, clothing, and money. Such a prayer request is characteristic of this maritime city, where the precariousness of human life is never far from the minds of its citizens.

Housing shortages and sickness, hunger and epidemics go together. In the nineteenth century the plight of the homeless is repeatedly exposed, as can be seen here in a sketch of the Berlin Workhouse published in "Gartenlaube" in 1858.

In 1683 Hieronymus Passmann opens a poor-school in Hamburg that is attended by some 300 children. Subsequently three more such schools are founded. August Hermann Francke becomes acquainted with the work, and when in Hamburg he teaches at Passmann's school. The city's close ties with the Netherlands certainly had a bearing on the founding of such institutions; there is no doubt that ideas entering Germany via Hamburg from Holland blend in with Francke's own ideas.

Soon Hamburg becomes famous for the philanthropy of its citizens. But what comes to light during a city poverty survey in 1785 is alarming. Although not a few of the poor forego the assistance they have been receiving rather than report their financial status to the canvassers, hundreds of others are found to be living in the most abject poverty, without anyone's having known. Most of these have no bed of their own; close to two thousand have no clothing of their own. And those who canvass the rural flatlands surrounding the city find more hardship than was ever suspected.

The new awareness of need, along with the example set by his friend Mayor Alemann, bring Prof. Johann G. Büsch, an economist, on the scene. Büsch and Caspar Voght, a Hamburg merchant, are instrumental in stirring up interest in poor relief in the city's Patriotic Society. Their first accomplishment is the founding of a medical institute where the poor can receive treatment and assistance. Meanwhile the real extent of poverty in the city is being more fully exposed all the time, and Büsch sets about drawing up plans for a comprehensive welfare program. On November 2, 1788, Hamburg gets its Municipal Poorhouse. The city is divided into a number of districts, to which a total of 180 workers are assigned. This is a surprisingly large number, considering Hamburg's modest size at the time, and it clearly shows that the sponsors of the legislation mean business and are trying to help everyone in need.

Hamburg is also the home of Amalie Sieveking, who without training starts teaching a small class of children. During the great cholera epidemic of 1831 she goes into full-time nursing work, undeterred by the prejudice she encounters, and becomes an indispensable assistant to the doctors.

Fliedner wants her to take charge of his motherhouse in Kaiserswerth, but she stays in Hamburg. And although she doesn't succeed in starting a Protestant sisterhood, her society of nurses and poverty workers, which begins with only twelve women, is able to alleviate a great deal of want and hardship. She is one of the first to recognize the urgency of the housing crisis and its potential for harming body and soul. In the eighteen-family settlement she founds, pale city children begin to blossom in the fresh air. Amalie Sieveking is also happy to see a change in the life of a number of drinkers and unfaithful husbands.

Eight years before the cholera epidemic, Johann Gerhard Oncken lands at Hamburg. At the age of fourteen, Oncken had left his home in Oldenburg (an old German state that bordered on the North Sea), traveled to Scotland and England, and was converted to Christianity through a Methodist minister. Oncken comes to Hamburg as a missionary of the Continental (Bible)

Society, an English organization. In 1824 he is instrumental in starting a Sunday school in Hamburg. The sponsor of this venture is Pastor Johann W. Rautenberg, an active booster of all home missions work and a friend of Amalie Sieveking's. Later, Oncken goes on to found the German Baptist movement; out of Pastor Rautenberg's Sunday school will emerge the vision for a new ministry of practical Samaritan love, as we shall see.

Wichern and the Inner Mission

One day a young man named Johann Hinrich Wichern is engaged to teach in Rautenberg's Sunday school. Wichern knows hardship at first hand. Born in 1808, the oldest of seven children, Johann is just sixteen years old when his father dies and he is faced with the task of supporting the family. The Latin lessons he gives in order to put himself through school do not pay enough, so he takes a job teaching in a boarding school run by Wilhelm Plun. Here he discovers his love for children; and the change of course he has made in order to ease his mother's burdens turns out not to be a detour after all. By dint of hard work he is able to prepare himself for the university where he studies theology. But he never forgets what he first discovered at Plun's school: his real work will be to serve his neighbor.

Wichern finds plenty of opportunity for service in the Sunday school. It is located in St. Georg, a laborers' settlement on Hamburg's outskirts which has its share of saloons and shanties. Wichern sees that education alone isn't going to help the children. As soon as school is over they are back in the streets, where they started. He follows them to their sad little hovels and tries to do something about their neglect, but he gets nowhere. At that point the idea of a rescue-home comes to him. The children would move out of their demoralizing milieu into a home of their own, where the facilities are clean and the atmosphere wholesome.

Wichern calls on his home town for help, and Hamburg's citizens show themselves receptive. An old farmhouse in Horn, another nearby village, is turned over to him. Called *Ruges Haus* after a previous owner, it will now become world famous under the name of *Rauhes Haus* (literally, "rough house"). Wichern moves in on October 31, 1833. His mother and the other children help him with the furnishings, and before the year is out, fourteen

The old "Rauhes Haus" in Hamburg, where neglected boys first find a home.

Hamburg Rauhes Haus

delinquent boys are welcomed into the house. (By now Wichern is thinking of a whole youth village where young people can grow up in families, free of any constraint, held only by the bonds of love: something like Pestalozzi's venture in Stans.) He gives the boys plenty to do, so as to channel their excess energy. There is a woodworking shop, a cobbler's shop, a book bindery, and the farm itself, all of which offer plenty of opportunity for exercise and activity.

Like all doers of good works, Pastor Wichern is not spared disappointment. But a spirit of humble waiting on God carries him through the hard beginning stages and the many setbacks. Once he goes after a boy who had run away several times. He finds him in a tavern, miserable and alone, and takes him by the hand. "You must be hungry," he says. Taking him to a bakery, he has the boy eat as much as he wants. Then he takes him back to the Rauhes Haus and talks him into staying. No angry words, no punishment.

It is not long before Wichern needs some assistants. He addresses an inquiry to C. H. Zeller, who since 1820 has been in charge of a home for underprivileged children and a teacher training school, both located in a former lodge of the Teutonic Knights in Beuggen, near Basel, Switzerland. Zeller sends him an alumnus of his institution, a baker's assistant named Baumgartner, who hikes to Hamburg to become the first "Brother" (as Wichern's assistants come to be known) of the Rauhes Haus.

In 1844 a small training school for these Brothers is opened, which enables Wichern to train his own assistants. Soon Brothers from Hamburg are being sent to most European countries and to the United States, where they work as housefathers in rescue-homes, preachers, hostel managers, and prisoner-welfare workers. These missions reflect Wichern's major accomplishment in the Protestant church: after centuries of struggle and controversy over doctrinal purity, which often left little room for helping one's neighbor, Wichern combines the two main tasks of the Christian—evangelization and the ministry of love—in what comes to be known as the Inner Mission.

In 1848, the year of the liberal-nationalist revolution in Germany, Wichern appeals to the General Conference of the Protestant church at Wittenberg: "One thing is needful, that the Protestant church as a whole acknowledge for itself: *The work of the Inner Mission is mine*; and that it seal the whole of this work with one great proclamation: *Mine is to love as well as believe.* Love must burn in the church as a bright torch of God, proclaiming that Christ has become incarnate in his people. As Christ reveals himself in the living word of God, so he must also proclaim himself in the works of God; and the loftiest and purest of these works, that which is most intrinsically the work of the church, is saving love." The appeal is heard, and now the Hamburg pastor is called upon everywhere for aid and counsel.

After barely a year it is resolved to form a Central Committee of the Inner Mission, which is to integrate all the ministries of the diaconate in Protestant regions. The first of the Committee's bylaws clearly shows the intention of Wichern and of all those who have responded to his call: "The purpose of the Inner Mission is to deliver the Protestant community from its distress of body and spirit through the proclamation of the Gospel and the brotherly ministry of love."

The Rauhes Haus is now only part of his work. He has already been called to Upper Silesia, where an epidemic of typhus has broken out (in 1847). Great numbers of people have succumbed, and the local authorities have done nothing. Not until the press raises an outcry is Berlin moved to act. In February 1848 a commission is dispatched to the area, and Wichern is on it. Another member, a physician named Rudolf Virchow, is one of the few people on the commission who are unafraid to get to the roots of the matter. He does not turn away from the most wretched-looking shanty, and he comes to see that the needs being uncovered are social rather than purely medical.

The epidemic in Upper Silesia motivates Dr. Virchow to political activity as a means of doing something about the social problems of the day. Wichern, however, sticks to on-the-spot aid. Constantly on the go, he helps to save numbers of orphans from certain disaster.

In Hamburg, the founder of the Inner Mission is able to realize one of his goals himself by starting a city mission. The mission combines the proclamation of the word of God with practical deeds of Christian love—a combination which is used to attack the growing urban crisis and which soon proves effective in other large cities as well. The wayside hostels for journeymen-craftsmen also grow out of a suggestion of Wichern's. In 1854 Professor Clemens Perthes founds the first of these in Bonn. A promotional article he writes on the project sounds the call to action.

It is not long before the king of Prussia commissions Wichern to launch a national penal reform program. But bureaucratic opposition and widespread prejudice make his task a very hard one, and although he does manage to incorporate the work of Howard, Mrs. Fry, and Fliedner into the machinery of the Prussian government and to prepare the way for a thoroughgoing penal reform, it is preeminently this assignment that saps his strength. During the war which Prussia and Austria fight against Denmark in 1864, he is still able to work with twelve of his Brothers in attending the casualties under the auspices of the Red Cross. When war breaks out again in 1866 and 1870, Wichern and 1,360 Brothers are able to aid many more thousands of soldiers, but thereafter he becomes crippled by paralysis. The following years find him progressively weaker, and in 1881 he dies.

Six years later he is followed in death by Gustav Werner, the father of the Swabian Inner Mission and founder of the Reutlingen training center for Rauhes Haus Brothers, a large complex that is still in existence today. Werner, who as a young vicar in Strasbourg is one of a group engaged in a new translation of the Bible, is profoundly stirred by the ministry of Johann Oberlin. Some time later, in the small community of Walddorf bei Tübingen, as he is standing beside the grave of a mother of six small children, he is obliged to recognize how little willingness there is on the part of the parish to alleviate need. No longer able to ignore the call to compassion, he finds room for one of the orphans in his home; and that is how his children's rescue work begins. It eventually takes him out of the ministry in the Württemberg church and becomes his life vocation. Faithful to his motto, "If it doesn't produce action, it doesn't count," he joins the attack on want and misery.

On one front Werner dares to advance further than any of the other leaders of the Inner Mission. He sees the implications of the revolution brought about by the machine; and after working his way through to a creed of Christian socialism, he attempts a factory evangelization program. His own factories not only finance his training centers; they also become the home base of a Christian worker-class. His smaller business operations succeed; the larger ones run into serious financial trouble, and of the latter only one survives. But Werner acted rightly in addressing himself to social issues—issues whose dominance of the nineteenth century would continue to grow.

9. Industry and War

Lord Shaftesbury and the Struggle in Parliament

Baron von Kottwitz's experiences with the weavers; the lesson Dr. Virchow reads in the typhus epidemic in Upper Silesia; the growing urban and human crisis in the larger cities—all these are signs of the times. Monumental tasks are piling up, and in these years of beginnings, no one can see how they might be dealt with. Since the invention of printing at the beginning of the modern era, no invention has so transformed man's way of life as the steam engine, the magic wand of the Industrial Age. Factories are mushrooming, and the cities are drawing the people like magnets away from the farms and the village workshops into their own sphere of influence. The plight of the weavers, which von Kottwitz is able to alleviate, is only one illustration of a trend: people are being cut off from their roots. The urban migration has begun, and since that migration is both chaotic and precipitous, the results are often tragic. Since the factories are turning out products that are much cheaper than handmade goods, craftsmen begin to lose their needful share of the market and many are reduced to begging.

The first to feel this squeeze are the textile workers. The man out of work who doesn't want to starve moves to the city and tries to get a job in a mill or factory. He doesn't always succeed, but if there is a job to be had anywhere, no questions are asked about the pay scale. The main thing is to make enough money to keep the wolf from the door.

Finding a job is one thing; finding a place to live is quite another. The housing problem, already cause for alarm in some cities, now becomes a major crisis. Soon primitive shanties are huddled around the factories, or barracklike tenements are built in which the inhabitants barely have room to breathe. Often several families must live in one room. The conditions are indescribable.

But there is something even worse than cultural displacement and the housing crisis, and that is the callous exploitation of the worker by the factory owners. True, the offenses are not always committed deliberately. Often the factories are simply caught up and swept along in the breaking tide of industrial change. The new situation is impossible to cope with. Questions of working hours, working conditions, and job security (to say nothing of labor having a share in management decisions), just do not arise. The French Revolution has sounded the call for human rights, and the echoes are still reverberating; but who thinks of applying the principle of human rights to the new social order? No one had foreseen the impact that industrialization would have upon society; no one had dreamed of the sudden emergence of a new "fourth class"—the proletariat. In the machine age, who looks beyond the machine? A few people, perhaps. It is said that George Stephenson, builder of the first steam-blast locomotive, was concerned about occupational hazards and industrial safety precautions, but Stephenson is an exception. Most manufacturers who have invested heavily in the new machines are thinking about one thing: how to get the most out of the investment. The investment must pay off. The new products are selling, and workers can be had at any price—that is how people are now converted into ciphers. Women and children are hired because they come cheaper; and they are worked from early until late. The main thing is to keep the machines running and business booming.

No one shows any concern about adequate working conditions. The spotlight is on the product, not on the man who does the work. And the result is that working conditions in industry are not much different from working conditions under slavery.

The demand for coal and iron in the new factories soars; the development of new methods of materials-transport within the mines is not rapid enough to keep pace with it. Consequently, the conditions in the mines grow worse. Women and children are harassed and driven. One has to look at some of the pictures of those times—the first half of the nineteenth century—and read the accounts of the first reformers to get an idea of the kind of inhumanity and virtual slavery that was possible in those days, to some extent on the Continent but notably in England, the cradle of industry. And this at a time when Parliament is denouncing real slavery and the African slave trade. "Yorkshire Slavery" reads the accusing caption over a letter written by Richard Oastler to the "Leeds Mercury." Yorkshire is William Wilberforce's old constituency, and in 1830 (Wilberforce having retired by then) one of its representatives in Parliament is Henry Brougham, whom Oastler calls a "giant of antislavery principles." Oastler too had emphatically espoused the cause of the Negroes. So had all Bradford, a town of conspicuous piety, which had been outraged that Negroes on faraway islands should be lashed like animals. But Oastler discovers a scarcely less reprehensible form of slavery flourishing right under the noses of Bradford's residents. Children are being forced to work at machines thirteen hours a day under the constant threat of the overseer's strap. In most cases they are obliged to wolf down their meager rations on the job. Some of them are so small that they have to be carried to work. At the instigation of Antony Ashley-Cooper (later Lord Shaftesbury) a commission is formed to investigate the question of child labor in mines and collieries; and when its report is issued in 1842, the shock waves reverberate throughout England. The physical conditions and the psychological and moral climate have combined to produce an appalling and previously unsuspected state of affairs. Seventeen-year-old Anne Hamilton testifies:

> I have repeatedly wrought the twenty-four hours, and after two hours of rest and my peas [soup] have returned to the pit and worked another twelve hours.

Frequently, boys and girls between seven and twenty-one work in rags or almost stripped. "Hewers" lie on the ground, naked, breaking up the coal, with girls assigned to help them. Women and girls often trudge along ten miles of slippery paths a day, heavy loads of coal on their backs. The women, used as beasts of

Silesian weavers, in misery and desperation, rise up en masse to protest their brutalizing conditions.

This political cartoon from the "Fliegende Blätter," 1848, shows what the "official remedy" for such "revolts" was like.

burden, are actually much worse off than the pit ponies, which pull their carts over iron rails. Other coal sleds are pulled by pregnant women working on hands and knees; a chain hooked to the sled is fastened to a belt or girdle around their waist. Within hours after they have given birth, they are back in the mines. Ignorance, alcoholism, brutality, and immorality proliferate in such conditions and among those who work under them; if the workers survive at all they will see nothing but this incomprehensible misery from childhood on.

It is impossible to get a true picture of the times in all their detail, even though they are separated from our own times by little more than a century. It is also impossible to record all the individual and collective efforts at reform. The inhumanity that is exposed on the one hand, and the humanity that emerges on the other, constitute the beginnings of modern social history. Among other names and events, Robert Owen, the English social reformer, and his "Institution for the Formation of Character" in New Lanark belong here. Owen must at least be given credit for ideas that were in advance of his time: preschools, adult education, and social activities centers. It might be noted, by the way, that Owen soon becomes involved in the emerging labor union movement—a reminder that from this point on, social history is going to be made on more and more fronts.

The history of socialism is worth studying in its own right, of course, and we cannot do it justice here. Oastler and Shaftesbury may stand as representative of many other champions of labor, and of their struggles to achieve adequate living and working conditions, justice, and humanity.

Particularly in the case of Lord Shaftesbury, one can detect something of the selfless dedication that has its roots in Christianity, showing that even in times of upheaval Christians are given a clear vision of the new and urgent challenges that are emerging. At the same time it cannot be gainsaid that the church (like most governments) is frighteningly dilatory in facing up to these challenges. The reaction of all the established institutions, ecclesiastical and secular, is one either of indifference or of hostility. This seems to be a law of history borne out even at a time when the consciences of men are being stirred by the French and American Revolutions. The demand for universal human rights is no mere slogan yet men are reluctant to draw the corresponding implications; and in comparison with the rapid pace of developments, the changes that are put through are too little and too late. The serfdom of the peasantry is largely ended, freedom of speech and of the press are beginning to be taken seriously, and yet it is still true that countless Europeans are forced to emigrate in order to live. And many of the peasants, barely free of their old indenture, are compelled to live under the new oppression of the machine if they do not want to starve.

As a politician, Lord Shaftesbury himself has to shake off the insularity of his education and his class before he is able to see the need around him. At that point he perceives where his place is: at the side of the poor.

Born in 1801 in London, of aristocratic heritage but the child of tyrannical parents, Antony Ashley-Cooper becomes the champion of the poor by reason of the tragedy of his own childhood, in which he had known loneliness, cold, and hunger, but little love. Elected to the House of Commons at the age of twenty-five, for a time he pursues his own interests. His first parliamentary move for human rights is, so far as he is concerned, little more than a routine matter during his tenure as a commissioner on the India Board of Control. To the horror of all the specialists on India, he calls for a ban on the Indian custom of suttee—the ritual burning of a widow on the funeral pyre of her husband. During his two-year tenure, he develops a keen interest in missionary work in India and becomes an enthusiastic advocate of a colonial policy based on Christian principles, whose objective would be to prepare the colonies and their peoples through a gradual process of education for eventual independence.

Ashley next turns to the care of the insane. He supports and helps pass a bill to improve the system of regulating the asylums and thus to reform what are, by and large, scandalous and prisonlike conditions. The main provision of the bill is a new regulatory commission. Lord Ashley becomes one of its members and, after a year, its chairman. For fifty-seven years he is active on this watchdog committee.

Initially he attaches little importance to the growing ferment among England's working classes. He has no plans in mind for the new labor movement, and the rational-socialist thought of an Owen repels him. But one day there is a change.

It is precipitated by Oastler. Ever since his opening salvo in the "Leeds Mercury," Oastler, a born agitator, has kept up his efforts to din it into Parliament and the public that England must put a stop to its own brand of slavery. Taking a cue from Clarkson and his abolitionist crusade, Oastler continues the attack with public meetings, petitions, appeals, and exposés. His short-range objective is to curtail the working hours of children; later he hopes to win a ten-hour day for adults, and finally to get child labor abolished altogether. Michael Sadler, a Leeds importer who successfully stands for Parliament, undertakes to lead the attack in

Women and girls, often clad in scanty rags, may have to work in the mines for twenty hours a day and more.

the House of Commons, but all he accomplishes initially is the appointment of a Select (investigative) Committee. Under Sadler's leadership, however, this committee does some thorough work. In many ways its report is a counterpart to the evidence amassed against the slave trade. Ashley first learns of the affair when he reads extracts of the report in the (London) "Times," and he is immediately aroused. When Sadler loses his seat in the Commons, Ashley volunteers to take up the issue. And this decision sets his political course. He has rejected a comfortable and successful career in favor of controversy and unpopularity, for he knows the cause is humanity.

Ashley now becomes the spokesman in the Commons for the "short-time" legislation. He puts forward no political platform; he wants only to defend the interests of the workers: men, women, and children. Especially the children. The manufacturers are conducting an unprincipled whitewash campaign, dismissing child labor as light exercise. Factory work, they say, is the best way to protect the children from idleness. They protest that the curtailment of child labor would spell the ruin of the factories. And they are unanimous in their opinion that too much work is better than no work at all. Evil deeds are thus cloaked in goodwill.

Children assigned to the "hewers" working the seams must perform hard labor.

But there is the committee's report, and the evidence, in black and white; and more evidence is being collected, for Ashley is now inspecting the mines and factories himself, just as Clarkson inspected the conditions on the slave ships. Ashley sees what the light exercise is really like. According to careful calculations he has made, he estimates that, in terms of performance and physical strain, the work performed by a child in the mines is more grueling than the forced marches soldiers are put through.

Robert Southey, the English poet, writes to Lord Ashley:

> They who grow cotton are merciful taskmasters in comparison with those who manufacture it. I know not how a cotton-mill can be otherwise than an abomination to God and man. . . . Moloch is a more merciful friend than Mammon.

Ashley elaborates the thought in a speech in Parliament, in which he says in effect:

> I have heard of people who sacrificed their children to Moloch, but they were merciful compared with the English of the nineteenth century. I have heard of the infanticide of the Indians, but even they are merciful compared with the English of the nineteenth century. For these nations killed their unhappy young at once, thus obviating a long course of suffering and crime. But we, after we have utterly sapped their bodies and souls, fling them out

into the world: mere hulks of skin and bones, incapable of work, corrupted in their minds, and defrauded of the immortality of their souls.

During an investigation of factory conditions, one cotton-mill owner testified calmly that most of the children contracted lung disease from the dust and that many died before their twentieth year. Nonetheless, the House of Commons temporizes once more, voting merely to establish a Royal Commission of Inquiry on child labor in the factories. The report of that commission is impossible to ignore; but the resulting legislation is only a feeble attempt at redress. Children under nine may not be employed in textile mills (except silk mills). Children from nine through eleven years old may work no more than nine hours a day and forty-eight hours a week. Children working in factories are required to attend school two hours a day.

The best feature of the new law is the system of inspection it establishes, but there are loopholes. By and large, the new provisions are more than inadequate. The advocates of the reform of working conditions and of poor relief are indignant both at the factory law and the new poor law of 1834; for neither keeps the employers from exploiting the workers. According to the poor law, for example, a man who is out of work (and layoffs during slack periods are common) is not to get "home assistance." If he wants relief, he is to live in a workhouse under deliberately inferior conditions. No wonder that such a man would put up with the poorest factory job and endure the harassment of his employers in silence rather than go to the workhouse. A character in Charles Dickens perfectly illustrates the situation: Oliver Twist, a poor, half-starved orphan whom everyone spurns and no one pities, is knocked about in the world, nowhere treated as a human being, universally regarded as a burden. The poor wander about England just like Oliver, begging for a job so as to escape the workhouse.

Oastler is financially ruined in his fight for the rights of workers. He loses his whole fortune, eventually lands in debtors' prison, and is thus effectively silenced. But Ashley fights stoutly on. In 1840 he succeeds in getting two more inquiries going. One deals further with the employment of women and children in the mills and factories. The other one, conducted by a Royal Commission, takes up child labor in the mines and collieries, as well as in industries not yet covered by the factory acts. This commisson's first report, which appears two years later, is a chronicle of horror. Introducing it to the Commons, Ashley says:

> Sir, it is not possible for any man, whatever be his station, if he have but a heart within his bosom, to read the details of this awful document without a combined feeling of shame, terror, and indignation.

The undertone running through the whole speech is: Do not forget that these people are human beings, like ourselves.

For Ashley there can now be no more holding back. Halfway measures will not do. He moves to abolish employment in the mines of women and girls, and of boys under thirteen. The bill passes the Commons easily; the House of Lords, a number of whose members are in the mining business, manage to weaken it slightly (lowering the minimum age for boys to ten), but in the main it is unimpaired.

In 1843 the commission's second report is published. Among its disclosures: seasonal factories often work their children from four a.m. to eleven p.m. Parents stay awake nights in order to get their children up in time for work. Again Ashley decides to go the whole way. Only one thing will put an end to such indignities: a compulsory education plan.

But the government finds an interim solution with a bill that, as enacted, provides for a half-time system for children: six and a half hours of work a day and about fifteen hours of school a week. Young persons' hours continue at twelve a day (women of all ages now being protected as young persons). Ashley sees nothing to do but continue to push for a ten-hour bill. A hard battle ensues, one of Shaftesbury's chief opponents being Prime Minister Robert Peel, who believes that humanitarian feelings blind men to economic necessities.

In 1846 Ashley resigns his seat over another issue, leaving the Ten Hours Bill in the hands of John Fielden, a member of the House of Commons. Fielden's measure, which passes, stipulates a ten-hour day for young persons and women. The laborers, thinking they have won a total victory, cheer Oastler, Ashley and Fielden. It is generally assumed that the Ten Hours Law applies to adult males too. But everything is thrown into question again when it becomes apparent that the new law has loopholes. There is no provision saying that the ten hours must be consecutive, and thus many employers use a system of "relays" and "shifts" making it possible for them to work their people for more than ten hours and still escape the eye of the inspectors.

Ashley is not satisfied. He has returned to Parliament in the meantime (taking his seat in the upper house as Lord Shaftesbury in 1851), and in the laws passed in the 1850s and in 1874 and 1878 his aims—an effective Ten Hours Law and the necessary protective measures for women, children, and young people—are realized. They are not his triumph alone, and it would be historically inaccurate to give him and his handful of allies all the credit for the legislation. Neither their action nor the exposure of the shocking conditions that prevailed in the beginning years of the big industries could have won the day alone. The evolution of the industries themselves also contributed something, especially the continuing trend toward consolidation and bigness. Labor now begins to organize, and as the unions achieve equal status with management, it wins an important franchise: a voice in its own affairs. The emergence of class struggle, violence, strikes, and other new methods cannot obscure the significant role that the militant proletariat wins for itself in this age of social upheaval.

Though never a union backer, Shaftesbury is totally faithful to the cause of the workers. What he sees first in any task facing him is always the human side; the everyday worries of the flower girl weigh just as much as the fight for the welfare of hundreds of thousands. When he goes for a walk in the slums of London one day, he does not hesitate to add one more task to his work load.

"What a perambulation have I taken to-day in company with Dr. Southwood Smith!" he writes in his diary in 1841. "What scenes of filth, discomfort, disease! What scenes of moral and mental ill!" He goes on more of these walks, with Dr. Smith and other companions. As a result he becomes one of the early fighters for public health and sanitation, which at that time interest few people. His concern is that the "domiciliary condition" of the working classes should be "Christianized." He recognizes as few others that it is impossible to save the souls of men and ignore the needs of their bodies.

Seven years after that perambulation with Dr. Smith, a Central Board of Health is established in London. Ashley is the chairman and his associates are Dr. Smith and Edwin Chadwick, both public health reformers. The Board is abolished in six years, but Ashley has seen what needs to be done and he follows through on it. London gets a drainage system, and other cities follow its lead. Finally the "window tax" is repealed. In consequence of this bizarre regulation, which assessed dwellings according to the number of their windows or lights, many people preferred to do without a normal number of windows rather than pay the tax involved.

Ashley also sees to it that the poorhouses are regulated. Model institutions are built, in which a private room—not large, but neat and clean—can be had for fourpence. Up to then, one could pay that much for a place on the floor of a pub, where forty or more people, lying side by side, would try to sleep. Now, a "Society for Improving the Condition of the Labouring Classes" provides inexpensive three-room flats, and eventually entire workers' housing developments are built. One of these still bears Lord Shaftesbury's name.

All this is the beginning of a struggle that is still going on today. The glittering fronts of the big cities hide slums—back alleys, tenements, hovels, in which poverty and crime are equally commonplace—and London is no exception, as the shocking reports of the London City Mission attest. Founded in 1835 by a Scotsman named David Nasmith, the London City Mission regularly sends its men into the slums to preach the gospel in urban backyards, seeking to bring light to those living in darkness. The work not only requires total dedication; it also requires courage. This is borne out by an experience of Dr. Thomas Barnardo, later to be known as the "father of nobody's children." Early in his ministry Barnardo is distributing Bibles in the slums

A working-class home in London, about 1850. Homes like this are found in all European cities during the Industrial Age.

one day when a group of young toughs break two of his ribs. He decides not to prosecute and is thus able to win the confidence and friendship of his assailants.

Dr. Barnardo is also one of those assisted by Lord Shaftesbury, as is a crippled shoemaker named John Pounds, who founds one of the first "Ragged Schools." Pounds opens his doors to the city's juvenile delinquents and attempts to provide a home for them. He also wants them to get some education. Pounds is not able himself to provide anything very solid along these lines, but when Ashley finds out about the Ragged Schools through an article in the "Times," he lends his support. More schools are established, and Ashley becomes president of the Ragged School Union. No task moves him so much as this one, though it appears at first glance one of the humblest.

Schooling turns out to be the only means of reaching the people in this urban jungle, especially the children. Manual arts courses for the boys and homemaking courses for the girls enable the children of derelicts to rise above their circumstances and grow up to be responsible adults. The schools are founded on the premise that it is futile to build better homes and create better living conditions if the people that are to enjoy them are not helped to come alive in mind and spirit. The Ragged Schools prove their worth, and they are continued even after compulsory education goes into effect.

There is hardly a sector of human life in which Lord Shaftesbury does not take an active part in organizing or supporting reform. He makes it possible for discharged convicts to emigrate, and he starts a loan fund for flower girls. He is active in the planning of parks and playgrounds, and he raises money for the Jewish victims of the pogroms in Russia in 1882. He supports the Zionists' efforts toward unity; and among his papers are found plans for the settlement of Palestine that are far in advance of their time. Although human needs are always his central concern, his Christian charity extends beyond man to include all creatures. He urges the "costermongers" (fruit and vegetable sellers) driving their donkey-carts through the streets to treat their animals properly. Before his death in 1885 at the age of eighty-four, Lord Shaftesbury can look back on a life whose strength came from a firm, clear-cut Christian faith, a life which was sweeping in its breadth and dedicated to the inner strength and health of all the people.

Meanwhile, crusaders for social justice are active in other countries as well. On one front the battle is led by District Governor Friedrich Wilhelm Raiffeisen of Westerwald in northwest Germany. As a child Raiffeisen was taught the practical meaning of loving one's neighbor, and—like Oberlin in Alsace—he pitches in to help the impoverished rural population of his district. Raiffeisen has seen clearly that hunger spells national emergency, and that therefore the national welfare is dependent on a farming constituency that is well off and crisis-proof. When crop failures one year threaten to plunge the struggling Westerwald farmers into further misfortune, Raiffeisen plans relief action. From 1847 to 1854 he founds a number of service organizations: the consumer cooperative in Weyerbusch, the "Flammersfeld Relief

Society for the Assistance of Needy Farmers," and the Heddesdorf Philanthropic Society. Out of the last of these will evolve, years later, the first savings and loan institution. With its founding Raiffeisen takes the decisive step away from welfare and toward the kind of self-help that characterizes the agricultural cooperatives that still bear his name today. He has come to see that "direct help without some corresponding effort on the part of the people themselves is manifesting its drawbacks everywhere." Self-help plus cooperative resources and strength are his formula. From 1866 until his death in 1888 he dedicates himself to boosting the cooperatives.

The Prussian legislator Hermann Schulze-Delitzsch is a leader in similar movements in the crafts and small business enterprises. The eventual results of his efforts are the middle-class cooperatives.

Kolping, Father to the Rhineland Journeymen

Especially menaced by the Industrial Revolution are the crafts. The plight of the weavers is revealed in all its appalling depths by Gerhart Hauptmann's play, "The Weavers," and by the etchings of Käthe Kollwitz. But the problem cuts deeper and wider than just the weavers, as we shall see by looking at the life of Adolf Kolping, "father to the Rhineland journeymen."

In 1837 the Marzellengymnasium, a preparatory school in Cologne, enrolls in one of its middle forms a shoemaker's apprentice who has acquired the basics of Latin in his few spare hours (mostly at night) in order to prepare himself for the Catholic priesthood. His name is Adolf Kolping and he is twenty-four years old. Why doesn't he want to stick to his shoemaker's last? He began his apprenticeship in his home town of Kerpen, in the Rhineland, at the age of thirteen. After that he made his way around neighboring towns as a journeyman and ended up in Cologne. There he was plunged into the middle of the seamy life of the journeyman-craftsman. He worked in many shops and went through hell in all of them. His fellow journeymen were reprobates, not one of them respectable or clean inside or outside. Their life was a wild carouse of drinking, cursing, and wenching; and no master ever showed any concern or took any action. Kolping couldn't get over it. What mattered to him was people, human beings, and in such conditions the human element was not to be found. And so he made up his mind to become a priest.

He attends the Gymnasium for four years, graduates, and enrolls in the University of Munich. After his ordination he goes to Elberfeld as a curate and becomes the president of a young bachelor's club. He now sees his calling and his course. Two years later we find him working as a vicar in the Cologne Cathedral, the construction of which is finally being resumed. The beginnings of the Cologne youth work are modest to the point of being pathetic. His first group of apprentices meet in a school. Soon they have to move to larger quarters in an inn, and when they outgrow the accommodations there, they move to a large house, the first of the many Kolping Houses that are in operation all over the world today.

What is Kolping trying to do? He wants to see that young apprentices are not left to face temptation alone. He knows what goes on in the shops: the contaminated atmosphere, the smoldering passions. How is a young man to avoid being swept along with the tide under such circumstances? What kind of journeymen, what kind of masters, are these boys going to make? And in the factories, which are growing more and more numerous, it is even worse. The people there drift about like flotsam, and are drawn down into vice. Ringleaders plant their ideas in the minds of the others, luring them with seductive prospects.

Kolping sees and plans his work as a counteroffensive against the erupting covetousness of the proletariat, which is now beginning to emerge as a political force. He has no sympathy for the slogans of Karl Marx and other socialists. However imperfect the order, he sees God at work in it, and for him God comes first. In these turbulent years, wherever revolutionary movements aim at dealing with the malaise by destroying the sick organism, he proceeds nonviolently, seeking rather to heal. He is not a disrupter; he is a healer and shepherd of the endangered flock.

He sees the family—so often dismembered in those years of urban and industrial upheaval—as the divine order that must be maintained. And by watching out for these morally imperiled youths in his homes, he aims to preserve in them the inner resources that once enabled journeymen to become good craftsmen and good fathers and providers. Thus he cannot preach hate—as so many do in those days—or agitation, or the overthrow of the existing order, or class war. And he may well be more farsighted than many labor leaders who are steering straight for the radical transformation of the social structure. He sees that labor and management are dependent on each other and that they must not be allowed to work at cross purposes; he also knows that every ship needs a captain and pilot as well as a crew.

The foundations of his work—soon to spread beyond the Rhineland and Germany—are laid in the Cologne Journeymen's Association, which meets in an inn called the Brabänter Hof. Hundreds of journeymen spend their free time at this center. They use it to further their education and training, for Kolping believes that one can never be too well prepared for the competitive world he will soon be facing. There are lectures, there are courses in math and drawing and writing. Members talk to each other about anything on their mind: home, family, love. They pray together and seek answers to questions of faith. And they explore avenues of mutual aid: a sick fund, savings clubs, homes and centers. Kolping disagrees at many points with Wichern, holding that Wichern stops with reminding Christian craftsmen of their sinfulness, and the two men often dispute with each other. But basically, both are actively concerned for the morally and economically precarious state of the crafts, and both are effective in their efforts. Both see the human being first and the craftsman second; and the work of both is oriented on that principle.

Kolping wants to "re-establish on firm ground the class of the craftsman, which has been crushed and torn to pieces." Many of his ideas seem quite contemporary today; and in a way his "homes" are the predecessors of adult education in modern Germany. He tries to reach his objectives by preparing his journeymen for their occupations; but he also wants them to become good citizens of their country and loyal members of their craft, their professional "family." Kolping does not discount the value of technological innovation, but he wants to preserve the best of the old as well. The way he goes about his task evokes admiration to this day.

In 1849 Kolping opens his "Columbus School" with seven journeymen enrolled. Today there are over 2,500 "Kolping Families," as the associations are called. The program of all of them is, as Kolping's motto has it, "religion and virtue, industry and diligence, harmony and love, good fun and sport."

In Germany, Kolping's aim is to preserve the heritage of the past through education and character formation. Meanwhile, in Italy, a Catholic priest named Giovanni Bosco is building up a similar work, whose influence has likewise endured to our own time.

Don Bosco and the Bricklayers' Helpers

Two years younger than Kolping, Bosco has the same kind of unpampered childhood behind him. In his native Piedmont, he used to herd the cows and do the chores. But his great ambition was to become a priest. And he does. He is ordained at the age of twenty-six, and soon thereafter finds his vocation in life. In Turin he discovers young boys who have neither home nor family. They sleep underneath bridges or in the dirty backyards of the city. Sometimes they work as bricklayer's helpers, carrying bricks and mortar, earning little love and less money and learning nothing worthwhile. None of them can read or write. Repeatedly they fall for the blandishments of the first con man who comes their way. These are the boys whom Don Bosco seeks to befriend.

He knows it is not enough just to gather the boys together; he must help them get a new start, and the help must be organized. What he offers the boys is the chance of their lifetime. He sets up an evening school in a flat in the house of Joseph Pinardi, a house he is later able to buy outright. Those of the boys who are not totally apathetic flock to the school. Soon they have outgrown their quarters, and from this point on Don Bosco is constantly running out of space. Even his bold and sometimes unsuccessful building projects do not solve the problem, for the number of boys who are eager for an education grows to many hundreds. Before long this unfailingly cheery and enterprising priest has to open "extension schools" in other cities.

By 1857 the two-room school in Turin has become a large new house (the old one having been torn down) and an adjoining church. Many hundreds of "mortar boys" and journeymen-bricklayers have found a home here. And now Don Bosco is becoming known. Not simply the work itself but also his methods

The young Italian priest Giovanni Bosco finds a vocation in helping neglected youth, especially apprentice craftsmen. In Turin he opens the first home for "mortar boys." It includes an evening school.

Herder Verlag, Freiburg

and his carefree, cheery spirit give the work a style that inspires emulation. Whereas at the beginning even his sanity was questioned and there was talk of having him put in a mental institution, now all Italy is looking to him. When he dies in 1888, his work goes on, taken over by the Salesians. Among Catholic youth today, he is just as highly honored as Adolf Kolping.

It would be unjust not to say something more about Dr. Barnardo, briefly mentioned in connection with Lord Shaftesbury. Thomas John Barnardo is a fine upstanding London student who pays very little attention to social problems until one day he discovers the street-arabs of London who are "nobody's children." The awful sights he sees stay with him; he cannot get them out of his mind. In 1867, he gives an extemporaneous speech in an agricultural hall in London about the plight of these waifs, and

Londoners prick up their ears. Once more they learn that while their gaze has been fixed on remote lands, appalling conditions have been breeding in their own backyards. The newspapers pick up Barnardo's appeal, and Lord Shaftesbury reads about it. He invites the student to dine, and that same evening the young man takes the aging earl and parliamentary leader to the slums and the homeless children—hidden on the roofs of fishmarkets, underneath bridges, or in a corner of some *cul de sac.* They are little troglodytes: delinquent, rudderless, yet full of longing for light, freedom, warmth, and a little love.

Barnardo is to these urchins what Don Bosco is to his protégés in Turin. He builds homes for them and sees to their education and training. He goes down into their ratholes, down where they live, so that they will come to trust him enough to let him bring them out.

Getting down to where one's fellowman lives—that is the secret of genuine love, the love that makes a difference. And there are many men and women in this so "progressive" nineteenth century who actually put it into practice. Ignoring the philosophical doctrine of the superman, and Nietzsche's dictum that whatever seems bent on falling should be given an extra push, they become living examples of love-in-action.

A Lady Who Knows What She Wants

While Dr. Barnardo is putting the spotlight on the darkest corners of London's slums, an upper-class Englishwoman takes a lamp into the military hospital of Scutari, the Asian quarter of Constantinople (Istanbul). The background of the story can be briefly told. The year is 1854, and the Crimean War is in progress. The "Times" of London has printed yet another disturbing report, this time on the intolerable conditions in the English barrack-hospital in Scutari. And once more Lord Shaftesbury is moved to action. The government has learned to listen when he talks, and public opinion tends to take its cues from him. When Shaftesbury calls for a commission to be sent to Scutari, the suggestion is immediately adopted. The "Times" correspondent has denounced the "manner in which the sick and wounded have been treated" in Scutari. The public is aroused; something had better happen.

Sidney Herbert, the English secretary at war, dispatches to the area a Commission of Enquiry into the State of the Hospitals. He also names as "Superintendent of the Female Nursing Establishment of the English General Military Hospitals in Turkey" a society lady, Florence Nightingale. Miss Nightingale knows what she wants. She always has. While still a girl she was sure of her vocation; it was going to be nursing. At first her family was horrified; for in those days a good proportion of nurses was still made up of former streetwalkers. But Florence will not be dissuaded. During trips to the Continent she visits hospitals wherever she can, becomes acquainted with St. Vincent's Daughters of Charity in Paris, and meets Theodor Fliedner in Kaiserswerth, remaining there for some time in order to prepare herself for the service she was eventually to render. She once writes of Kaiserwerth:

> There is my home; there are my brothers and sisters all at work; there my heart is.

Back in England, she studies the advances made in hygiene and assists the most prominent medical specialist of London, Sir William Bowman, during a cholera epidemic. Her reputation as an expert in all branches of nursing spreads throughout England, and so it is not surprising that Herbert, who has known her for years, should give her the Scutari assignment.

On November 4, 1854, Florence Nightingale arrives in Scutari with her friend, Mrs. Selina Bracebridge, and thirty-eight nurses. Their reception is unnerving. The doctors and hospital officials are outraged that the government should send a woman to inspect them. Some affect great cordiality; others greet her with irony or cold rebuffs.

They know they cannot simply tell her to go away; they are quite aware that she has been sent by Sidney Herbert with the sanction of the queen. But they intend to see to it that she will *want* to leave. The hospital and its vicinity is no place for the tender spirits of women more accustomed to places of quiet devotion. It is a mud-spattered tableau of tattered uniforms and

Florence Nightingale on her rounds in the Crimean War. Until her arrival in Scutari, the conditions in the military hospitals were monstrous: rotten straw, rats, stench, epidemics.

Historisches Bildarchiv Handke, Bad Berneck

amputated limbs. The stench is almost unbearable. And what will happen when these women appear in the crowded wards, surrounded by the wounded, brutalized, in many cases alcoholic soldiers driven half out of their minds by monotony or pain or both?

Florence is under no delusions. She immediately sees through the masks of kindness, irony, or obstinacy the hospital officials have donned. Behind the masks she sees laziness, arrogance, and malice. The nurses are billeted in three tiny rooms. Florence can get no supplies with her own money or the money that has been given her. The regulations do not allow this. The nurses get no authorization from the doctors to go into the wards. The state of the latrines is unspeakable. Rats scurry about everywhere. Men who could actually be saved are dying on their straw sacks. Every day more casualties arrive, often on overcrowded ships carrying highly contagious diseases, notably cholera.

For a few days the doctors and officials bide their time. The delicate likes of a lady won't be able to take this, they think, waiting for the rout of the nursing corps. But here as well, Miss Nightingale knows what she wants. She doesn't give up. If there is no other way, she will just have to deal first with the official stupidity of the staff before turning to the wounded. Of course she will purchase beds, covers, chamberpots, bandaging, sheets, and everything else. Of course her nurses would go into the wards and attend the men. She would see that the latrines and wards were cleaned and that the rats were eliminated. And she would do her best to see that no more of these unfortunate men would die helpless and alone.

Her light flashing to and fro, she goes through the wards at night, holding the hands of the dying, dispensing what relief she can, and working as long as her strength lasts. She can be found in the wards in the daytime as well. Her quiet work revives the hopes of the patients, and eventually even her antagonists realize that she is the only person who will be able to do anything about the chaos to which overcrowded conditions and negligence have reduced this hospital. Soon the mortality rate goes down. Formerly as high as seventy percent, it now drops to below ten percent. Clean floors, ventilated and improved sewers, new drainage facilities, cleaned water reservoirs, and a well-run kitchen (presided over by a French chef who has volunteered his services) — these are the results of her work after a short time. The piles of offal are removed. Beds replace the straw sacks. The nurses are at last allowed to get to work, not only tending the patients but also assisting the doctors. The patients are amazed to find they are human beings once more and are treated as such—even by the doctors, whose attitude up to now has been rather different.

Before she came—the soldiers would say—we all cursed like the devil, but since she's been here it's as pious as a church. They call her the "angel of Scutari," and seldom has such a tribute been so accurately and justly accorded.

When the mess in Scutari has been cleaned up, Miss Nightingale goes to the Crimea to survey at first hand and to deal with the equally intolerable conditions on the front. Dr. John Hall, chief of the medical staff of the British forces, doesn't make it easy for her. Things look especially bad in the epidemic-ridden city of Balaclava. Miss Nightingale herself comes down with fever and for two weeks is close to death. The men in the Scutari hospital actually cry when they hear the news. She is barely out of danger when Dr. Hall and a colleague of his arrange for her to be put on a ship that is supposedly to carry her to Scutari, where she is to take a kind of rest-leave in a house that has been found for her. In actual fact, the ship in question is not even scheduled to call at Scutari; Dr. Hall has simply seized a convenient opportunity to get rid of this strong-minded lady. Fortunately, a friend of Miss Nightingale's finds out about the situation in time to have her transferred to another ship, which does land her in Scutari.

Miss Nightingale does not return to England until the end of 1856. She is now thirty-six years old. Her name, now known far beyond England's borders, has become a symbol of humanitarian concern. She continues to be active for another half-century. Even when failing health confines her to her home, she successfully campaigns for higher public health standards, nurses' training, and effective ways to relieve human misery. She continues to counsel and write until she dies in the year 1910 at the age of ninety-one.

What Florence Nightingale did in Scutari would soon become an international endeavor: to do everything humanly possible to mitigate the suffering of men wounded in combat. Her example undoubtedly made a profound impression on a young Geneva businessman named Henri Dunant.

The Birth of the Red Cross

Dunant's family background is wholly that of the religious bourgeoisie in Geneva that since Calvin's day has considered good works an indispensable duty and that fulfills this duty with faithfulness and integrity. Business acumen is put to work for God: talent is turned into money, and money is used to provide a variety of welfare services for the poor, the sick, and the neglected, as well as prisoners and orphans.

A formative influence upon the young Dunant is that of his mother. While quite young he is allowed to accompany and assist her on her charitable visits to poor invalids, lonely old folk, and people who need cheering up. He does not probe critically for the causes of misery; he is glad to be able to help. This attitude remains with him. On one occasion his father goes to Toulon to visit the prisoners there; and Henri, who is allowed to go along, is shaken at the sight of the chain gangs who are conscripted to work on the roads. At the age of eighteen he joins the "League of Alms" and visits the poorest sections of Geneva with his fellow members, distributing alms and cheer. He puts all his pocket money into this project, and works at it day and night. In 1847 Dunant, always looking for new challenges, takes a leading hand in organizing a group that a few years later will become the Geneva chapter of the Young Men's Christian Association.

A passionate supporter of the international abolitionist cause, Dunant meets Harriet Beecher Stowe, whose novel *Uncle Tom's Cabin* has focused world attention on the plight of the slaves in the American South, and who is now bringing her message to Europe. This meeting intensifies Dunant's desire to be of help to the suffering.

Dunant also becomes one of the most active boosters of an international YMCA. His efforts are rewarded in 1855, when the first YMCA World Conference is held in Paris. Here, as in the case of the subsequent founding of the Red Cross, a movement in which Dunant is a leading force will go its way without him.

These formative experiences do not prevent Dunant from pursuing a promising-looking career, true to the Calvinistic traditions of his family and his native city. He goes into business, and in 1859 a business trip takes him to northern Italy. He has in mind a large mill operation in Algeria, which is under French control, and he has mapped out an involved strategy to get it going. First, he needs some large land grants from Napoleon III. Napoleon is somewhere in Italy, trying to keep the Austrians out of that country. A friend of Dunant's, General de Beaufort, is also in Italy, so Dunant tries going through him. De Beaufort has already given him a letter of introduction to the French marshal, Maurice de MacMahon, who has just won a crucial victory in northern Italy.

De Beaufort suggests trying to find MacMahon. Armed with this letter, and still in pursuit of Napoleon, Dunant sets out for MacMahon's headquarters.

While Dunant is quartered at an inn in Castiglione, the French meet the Austrians at nearby Solferino. Austrian troops hold the hills as the French attack. A murderous fifteen-hour battle ensues. What starts out as war as usual turns into a barbaric orgy of blood; and when a severe storm finally ends it, thirty thousand men are lying dead or wounded on the battlefield, which Dunant in a subsequent account calls a "vast field of carnage." The Algerian mills are forgotten, the letter of introduction to MacMahon has lost its importance, the emperor is suddenly a remote figure. All that matters at the moment are the agonized victims of a senseless battle. Dunant will never forget the cries and groans of a poor Tyrolese soldier of the Imperial Austrian Army, his fingernails bent back in the last convulsions of pain and thirst, his mouth crammed with earth, his face swollen beyond recognition, a ghastly mottle of green and black.

Dunant sees that the medical aid for the wounded is wholly inadequate. He wastes no time wondering whether a lone individual can accomplish anything; he simply begins helping. He passes water around, and he murmurs words of consolation. He also manages to save the lives of a couple of Hungarian peasants who have been taken for Croats (to whom no quarter is given by the French) and who are about to be killed. A drop in the ocean, to be sure, but this is how the vast worldwide work of the international Red Cross begins.

Dunant goes through the motions of pursuing his original errand. He finds MacMahon, and he gets as far as stating his business to an imperial attaché at Napoleon's headquarters. But he gets no further. He leaves a copy of a book he has written, dedicated to the emperor, which he hopes will be his entrée. The imperial reply, a polite note turning down the dedication, merely writes a formal *finis* to the episode. Though it has a later sequel, its importance is eclipsed by what Dunant has been through; the die has long since been cast.

He now goes about visiting hospitals in Brescia and Milan, handing out small gifts and doing what he can for the soldiers' welfare and morale. Then while numbers of people from all levels of society are volunteering to help in the hospitals, Dunant turns up in the salons of the elite to tell of his experience and his reflections on it. The volunteer becomes the voice crying in the wilderness. How different would the battlefields look, he asks, if the armies of combatants were backed up by armies of volunteer relief workers? He urges that such volunteers be trained now, in peacetime, and that they be given neutral status to enable them to attend the wounded.

In the fall of 1862, three years after Solferino, a small book is published bearing the title *Un Souvenir de Solferino,* "A Memory of Solferino." This is Dunant's candid portrayal of the horror of that battle, together with his proposals for medical aid on the battlefield. The book is not an impassioned polemic against war; it deals realistically with things as they are, and it is written to further the one purpose Dunant has resolved upon: rescuing the wounded. He gives a reprise of Solferino as it looked after the battle, without retouching the hideous scene. Then he turns to his conclusions. Would it not be possible, he asks the reader, to begin in peacetime to found relief organizations that would tend the wounded in future wars? In the same reasonable, shrewdly tactful manner he asks: would it not be desirable to convene a congress with the aim of reaching agreement on certain principles that would then be internationally honored?

Behind the tact and the reasonableness, however, are images of horror; and these turn Dunant's questions into moral imperatives. It sounds paradoxical to appeal for love on the battlefields instead of ridding the world of battlefields altogether. But Dunant is feeling his way along. Man must first learn to see that "the enemy" is his suffering brother before man can see the necessity for settling international disputes by some means other than mass murder. Hate must be overcome by love.

Soon Dunant goes a step further. If relief organizations are going to be started, why should they be active only in wartime? Since they will have to be on constant alert anyway, couldn't their people be sent where needed during epidemics and disasters, too? Here again, as in the case of the YMCA world alliance in Paris, Dunant's perspective is international.

Dunant's book is almost universally acclaimed. World leaders are stirred. The courteously noncommittal response of Napoleon III is an exception, and it is probably politically motivated. A French marshal bemoans the fact that the day is gone when one could burn enemy cities to the ground, but his statement finds no support—not until subsequent wars in our own times. But even Dunant is surprised to note that the response that really makes the difference comes from his native Geneva. Gustave Moynier, president of a philanthropic society in Geneva, asks Dunant how he intends to turn his proposals into reality. The result is that the Dunant proposals are discussed at a meeting of the society, while their author, who is present, listens in silence. A "Committee of Five" is formed. Dunant is named secretary, Moynier vice-chairman. The chairman is the Swiss general, Guillaume Dufour, who attracted public notice during the Swiss civil war of 1845–47 when he impressed upon his troops that military brutality is a disgrace to the uniform of the soldier. Dufour will also preside over the first International Congress in 1863. Two physicians, Theodore Maunoir and Louis Appia, complete the committee.

The moving spirits are Dunant and Moynier: the one eager and exuberant, the other methodical and levelheaded. The juxtaposition of these contrasting temperaments creates problems, especially as neither is free from personal vanity. From his experience in legal matters, Moynier knows that they must make haste slowly, while Dunant is already broaching plans that are absolutely unfeasible at this early stage. But their combined efforts are highly effective.

The first congress in Geneva is held in October 1863. Dunant has worked hard to bring it about. Appointing himself the International Committee's roving ambassador, he tours Europe, soliciting the support of leading statesmen. The result is that sixteen governments send delegates to a congress at the behest of five persons calling themselves an International Committee. Dunant did the spadework, but the negotiations themselves attest the adroitness and tact of Moynier. The delegates vote to accept the ten points of the draft convention. As they are not authorized to act in the name of their governments, however, the resolutions have the force only of recommendations.

La Charité sur les champs de bataille.

The first Red Cross teams go into action in 1864 when Prussia and Austria wage war against Denmark.

International Committee of the Red Cross, Geneva

But in 1864 Prussia and Denmark officially ratify the resolutions. Dubbed the "Red Cross" (after its insignia), the international organization gets its baptism of fire that same year, when Prussia and Austria wage war with Denmark over Schleswig-Holstein. In the test Dunant's ideas prove their feasibility.

But nothing can be accomplished without a binding convention having diplomatic status, as everything still depends on the willingness of the belligerents. And so on August 8, 1864 what comes to be known as the first Geneva Convention is held in Geneva's *Hôtel de Ville*. It is attended by delegates from sixteen states. Two weeks later the ten articles of the so-called Geneva Convention are signed by twelve states. Two years after the appearance of Dunant's book, the goal of international agreement is achieved, and Dunant is there to see it. The end of the conference is an unpleasant anticlimax—outside, crowds of angry demonstrators are talking about irregularities in the recently held local elections—but the breakthrough has been scored. In the years that follow other nations sign the Convention, and soon the Red Cross becomes a worldwide symbol of mercy. (Its counterpart among the nations of Islam is the red crescent.) Contemporary historians and a large part of the public take little or no notice of these developments, however. The "Times" of London, capable of courageous reports on human misery, as it proved in the Crimean war, says something about the undoubtedly well-meaning Geneva philanthropists, describing them as people who want to humanize war. Along with many contemporaries, the "Times" holds that the more violent the destruction and the bloodier the battles, the shorter the duration of the wars. In other words, getting wars over with quickly is more humane than all efforts to humanize war.

These beginnings are wrapped in much confusion, and the leaders of the Red Cross are initially beset by much uncertainty. Only Henri Dunant is absolutely sure; he pursues his ideas almost with the unswerving direction of a man in a trance. The course of the Red Cross to the present day, including the later conventions and the other milestones in its history, shows how right Dunant's own course was. Instead of promising the "abolition of war" in lofty phrases or assuring the world that war had been done away by the advent of new and more terrible weapons, Dunant confronts directly the inhumanity of war by taking Christian love to the battlefields. Alfred Nobel was wrong, as we shall see. Henry Dunant was not.

The honor that is justly his is not mitigated by the tragedy of his personal life. His bankruptcy brands him as an imprudent speculator. A Geneva newspaper even accuses him of having "knowingly deceived" his associates in his abortive Algerian enterprise, a charge hotly denied by Dunant. Eventually he rallies from the despair he keeps hidden from public view, being well aware of

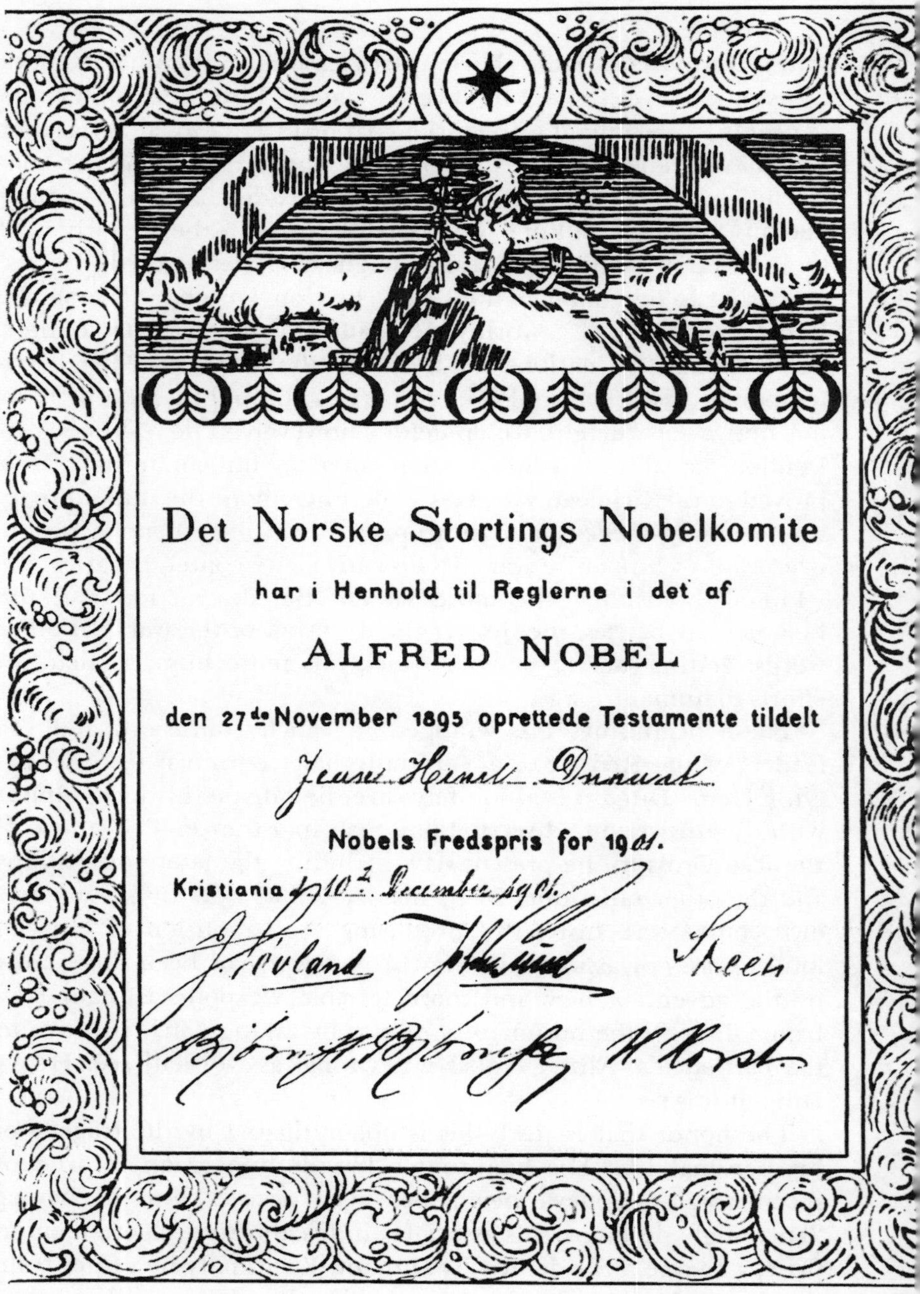
Det Norske Stortings Nobelkomite

har i Henhold til Reglerne i det af

ALFRED NOBEL

den 27de November 1895 oprettede Testamente tildelt

Jean Henri Dunant

Nobels Fredspris for 1901.

Kristiania d. 10de December 1901.

The Nobel Peace Prize of 1901 is awarded to Henri Dunant, who dedicated his life to serving the wounded on the battlefields after having witnessed the horrors of Solferino.

International Committee of the Red Cross, Geneva

his place in history as the founder of the Red Cross. He conceives new projects: an international university, for example, and a "Universal International Society for the Renewal of the Near East," with the aim of making Palestine a new Canaan for the Jews. This idea, which also circulates among Christians in England, should be given its due in any discussion of the complicity of the Christians in the persecution of the Jews throughout the centuries. The Franco-Prussian War demolishes these plans, however, as well as the world in which Dunant lives. His appeals for "neutral zones" are in vain. This time he is not heeded. So once more he resorts to direct action. He raises money by fund drives for soldiers and by benefit programs. His Swiss passport enables him to spirit a number of captured French guerrilla fighters out of Paris and thus to save their lives. But France is now vanquished; she can give him no more support.

So Dunant goes to England to promote his ideas: the return of the Jews to Palestine, a "world alliance for order and civilization," international courts of arbitration, and a convention to cover the treatment of prisoners of war—this last idea putting him years ahead of his time. He himself lives in abject poverty and want, staying for a while in the Swiss village of Heiden, near the Appenzell Alps, forgotten by the world and deserted by his friends. Only Wilhelm Sonderegger, a young schoolmaster, and Frau Sonderegger are true companions to him. It is through their efforts that the world again becomes aware of Dunant. One day the international press breaks the news that the founder of the Red Cross is living in poverty.

When Bertha von Suttner begins her crusade against war, Dunant takes up his pen again. In this case he feels called to. In 1901 he and Frédéric Passy are awarded the Nobel Peace Prize. Dunant does not use a penny of the money for himself. He dies in 1910—the same year as Florence Nightingale—at the age of eighty-two. In one of his letters he expresses his "last will," an outcry against all the hypocrisy and mendacity of men: "It is my wish to be carried to my grave like a dog."

10. Into the Breach

The Caritas Union

The nineteenth century produces a number of international movements. The Age of Industrialization, now in full swing, presents very different countries with the same problems. For a long time the authorities in these countries are helpless, and hence inactive, in the face of the new order; thus it is natural that protest and bootstraps movements should forge common bonds among the peoples of very different nationalities. In spite of all nationalism—and this century is definitely not lacking in nationalism—and in spite of various reactionary tendencies, a new feeling of international solidarity is spreading. This is apparent in the common fight against slavery, it is apparent in the life and work of such individuals as John Howard and Elizabeth Fry, and it is apparent in a host of public-spirited movements, such as the educational reforms initiated by Pestalozzi, and Fröbel's kindergarten program. First and foremost, however, it is apparent in the rise of the unions—the bootstraps movement of the international proletariat.

What Karl Marx and Friedrich Engels proclaim in their speeches and writings is quickly crystallized into a single summons: proletarians of the world, unite! Although the tendency of the emerging socialism is not so much toward philanthropy as class struggle, the achievements of the international labor union movement cannot be overlooked. These achievements are in the social sector, and they are partly won by means that are not available to the humanitarian leaders we have been talking about in these pages. But despite many wrong roads taken and right roads not taken, an integral part of such achievements consists in this international solidarity of humanness that characterizes the nineteenth century and continues into the present.

Admittedly, the age is also characterized by a great deal of confusion. The quarrels between various movements arouse more than our distaste; and some one-man crusades run parallel to each other without ever meeting. But taken together, events show that all mankind is endeavoring to break through to a new unity under the banner of genuine humanitarianism.

It is true that these endeavors must be seen together with the inhumanity that is also apparent, even in this progressive age. But one should also note that it is primarily this inhumanity that acts as a constant spur to good works on the part of those who take an optimistic view of the nature of man. Their belief in "progress" is really an unshakable hope that mankind can learn better conduct and better attitudes through education. Rousseau, who predicates his ideas upon the "natural man," has a different perspective on the matter from that of Christians, who know of man's sinfulness and his need of redemption. But in terms of their practical concerns, these two viewpoints can benefit greatly by cross-fertilization, as is shown in the case of Pestalozzi, and of the Red Cross as well.

The major development in the Christian world is unquestionably the revival of the diaconate in the form of the Inner Mission, a movement that spreads from the established Protestant church to many free churches and independent societies. The Mennonites' centuries-old ministry of active caring, which so greatly impressed the fathers of the Inner Mission, is now reorganized along the lines of the new movement. One notes the same kind of interaction among the Quakers, the Baptists, and especially the Methodists.

In terms of internationalism, the impact of the Inner Mission upon the Roman Catholic church seems of special significance. For centuries the Catholics have been fostering a spirit of interdiocesan cooperation in charitable ministries; and their motives have not only been the propagation of the faith but also purely and simply the practice of Christian charity. What was said about an emerging ecumenical diaconate in connection with Francke and Zinzendorf needs no special emphasis in the case of Rome; for the Catholics, such a spirit was and is axiomatic. The international impact made by Kolping and Don Bosco are two of many cases in point. Even so, the second half of the nineteenth century produces a new movement in the Catholic world that unquestionably derives its impetus from the consolidation of the Protestant diaconate into the Inner Mission.

As we survey the Catholic works of charity, we must turn again to France. Perhaps it is due to the life and work of Vincent de Paul that charity in France leads that of all other Catholic countries in the nineteenth century, the century after the French Revolution. But perhaps it is also a result of that revolution. At any rate, the fact is that in no country are there as many hospitals, day nurseries, institutions, asylums, hospices, welfare organizations, confraternities, and "congregations" (in the Roman Catholic sense) as in France. The statistics for Paris and the whole country speak for themselves. Moreover, wholly apart from the money that is gladly, sacrificially, and repeatedly given, it is also a fact that in no other country do so many people feel personally called to the ministry of mercy. We may also note that in all likelihood, no other Catholic country has let its light of charity shine so brightly on other countries as has France. French Daughters of Charity are at work in almost every country in the world; and they are now drawing our attention to needy regions that have heretofore been overlooked. They are in Mexico and South America as well as in the Philippines and the Levant. And it is from France that Catholicism in various lands receives its impetus for new works of charity.

Notable among the Catholic ministries of the nineteenth century are the "congregations" engaged in rescue work for prostitutes and morally endangered girls and children. The moral pitfalls facing youth, which have always been far greater than admitted in any age, are continuing to increase with the growing trend toward industrialization; and children are exposed to countless additional dangers to body and soul. The most significant new charitable movement serving in this and in other fields, however, originates in Germany, not France.

The example set by the Inner Mission is bothering the consciences of some Catholic men. Prominent among these is Father Cyprian Fröhlich, who in Munich in 1889 founds the Catholic Society for the Protection of Young Girls, and who in his later years takes care of German orphans in Carpatho-Ukraine. Pointing to the Inner Mission, Father Fröhlich urges that Catholic groups and programs be similarly consolidated. On November 9, 1897 a Catholic prelate, Dr. Lorenz Werthmann, and a few energetic friends, including Father Fröhlich, lay the foundations of the German Caritas Union in Cologne. At first the official church institutions pay little attention to it; in a few cases they are actually hostile. But in a short time the Union is granted full recognition by the bishops, and all Catholic charities are consolidated under its banner. Freiburg becomes its headquarters, and Werthmann—whose importance in many respects equals that of Wichern—is its first president. Like Wichern, Werthmann does not look on his work in the new organization as his whole vocation; he is also active in other social welfare projects, large and small, faithfully giving his time and energy to them. He founds homes for saleswomen and retired maids who are living alone and in need; and he pays special attention to the care of unwed mothers. Much younger than Wichern, Werthmann is able to carry on long after the end of World War I and has an important part in framing new public welfare legislation before he dies in 1921.

Among the chief objectives of the German Caritas Union are: surveying and thoroughly analyzing all welfare programs and welfare laws; coordinating the various works of charity; and training full-time and part-time volunteers and staff members. The Union also puts on large fund drives and makes special appeals for cooperative relief action during emergencies and disasters. Finally it functions as the liaison between Catholic and non-Catholic charities and welfare organizations in Germany and other countries. From the outset, certain categories of mission work are coordinated on an international level, and three years after Werthmann's death a coordinating committee made up of delegates from twenty-two countries is formed at the International Caritas Congress in Amsterdam. This committee marks the real beginning of the international work of Caritas, which today

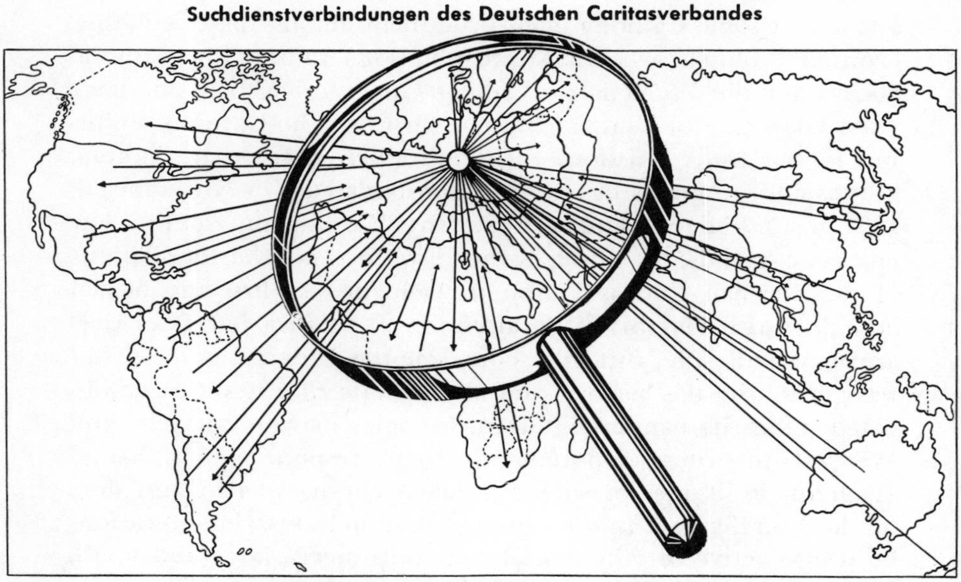

Today Caritas is at work all over the world. The Missing Persons Service of the German Caritas becomes especially important after World War II, when it helps to put many thousands of people in touch with their families.

embraces all Catholic countries. Such necessary organizational planning always goes hand in hand with direct-action ministries to the poor. A prime example of such Caritas action is provided by Wilhelm Emmanuel von Ketteler, the archbishop of Mainz. Von Ketteler is one of those great bishops who have been given to the church time and again since the days of Cyprian: a proclaimer of the gospel, a shepherd to his flock, and a true servant of the poor. In him are joined the charitable and social concerns of the times. He is constantly promoting the works of ministering love in his diocese, often being actively involved in them himself; and during the aftermath of reaction to the liberal-nationalist revolution of 1848, he becomes the champion of the proletariat, which has now lost even its political friends. Far ahead of his time, Ketteler attempts to find Christian answers to social problems and issues;

own personal example, he shows how great the
e. Although he does not live to see the results of his
rk on behalf of the laborer, he is able to open hearts
the question of social outreach; and in later years
who follow his lead.

of note are two Protestant pastors, Adolf Stöcker
Naumann, who find a Christian approach to the
s of their times. Naumann, who is familiar with the
from his work in the Rauhes Haus movement and
background comes to the matter of social reform,
that "love on a grand scale will always involve
n on the part of a compassionate state."

T ARMY IN THE WORLD

an Englishman named William Booth founds
ation devoted to social outreach, but totally differ-
nternational Caritas movement. This is, of course,
rmy, often laughed at, often mocked, yet of great
ectiveness.

am Booth? In his youth he is one of the have-nots
lums of England. As a laborer in the industrial
ngham, he finds out at firsthand what hardship is
is apprenticed to a pawnbroker, in whose shop he
the effects of misery and vice. But while untold
ople come to grief in similar circumstances, Booth
o God. He attends a Methodist chapel, and one day
ng services of his own. He begins as a street preacher,
ns are full of fire and conviction. Opposition to
causes him to break with the "Methodists of the
on" (which was itself a breakaway movement from
Church). He goes on preaching, and the power of
ems to grow. Gradually he forms a group of associ-
e Booth himself is an aggressive personality, the
comes a militant corps, an army, dedicated not to
t to salvation. This truly bizarre "Salvation Army,"
uch then as now, begins a fight that is more sig-
ll the wars ever fought. The Army is continuously
he front is everywhere. From England it exports its

war on misery to all the countries of the world; and it is always expanding. Instead of reporting the dead, wounded, and missing, its communiqués list the number of the rescued. The combatants are men and women, young and old, fighting side by side; and those they overcome immediately join the Army's front ranks—none is denied a place of honor in the continuing battle.

William Booth is the General of the Army. His wife Catherine, still fondly remembered, is his helpmeet and faithful companion in arms. She gives up the security and advantages of a good home to travel around England with Booth, sharing the uncertain existence of a roving evangelist. She is a loving mother to her children, but her heart is still large enough to embrace the countless numbers of people whom she and the general seek to reach in the slums of East London. William and Catherine Booth see their marriage as a joint ministry to their poorer fellowmen about them. How much the ministry of so many men and women in our story owes to the burden-sharing and understanding of a life-partner!

The number of volunteers Booth enlists grows steadily. Substantial amounts of money are coming in from affluent sources, and one day he decides the time has come to mobilize his army for a major offensive. It is June, 1882 and the attack is to be mounted against a large and notorious East London "public house," a king-sized tavern called the Eagle. There are no tables; the customers stand at the bar and put down dram after dram of spirits. Drinking while in a standing position is not very cozy, so it is done as fast as possible, and the Eagle's guests are soon drunk. But who cares? The main thing is that they pay. The bouncer is always standing by; drunks are grabbed by the collar and shoved out the door. Sometimes the whole visit lasts but half an hour. The Eagle is a gold mine for its owner, and his profits are not only from alcohol. The place is also the preserve of a bevy of tarts, who select their quarry from among the tipsier guests. Liquor, immorality, crime—it all goes together. The foulest of it collects at the Eagle.

This is William Booth's target. He buys up the whole business—tavern, gardens, music hall, and Grecian theater—by proxy, paying twenty thousand pounds for it. And then the

William Booth, founder and first general of the Salvation Army.

The Salvation Army, Berlin

inhabitants of East London are presented with a remarkable parade: Three thousand Salvation Army soldiers, their music blaring, march on the Eagle and occupy it. This causes an immediate uproar. The mob—hordes of the prodigal, the degenerate, and the debauched—will not have their amusement hall taken from them. For months they lay siege to the place, screaming and throwing whatever comes to hand; and the police are hard-pressed to keep them from storming the premises. Gangs armed with rocks and sticks try to retake what has been converted from a tavern and brothel into a rescue home. Several times Booth is in mortal danger, but he does not panic easily, and his blithe, unruffled good cheer helps him to handle any situation; the animosity and catcalls simply bounce off him. Booth also has a broad humor that can bring down the house, and this gift defuses many a tense confrontation.

The Eagle becomes the citadel of the Salvation Army; and a new spirit comes over the establishment. Girl volunteers, who were walking the streets not long before, now march to the houses of the poor and go to work with brooms and cleaning rags. Once they have things cleaned up and in order, they stay to preach the gospel to the people. Regular brigades of men proceed from headquarters to the slums, collect the drunks from the streets, and bring them back with them. Here the new guests sleep off their stupor, and then are given a meal. They cannot leave before hearing the word of God. There is also the "prison-gate brigade," members of which take up their posts in front of London's jails. They are not there to prevent breakouts; they are waiting for prisoners to be discharged, in order that they can help the former inmates in getting a fresh start.

The remarkable effectiveness of the Salvation Army should give pause to anyone who finds its methods peculiar. Nearly the whole Army is recruited from prodigal sons, degenerates, and washouts. One-time drunkards, criminals, dissolute vagabonds, pimps, prostitutes—these are William Booth's soldiers. Those who have come from the gutter know best how to help those who are still in it. And those with the most dubious reputations are the ones Booth trusts the most. His confidence is seldom misplaced.

In 1885 when Booth's son Bramwell gives an interview to the "Pall Mall Gazette" and discloses the shocking evidence he has amassed on prostitution and the growing white slave traffic, the government and the public are aghast. Bramwell makes his point well, and the government has to act. The age of consent is raised to sixteen. More lodges and "soup kitchens" are established. But that is only a start. On her deathbed, Catherine Booth discusses with her husband a manuscript that, when it is finally published, becomes a best seller. This time the English public is really stirred up. Booth calls the book *In Darkest England and the Way Out*—an obvious allusion to Stanley's *In Darkest Africa.* Critics are goaded to fierce rebuttals, but they cannot stop the wave of public tribute and donations. Factories and stores, founded under autonomous management, provide additional funds for the all-out attack on social evils which the Salvation Army now launches. Pauper colonies and pauper transportation overseas supplement a program through which untold numbers of lives are salvaged. Booth's program embraces more than the "seven works of mercy"; there is also a missing persons bureau and a counseling program for potential suicides.

Meanwhile, the movement has spread to other countries in Europe and elsewhere. Booth goes on long trips, becoming like Howard a "circumnavigator of charity." But unlike Howard, Booth does more than record facts; he takes action.

When he dies in 1912, the funeral procession through London halts traffic for hours. According to Harold Begbie, Booth's biographer, "the densest multitude ever seen in the streets of London" followed the body of one who became a fool for the sake of Christ's love. This poor, penniless lad from Nottingham, this frail pawnbroker's apprentice, has made the world rich in loving-kindness.

No episode from his life testifies more clearly to his attitude and his deep sympathy and understanding, or better confirms his identification with the outcast, than an incident that occurs one Sunday morning: Booth, at the time a young man, leads a group of shambling figures—ragged, filthy, evil-smelling—out of the slums of his native Nottingham into Wesley Chapel and down the aisle to the best seats available. One is reminded of the story told of St. Laurence, the Roman deacon who, on being asked by the prefect to produce the treasure of the church, presented to him the city's poor. The authorities in Wesley Chapel, less perceptive than St. Laurence, tell Booth that next time he must take his people to less conspicuous benches. But during his whole life Booth is forever bringing the least of his brothers as close as possible to Christ—to the front pews. Who can look at the record and still ridicule the strange Army of this strong-willed pursuer of well-doing? Anyone who takes the plunge into human misery in order to extricate the miserable cannot afford to be fainthearted in his choice of means. Booth dared to take the plunge, and he rescued human beings from poverty, vice, and misery.

Critics have often said that the Army's success in soul-winning is due mainly to a temporary surge of emotion, and that Booth and his associates should really have taken a more sober view of conversion as a genuine redirection of life. Certainly there were converts who lapsed into their former way of life and whose conversion did not last (of course, this is true not only of the Salvation Army). But it is also true that many thousands of people saved through the Salvation Army began and continued to live a new life.

Alcohol addicts are a case in point. It is the belief and the experience of the Salvation Army that the chronic drinking habit can actually be broken by a direct attack; and, indeed, the history of all temperance movements has borne this out, time and time again. The reasons are plain: the person who becomes addicted to alcohol or something else is psychologically weak or unstable; he can only be dealt with by firmness. The cures used by alcoholic sanatoriums are also based on the principle of keeping a firm hand on the unstable addict.

The Fight against Alcoholism

The crusade against prostitution and other offenses against morals goes back to much earlier times; but the crusade against alcohol really begins at the end of the nineteenth century. Alcoholism is, of course, as old as alcohol itself. In decadent Rome, gluttony and drinking to excess were commonplace. In medieval Europe, some alcoholic beverages, especially beer, virtually became part of the traditional culture. Brandy, initially used for medicinal purposes, was often made by monks. Since the seventeenth century, when someone discovered how to distill spirits from potatoes, liquor of all kinds (often inferior) has been produced and consumed in large amounts.

The introduction of liquor into colonial lands by the white men who conquered them is one of the great evils perpetrated by the Europeans. "Firewater" wiped out entire Indian tribes; and in Africa liquor is regarded—with some justification—as the bane of the black man. In ancient India, Buddha forbade intoxicating drinks; gluttony is inimical to the ascetic ideal he wanted to establish. The drinking of wine was also forbidden by Mohammed.

In the Age of Industrialization, the menace of alcohol becomes so ominous that the most rigorous countermeasures are required to deal with it. As a result of the restructuring of society, the emergence of a proletarian class of slum-dwellers, and the temptations that come with hard cash received by the day or by the week, alcohol becomes a widespread social problem. Because its direct bearing on the general welfare and the wide variety of its consequences (not only physical and biological) are recognized, the counterattack is mounted on several fronts and in several ways. Booth's way is to fight desperate diseases with desperate remedies. The authorities too feel compelled to take effective action. Special tariffs, surtaxes, or liquor sales bans are aimed at keeping alcohol consumption within limits. But more important are the one-man crusades motivated by conscience. Notable among these temperance leaders are two Swiss pastors, Louis Lucien Rochat and Arnold Bovet, who found a temperance movement known in Europe as the Blue Cross. It is born in 1887 at a Congress for "moral uplift." Rochat and Bovet put it on firm footing, see that it is well organized, and give it its general shape and direction. Bovet in particular is an untiring field man, always on the go. He knows that full exposure to the facts is one of the most important means of prevention, and so he gives lectures wherever he goes, describing the pernicious effects of the abuse of alcohol. The homes that are established for withdrawal cures are also effective. Sanatoriums for alcoholics have been in existence since 1841, but it is through the "Blue Cross" that their importance and their necessity becomes generally recognized.

Several decades before the Blue Cross is founded, however, there is a priest named Theobald Mathew who leads the temperance movement in Ireland. A public-spirited man, Father Mathew is first engaged in caring for the victims of a cholera epidemic before founding a temperance league in 1838. He signs up many members and is able to see the consumption of spirits cut in half; the crime rate drops as well. The famine years of 1846 and 1847 reverse the trend, however: the people use alcohol to deaden their hunger pangs. Father Mathew is cut to heart by what he sees:

> Thousands upon thousands now pine in want and woe, because they did not take my advice. . . . Thousands are now perishing,

> who, if they had not had the folly to spend their hard-earned money in drink, in riot, and in debauchery, would now be safe from danger. . . . I will not upbraid such victims for the past, I would rather cheer and console; I would rather tell them that it is not yet too late.

Father Mathew visits thirty-six countries in two years. He makes his warning appeals especially vivid by the use of realistic pictures. Ultimately he sacrifices his health to this mission. The subsequent Catholic temperance movement, led principally by Father Anno Neumann and Father Elpidius, is based on Mathew's work.

Two Kinds of "Falling Sickness"

It is true that the urgent problem of alcoholism is closely tied up with industrialization; but there is another problem that can be linked even more directly with economic causes: the problem of the homeless and the unemployed. After the Franco-Prussian War of 1870–71, e.g., France is required to pay to Germany the sum of 5,000,000,000 francs. This huge sum gives the German economy a sudden and powerful boost. But many of the new business ventures turn out to be bad risks, many new companies have to close their doors, and many laborers, who had left their farms to work in the new factories, are not only jobless but homeless. A lot of smokestacks are smoking, but a lot of others are not; a lot of people have jobs, but a lot of others are left high and dry and very much in need of help.

They find a friend in Friedrich von Bodelschwingh, the founder of an entire community for the sick: Bethel, near the city of Bielefeld. "Father Bodelschwingh" sees the need and extends his ministry to include it.

Bethel is another of those works that begin small. At first its purpose is to serve just one special class among the unemployed—and, for centuries, among the sick as well—the epileptics. The advances of medical science have brought them no aid. Their symptoms, sudden and violent convulsions that shake the whole body, baffle doctors and frighten laymen. No one wants an epileptic in his workshop, or on his construction job, or running his machine. The attacks come too suddenly; and on the job they may

For a hundred years the Stetten castle in Remstal has been an asylum for the mentally deficient. It also includes facilities for physical therapy.

endanger not only the life of their victim but also the work itself, and possibly other workmen as well. No one is willing to take the risks involved. Nor do schoolteachers want epileptic children in their classes. As a result, epileptics, who appear perfectly normal except during their seizures, live in a no-man's-land of their own, excluded from a normal life, from school, from an occupation. Not until the increasing incidence of seizures over the years produces brain damage and mental incapacitation are some epileptics committed to an institution. The real nature of their trouble remains a mystery for a long time.

One of the first institutions for epileptics is opened in 1864 by a Dr. Moll in an idyllic region near Lake Constance. Dr. Moll particularly urges the Inner Mission to plan separate institutions for epileptics; and during the Mission's 1865 conference in Bruchsal, he is vigorously supported in this by a Pastor Balke from the Rhineland. Head of the Hephata Mental Institution in Mönchengladbach, Balke is also instrumental in the founding of Bethel. The Württemberg delegation immediately seizes upon Moll's suggestion; its members have just secured more space for their

Stetten Mental Institution in Remstal, enabling them to broaden its functions. Johannes Landenberger, one of the fathers of modern physical therapy, had proved at Stetten that providing schools for the mentally retarded was not enough, that manual arts programs were also needed. Thus Stetten had already become an institution of pilot projects. Now it adds to its facilities for the mentally retarded a home for epileptics which combines medical supervision with remedial training.

When the Bethel Epileptic Asylum is started in 1867 in a small farmhouse in the Teutoburg Forest, Stetten sends Johannes Unsöld, one of its staff members and Landenberger's son-in-law, to work there as a teacher and a housefather. Public-spirited citizens of Bielefeld help to build up the little home for epileptic children. Unsöld has charge of the few patients that come in the beginning. The work grows year by year, and when the Deaconess House in Bielefeld closes its doors, it sends its sisters to Bethel. At that point Pastor Friedrich Simon and a businessman named Gottfried Bansi set out to enlist the man who will take charge of both works. They go to the Ruhr village of Dellwig, where they know a pastor whom they consider the right man for the job. As an assistant pastor in Paris, he had proved his capabilities as a counselor and Good Samaritan to children working as scavengers in the streets. His name is Friedrich von Bodelschwingh.

The work in Paris has had a telling effect on Bodelschwingh's robust constitution, and his wife is glad that he can recuperate in this quiet spot in the Ruhr valley. The men from Bielefeld know that Bodelschwingh's first work of ministering love was among the poorest Germans in Paris, the ragpickers and scavengers. They also know of the tragedy that befell the Dellwig parsonage in 1869 when, within the short space of twelve days, whooping cough took the lives of the pastor's four children. He takes his visitors to the cemetery, shows them the four graves, and they understand why he and his wife feel bound to Dellwig. They return to Bielefeld without any promise from the pastor. But Bodelschwingh cannot get his mind off the plight of the epileptics whom his visitors have described to him; and so, before making up his mind, he visits Bethel to see the little home which by now shelters fifteen epileptics. He is gripped by what he sees: there are many more people like these, and they all need help badly. What are they to do? What is to become of them? Care, training, and help is waiting for them here at Bethel. Bodelschwingh says yes.

He takes charge of the home in January, 1872 and begins a work of unique dimensions which eventually becomes a modern city of many hundreds of houses, large hospitals, workshops, stores, invalid homes, and schools serving thousands of handicapped people. Bodelschwingh soon sees that epileptics need special care, but that they should not be isolated. He also sees that the people in Bethel who are *not* sick should become teachers; and so he begins a number of schools, the most important of which is a seminary. A seminary in the midst of a city of mercy seems to make even more sense than a seminary in the midst of a university. Above all, however, Bodelschwingh develops and puts into practice a principle of therapy without which we today could hardly imagine a program of care for the disadvantaged. Nothing is worse than the realization that one is literally good for nothing. In Bethel, even the most hopeless case is good for something. Encountering a man reduced to despair by the feeling that he is altogether superfluous, Bodelschwingh is able to help him see what a service he is performing by praying silently in his sickroom. That is why everyone in Bethel works according to his capacities. It is also why Bethel, the city of unspeakable suffering, is a happy place. And it is why Bethel can even send assistance to the people of Africa—an Inner Mission enterprise supporting its own foreign missions program! At Bethel no one is disqualified because of his condition from being in some way a helper of others.

Finally, anyone who is so deeply engaged in serving the unfortunate comes to have a keen eye for all need, even needs that do not come within the scope of his own institution and ministry. Bodelschwingh cannot ignore the social needs of his time. Before long the word gets around that people in need can always go to Bethel and not be turned away. You don't need an appointment, not even to see Pastor Bodelschwingh himself. "Enter without knocking" is the rule all over Bethel. And so the jobless and the homeless, the victims of what was—as far as they were concerned—an economic mirage, hike to Bethel to beg a piece of bread or a meal, or a bed for the night, or a bed for the winter when it is too cold to sleep outside. And they get a hearing.

One of these tramps, already two or three times in Bethel, approaches Bodelschwingh one spring day. Now that winter is over, he is supposed to move on, for Bethel cannot keep him. Only people with the falling sickness (as epilepsy was called) can stay in Bethel permanently. The falling sickness? The tramp says bitterly, "I've got the falling sickness too."

Bodelschwingh doesn't know what to say. He stands there, stricken. Isn't the man right? Aren't the people who are turned out onto the streets and jostled about by the vicissitudes of life really prone to another kind of "falling sickness"? Aren't they too in danger, abandoned, lost? After thinking it over, Bodelschwingh allows the man to stay. He lets others come as well. Instead of alms he gives them work.

South of the Teutoburg Forest lies the "Senne," a grim and arid moor. Here in the middle of this wasteland Bodelschwingh builds a home for poor vagrants, and the tramps come, stay, and fill the house. They set to work with picks and shovels, and they plow up the dry ground. The moor becomes a farmland. Soon more homesites for tramps are found, developed, and put to use.

Bodelschwingh knows he cannot fight the mounting social crises by himself. He needs resources—a great deal of money, and a great deal of help. So he becomes a "beggar" himself. He travels around, hat in hand, trying to unlock hearts for his crusade against want and misery. His almsgatherers go from house to house, up and down stairs; he himself keeps knocking at the doors of government officials, asking for a hearing and for assistance. One day he succeeds in gaining entrance to the imperial palace and wins the crown prince over to his ideas and plans.

Bodelschwingh is seventy-three years old when he is elected to the Prussian Diet. His concern is for the lower classes, and he is convinced that all welfare projects need to be regulated by law. While other members are debating armament questions, he asks the Diet to pass a law requiring new factories to arrange for their employees' housing: a cabin and a half-acre of land for every man with a family. Thus we find coexisting with the slogans of class war, as proclaimed by the labor unions and Marxist factions, the appeal of a Christian avant-gardist. The church as a whole does not yet perceive the signs of the times. But individuals like Bodelschwingh point the way that Christians should go.

An Experiment in Sharing

Anyone who surveys this period of social and economic upheaval can easily see the causes of the social injustices of the day: the selfishness of management, bourgeois apathy, ecclesiastical purblindness, and bureaucratic inertia. It would be unjust, however, to pass a blanket judgment on all of management. Some employers were men of vision, deeply concerned for social justice. As early as the nineteenth century one can find experimental profit sharing plans. E. J. Leclaire, a French businessman, regularly began sharing profits with some of his employees in 1842; later he institutes a Mutual Aid Society within the "Maison Leclaire" and makes all his employees eligible for benefits. The results are spectacular; business booms, and the employees become a real team. The method catches on. In 1847 Johann H. von Thünen, a German economist, experiments with a similar plan of profit sharing on his Mecklenburg estate; and a machine manufacturer named Borchert follows suit in 1867. One of the outstanding programs begun in the nineteenth century is still going today: the Zeiss Foundation.

The foundation is the work of Ernst Abbe, the senior scientist and later proprietor of the Carl Zeiss Works in Jena, Germany. The company's rise straight to the top in its field is due to the solid foundation of research laid by Abbe. He later concentrates on an employee benefit plan that provides for a substantial proportion of company dividends to be put in a pension fund for retired employees. Another provision is a reserve fund for severance pay. This protects employees who leave the company before retirement age against loss of what had been set aside for them each year. Finally, all employees receive a year-end dividend. It is deducted from company dividends and amounts to between six and ten percent of the employee's salary. Two of Abbe's innovations are especially important: First, he puts these provisions on a contractual basis, giving the employees a legal claim to them and the right to sue for redress. (The foundation's statutes have the force of law after 1896.) Secondly, in 1891, he deeds all of his holdings in the Zeiss Works to the Zeiss Foundation. This move puts the whole issue of property and ownership in new perspective.

The experiment has its flaws. The social program is not discussed with the employees beforehand; the decision is handed down, so to speak, from the top, whereas real person-to-person help would consist in giving the beneficiary a participating role. But the program does show that social justice is at least a possibility, even in industry.

Christian Love in the Eastern Church

The division between East and West, though much more evident now than ever before, did not come about yesterday. Nor is the dividing line between East and West equivalent to a line between Christianity and atheism; it is rather the result of a development within Christianity itself that dates from the early centuries of the church. The Westerner—whether in Europe or North America—has always tended to let his own worries overshadow the problems in other parts of the world. He is forever trapped in his peculiarly Western perspective; his own culture becomes the criterion, his own way of thinking the norm. But anyone wanting to survey the history of "people who care" must cross the frontiers and take a long, hard look at the East, where to a frightening extent need and misery are coming to constitute an indictment of a West that is success-oriented, industrialized, and drunk with progress. Thus we shall briefly survey the main currents in Russia, which have followed a rather different course from those in Western countries.

Christian love of neighbor as practiced in the Eastern church contrasts markedly with mercy in the Western churches. The differences become apparent as soon as we compare Eastern and Western monasticism. Western monasticism was shaped by Benedict of Nursia, whose twofold dictum, "Pray and work," ensures a balance of otherworldly devotion and this-worldly action. Helping one's neighbor becomes, therefore, a task whose fulfillment is simultaneously a way of fulfilling Christ's commands here on earth. By contrast, the monasticism of the Eastern church is preeminently that of hermits and anchorites, that is, solitaries who withdraw from the world and devote themselves wholly to prayer and meditation. Ernst Benz, an authority on the Eastern church, compares it to a turtle that has completely withdrawn into its shell and rarely sticks out its head. The Orthodox church, says Benz, has withdrawn into its liturgy and sacraments and has renounced the world, including the fulfillment of the Christian ethic in the social sector. Thus, suffering and identification with the suffering of others do not produce good works; they are seen as life itself. Living means suffering, renunciation means gain.

This may go some way toward explaining why the principle of loving one's neighbor is expressed more in pity, in identifying with the unfortunate, than in practical relief measures, despite the astonishing ventures in practical Christian service by the early bishops in Constantinople and in Caesarea of Cappadocia. This is not to deny that the identification-in-suffering practiced down through the centuries issued in much real help. But the help is usually anonymous, coming from the great host of believers. This makes it difficult to ascertain the historical facts. Moreover, the literature of the Orthodox church consists largely of praise and adoration, as does its representational art. Historical records are scanty. Also of relevance, perhaps, is the Orthodox conviction that the individual's good works do not need to be spoken or written about. Even so, it is still possible to say something about the history of Christian charity in the East.

In the Orthodox church, poverty means more than merely social inferiority. Poverty may be the life laid upon the traveler toward the Kingdom of God—just as riches may be. Poverty is accepted in humility. It is lived with. It is considered a means of achieving self-discipline and asceticism. An old Russian proverb says, "Do not eschew prison or the beggar's sack." Particularly in old Russia, beggars are considered the Blessed Poor, and consequently there seems to be no immediate reason to improve the social welfare of a class that is blessed in its poverty, and thereby risk impairing that blessedness. However, while no relief action is organized for them, the poor are commended to the protection of the church. Nowhere is the saying ascribed to St. Laurence—the poor are the treasure of the church—taken so seriously as in

Russia. The poor live in hovels surrounding the churches and subsist on alms. That is entirely in order, and there is no reason to deliberate about change. These beggars are known as "church people," and by virtue of the statute decreed in 1011 by St. Vladimir, Grand Duke of Kiev, all wandering pilgrims and all the blind and the lame are also considered "church people." A similar statute is decreed by Prince Vsevolod of Novgorod.

The feeling that poverty and suffering bring God's blessing becomes more pronounced when fear and want spread over a large part of Russia in the wake of the Mongolian invasion of 1224 and the conquest by Batu Khan in 1237. The Mongolian raids particularly bring such political and economic disaster that people are virtually compelled to doubt the value of earthly goods.

It is true that in some famine years there are not even enough crumbs left over for the beggar. Relief action is then undertaken, mainly by the large monasteries. As early as the eleventh century, St. Feodosi, abbot of the Monastery of the Caves (Percherskaya Laura) in Kiev, organizes help and care for the needy. The fifteenth-century abbot Pafnuti Borovski feeds as many as six hundred people a day, and about fifty years later, when crop failures result in urgent food shortages, Abbot Josif Volocki does likewise.

We learn nothing about orphan care until we come to the first half of the seventeenth century. Here the monasteries come in for mention once more, notably the Monastery of the Holy Trinity (Troitse Sergieva Laura), where orphans are not only fed and clothed but instructed in reading and writing and manual arts. Michael Romanov (Czar from 1613 to 1645) has a children's home built next to the Solovetski monastery on an island in the White Sea; and in the monastery at Kirillov, orphans in the care of an old monk are trained in special workshops. When they reach adulthood, there are plots of land available for them where they can start a home of their own.

The Chudov or Miracles' Monastery in Moscow distributes money and food in the prisons of the city every Christmas and Easter; and in the early eighteenth century one of the metropolitans of Novgorod builds a number of asylums, poorhouses, and hospitals, and promotes an extensive program of private good works.

Beginning with the reign of Peter the Great, charitable activity declines noticeably, and in the course of the general trend toward secularization it is arrested altogether. Not until the nineteenth century is the material situation of the monasteries sufficiently improved, through outside contributions, to permit them to resume their charitable activities, at which time poorhouses and other institutions are built again here and there, staffed mainly by nuns.

The Prophet of Yasnaya Polyana

The social conscience of Russia, however, is not the Orthodox church. Count Leo N. Tolstoy, the great prophet of the Russian people, is in fact excommunicated by that church. And Stalin and other militant socialists, most of whom owe their education to monastic schools, renounce God and the church altogether in favor of Marxist slogans; they seek to achieve social progress through class war.

It is not easy to do justice to Tolstoy. Tolstoy the novelist is honored by all, and he is without question one of the great writers of all time. But Tolstoy the social philosopher and religious critic meets with hostility and condemnation. There were too many harsh, gratuitous, Olympian, and—it is often said—unscholarly attacks by Tolstoy upon all churches in general and the Russian church in particular. He never got beyond half-truths, it is said; and he was able to practice nothing or pathetically little of what he preached. But most of those who make such charges have not even ventured as far as Tolstoy's half-truths; they have merely talked. Still another charge is that Tolstoy contributed materially to preparing the way for Bolshevism. So did others, and perhaps even more materially; for if the Bolshevists did learn anything from Tolstoy, they certainly betrayed a fundamental misunderstanding of his main concern. Tolstoy wanted no part in evil. He wanted no part in violence—which is expressly condoned in the socially revolutionary proletariat. It is indeed no easy task to understand and do justice to this great Russian thinker. But one thing should be clearly brought out: Tolstoy has a deep distrust of all organization. He despises the chiliastic dogmas of the politicians, and he dismisses as pharisaism all organized good works of the kind we have mentioned so often in this book. Behind this exaggerated dogmatism one can see the honest attempt of a man to live a life according to the Sermon on the Mount, as he himself says in his semiautobiographical play, "The Light Shines in the Darkness."

Tolstoy is born August 28, 1828, on the estate of Yasnaya Polyana, near Moscow. His teen-age and university years are tempestuous and hedonistic. At the age of nineteen he enlists in a Caucasian brigade and sees action in Sevastopol. In that embattled city, serfs—who at Yasnaya Polyana and on every other estate in Russia lead a subhuman existence—bravely fight side by side with freemen; and Tolstoy, observing this, finds his whole view of them changing. The peasant-serf is no longer the workhorse of human society; Tolstoy sees him as a brother.

Returning to Yasnaya Polyana, he begins to write. "Childhood," his first story, marks the beginning of a lifetime output that, when completed, would constitute a single autobiographical "confession." Afterward come the major novels *War and Peace* and *Anna Karenina.* At thirty-four Tolstoy marries an eighteen-year-old girl, Sofya Andreyevna Behrs, and his happiness seems complete. He idolizes his wife, he watches his children grow up, he manages his father's estate with skill and shrewdness, and he writes. His literary fame spreads, and soon he is one of the most celebrated writers in Russia. The insights he got as a soldier in the Caucasus remain with him, but they do not yet have any impact on his way of life. He is still too fond of the literary salons, the elegance and sparkle of high society. But there are signs that the turning point of his life is approaching. In 1865 he writes:

> One can only live when one is intoxicated with life. But as soon as the intoxication wears off, one sees that everything is phony. . . . Family, art, were not enough for me any more. The family were unhappy people, as I am. Art is the mirror of life, but when life has no meaning left the mirror game is no longer amusing.

And a little later:

> . . . at this thought [of God] the glad waves of life rose within me. All that was around me came to life and received a meaning. . . . I remembered that I only lived at those times when I believed in God. As it was before, so it was now; I need only be aware of God

> to live; I need only forget Him, or disbelieve Him, and I died. . . . "What more do you seek?" exclaimed a voice within me. . . . "To know God and to live is one and the same thing. God is life." . . . And more than ever before, all within me and around me lit up, and the light did not again abandon me.

Tolstoy's new life has begun. He begins to practice asceticism, dresses in workclothes, plows his fields, and stops to visit with his peasants. He instructs their children and talks over their troubles with them.

In 1881 he moves to Moscow so that his children can go to school there. During a census he volunteers to do canvassing in the slums, and he is shaken by what he discovers. He tries to raise money in order to do something about the conditions, but he is unsuccessful. *What Then Must We Do?* he asks urgently. The question becomes the title of one of his books. Looking the other way becomes culpable; good intentions do not eliminate social evil. To have no part in evil—that is the thing. To be truly human, one must be present to one's fellowman as a brother. In Tolstoy, the social conscience of mankind is awakened.

He embarks on his difficult journey, his revolution of renunciation, in order to be in all things and in the fullest sense a brother to his neighbor. He waives the literary rights to his works. He makes up his mind to renounce his property rights as well and to gives his land to the peasants. When his family, particularly his wife, intervenes (a friend tells him that they would try to have him pronounced mentally incompetent in order to nullify the terms of his will), he deeds over all his possessions to her. He wants no part of them any more, wants no part in injustice. He is dead-serious about following Christ. Does he fail? His marriage threatens to collapse, his family doesn't understand him any more, he is damned by church and state. It wouldn't take much more for him to be put away. People are determined not to hear his accusations.

How utterly new the trend of Tolstoy's thought is can be seen in the matter of nonresistance and conscientious objection to military service. Tolstoy recognizes that organized pacifism isn't the important thing; the czar's peace proposals, enthusiastically endorsed by Europe's pacifists, Tolstoy dismisses as flummery. His concern is to restore to man a sense of inner freedom, including the freedom to say no to murder in war, regardless of the consequences.

When the peace-loving czar stakes the lives of ten thousand Russian soldiers on a speculative bid for Manchuria, however, Tolstoy joins in the protest with his pamphlet "Bethink Yourselves!" a general appeal favoring conscientious objection. The appeal is printed abroad and distributed illegally in Russia; Tolstoy has no fear of man, hence no fear of the czar. Had Russia's czardom ever received a more audacious challenge? When defeat at the hands of the Japanese leads to the Russian Revolution of 1905, and the revolution to bloody repression, Tolstoy is equally sharp in his denunciation. "I Cannot Be Silent," he calls his protest, and those words are written large over his whole life.

Tolstoy and his friends proved their magnanimity in two great humanitarian acts; and if nothing else were known about Tolstoy, these two things alone would require us to pay tribute to him here. The crop failures of 1891 and 1892 result in widespread famine, particularly in the vicinity of Ryazan. When this news reaches Yasnaya Polyana, Tolstoy grumbles that people are hungry all over Russia. It is not enough to feed a horse that is ready to drop; one must get off its back. In other words, Tolstoy is sticking to his principles of avoiding organizations. He sees clearly that good works and philanthropy cannot undo the wrong inherent in the concentration of property in the hands of the rich. But when he visits the famine-stricken areas and becomes aware of the extent of the misery, he is moved to act. With the assistance of his family, repudiating all the attempts of the government to play down the situation, Tolstoy organizes a relief program that keeps him in the famine area for two years, almost without interruption. The experience brings out a practical bent in Tolstoy. The soup kitchens he sets up with the help of his two older daughters are highly effective in meeting the need. His sons also help out in the famine area, and his wife raises money in Moscow.

Hardly has a bumper harvest ended the famine when Tolstoy feels challenged to undertake a new and entirely different relief work. Religious sects have been persecuted in Russia in every age. By the end of the nineteenth century, the combined membership of these groups approaches twenty million, which means that a large part of the population is living in persecution or in constant fear of it. In Tolstoy's day, one such group is the Dukhobors, a Protestant community in the Caucasus who have refused to do military service and have destroyed their arms. Thousands of Dukhobors die in the savage reprisals that follow. Some four thousand of the survivors are shipped to Siberia, a large number of them dying on the way.

A manifesto is issued on behalf of the Dukhobors. It is signed by several brave men and includes a postscript by Tolstoy. It proposes that the Dukhobors be given a chance to emigrate instead of being exiled and killed. Copies are made and distributed. Even the czar receives one. The signers are sent into exile, but Tolstoy remains free. The authorities are afraid to do anything to him. He is thus able to resume the appeal, and after five years of lobbying, bargaining with ship lines, and wire-pulling he actually manages to get permission for the Dukhobors to emigrate to Canada. He also rallies popular support in other countries by further public appeals; and one of his sons goes to London to promote the cause. Finally the Dukhobors' way to freedom is clear. To swell the funds being raised to cover their considerable expenses, Tolstoy sells the first rights of his novel *Resurrection* to a magazine for 12,000 rubles, every kopeck of which goes to the emigrants.

11. The Gentle Force

Gandhi: A Life for India

The prophet of Yasnaya Polyana was able to move minds in Europe and Asia. As a young man, the Russian philosopher Nikolai Berdyaev feels the trenchant force of "Tolstoy's revolt against false standards of greatness and history's sacred cows, against the hypocrisy of the social structure and of all human social relations." Maxim Gorki looks up to him with love and admiration. The Frenchman Romain Rolland sees in him the "beacon for the younger generation of his times," and even Rainer Maria Rilke, so different in spirit from Tolstoy, says that he owes everything to him.

But above all, Mahatma Gandhi, who called himself a "humble follower" of Tolstoy, looked to him as one of his great guides. Thus we may well follow our discussion of Tolstoy with a look at Asia, where the nonviolent campaigns of the sage of India and the "gentle force" of Toyohiko Kagawa direct the currents of the times.

At this point the world of Asia and Africa, peopled by races that white westerners smugly refer to as "colored," emerges or reemerges within the scope of the history of good works and humanitarian concern. The responsibility for its absence heretofore must be shared by Europeans; for in the period of conquest and colonization—as well as of evangelization, the goals of which were not always selfless—Europeans made no efforts to win the friendship of the peoples they encountered.

To do no harm to any living thing is one of the most ancient Indian ideals—*ahimsa,* it is called. No wonder, then, that Mohandas Karamchand Gandhi, known and venerated as Mahatma ("great-souled"), finds his approach to the Christian doctrines of love and suffering by way of Tolstoy's precept of having no part in evil. Gandhi lives his whole life according to the Sermon on the Mount, without joining a Christian church, without renouncing his ancestral Hindu beliefs, and without discriminating against other religions.

Who is this Gandhi, whose name soon becomes known around the world? His family home is in Porbandar, on the Gulf of Oman, where he is born in 1869. The name should be remembered along with Yasnaya Polyana and Assisi. A Samaritan is born in Porbandar.

He studies in London and becomes an attorney in Bombay. From 1893 to 1914 he lives in South Africa, which has a sizable Indian population. He fights for his countrymen and suffers with them and finally, by dint of incredible effort, he is able to help them secure better living conditions and wring a fuller measure of justice from their English oppressors. His tenacity earns him several terms of prison and hard labor, but he achieves his goal.

After twenty years he returns home, puts his trust in the English promise of home rule, and initially supports the colonial powers. At length he grows disillusioned and organizes the strangest kind of resistance of all time: passive resistance. He proclaims civil disobedience; noncooperation with the British government; a boycott of English schools, courts, and goods; and above all the return to the simple, Indian way of life. For his part he renounces his titles and resolves to live the life of a farmer and weaver in spiritual fellowship with his disciples. He founds an "ashram," a kind of religious colony, in Sabarmati; and it too has a strange purpose: turning young people into freedom fighters. But far from being destructive, their weapons are the forces of truth, love, and the soul. The young men also learn the traditional Indian occupations of spinning, weaving and farming. Gandhi himself takes up spinning to pay his living expenses.

It may seem as though such things as looms and distaffs are poor weapons for a revolution. But Gandhi sees beyond what meets the eye. Like Tolstoy, he sees first the evil in his own ranks. "We must change," he says, and he doesn't mean it in Tolstoy's individualistic sense; he means the whole people must change. India has herself to blame for her troubles. She is suffering from her own divisions: the chasm between Moslem and Hindu, rich and poor, and the unbridgeable gulf between the various castes. Such division, he says, represents a lack of love. We Indians must learn to love—even our enemies. Although Gandhi himself belongs to the Vaisya caste, he breaks through to the "untouchables," the outcastes, the pariahs. We treat the pariahs like dogs, he says; that is why the world treats us like dogs. The injustices must be redressed, but one must not be unjust himself in redressing them; violence must not be fought with violence. The man who follows that course becomes the slave of violence and injustice.

Gandhi goes his quiet way with his band of disciples. He succeeds in eliminating the grossest of the inequities suffered by the poor indigo sharecroppers in Champaran. He goes to prison serenely when, despite his appeal for nonviolent resistance to English rule, Indians resort to violence. He believes that the poor, the meek, and the peacemakers will overcome; he believes in the power of the good in man. Unswervingly he pursues his goal: to get his people ready for independence. If the cause requires him to serve sentences in English prisons, he goes to prison; if it requires fasting, he fasts, adding the weight of personal example to his nonviolent principles. His hunger strikes are news all over the world.

Gandhi achieves his main goal after World War II, when England gives India her freedom. But he is deeply disappointed at the form that freedom takes. His dream of one nation of Moslems and Hindus is not fulfilled. England creates two states, and the polarities are intensified. As the factions become increasingly militant, Gandhi falls back on his most effective weapon: he begins a fast. Now approaching eighty, he tells his rioting countrymen that the only thing he can do for them is to suffer, that he will not eat until they end the fighting.

Five days later, the leaders of the opposing factions reach an accord. Gandhi has won. A week after that he is dead, felled by the bullet of a fanatical Brahman who considered him a menace to Hinduism.

But Gandhi's work lives on. His favorite disciple, Vinoba Bhave, consistently follows the path of his teacher. Bhave has already founded several ashrams and has made the simple life a blueprint for many young Indians. Now he launches a mission that quickly gets government support: land reform. He goes on marathon walks through India to beg land. He persuades rich landlords to give some of their holdings to him, and he in turn gives it to the landless poor. Others follow his example. They get and redistribute much land. But it is not enough.

Nor is it enough merely to give the land away. The pariahs must learn to farm it. Independence brings new challenges to India. Many mistakes must be made good. But there is no doubt that Gandhi, the apostle of nonviolence, did more for India than many leading statesmen. It is also certain that, although not a Christian evangelizer himself, Gandhi broke much ground for Christianity in India.

A Japanese Who "Cares"

What Gandhi does in India, a mission school graduate and converted Samurai named Toyohiko Kagawa (1888–1960) does in Japan. As a young man Kagawa is miraculously saved from dying of tuberculosis. In the last stages of the disease, given no hope of recovery, he vows that if he is spared, he will devote his life to the poor. When he does recover, Kagawa, just twenty-one, sets about redeeming his vow.

On Christmas Eve, 1909, the slum-dwellers of the metropolis of Kobe are treated to a curious sight. A frail young man, pushing a handcart containing his few earthly possessions, is making straight for an abandoned hut. Even though the slums of Kobe are desperately overcrowded—swarming with prostitutes, pimps, thieves, and drunks—and even though the space problem is acute, this hut has stood empty for years. No one wants to live in it because a murder was committed there years ago and it is said to be haunted by the dead man's ghost.

Undaunted, the young Kagawa moves in. He is alone only for the first night; after that he shares his shabby accommodations with anyone who ventures in. An old beggar-woman calls him her son, and when he would otherwise go hungry she picks through the garbage piles to find food for him. A drunk drives his fist into

Toyohiko Kagawa, 1888–1960.

DPA

Kagawa's face, knocking in several teeth. A transient houseguest infects him with trachoma, an eye disease, and Kagawa almost goes blind. But he stays. This brother-to-the-poorest sticks it out in the slums for fifteen years. He finds a life-partner who is in full sympathy with his work. And since, like Tolstoy whom he admires, he has a writer's soul, he unburdens himself by writing about the needs of the unfortunate. His writing is published, and he uses the money for his work. But during these years, living and loving and suffering as an urban St. Francis in Shinkawa, the "slough" of Kobe, Kagawa does not succeed in eliminating the slough itself, nor the misery of those who dwell there.

Aware that he cannot manage it single-handed, Kagawa departs from Tolstoy's course, and from that of Gandhi as well. He sees that he will have to equip himself thoroughly in order to attack the problem of human misery on another level. He goes to the United States and studies social problems and conditions. He gets acquainted with organizations in Europe and North America. His own country, where the people are going hungry, is now facing the onslaught of industrialization; and he sees no other way to help the farmers and the laborers than to help them organize, but without violence. He becomes the greatest social reformer of Japan. Despite his country's aristocratic traditions and militarism, he is able to secure for the downtrodden the kind of conditions for which many groups in Western countries had to crusade for decades.

Ignoring the government's legal prohibitions, Kagawa founds the Japan Federation of Labor, the Farmers' Union, and a fisherman's cooperative. He organizes schools and training programs, insurance plans, health plans, and counseling services. Government spies trail him everywhere, and once he is imprisoned. But to the proletariat he is a saint. When 18,000 dockworkers in Kobe are on the verge of destroying their own worksites in their utter frustration and despair, Kagawa interposes himself and begins to pray. He is successful in calming the workers, but this does not prevent him from fighting for their cause all the more intensely with his own weapons. He knows no feelings of revenge.

On September 1, 1923, Japan is hit by an earthquake. Tokyo, the capital, and Yokohama are buried in rubble and ashes. Earthquake, fire, and flood turn the cities into a wasteland. The death toll and the numbers of homeless and destitute reach staggering proportions, and there seems to be nothing that can be done about it. The government, powerless to act, puts itself in the hands of Kagawa, the workers' friend. The authorities get him out of prison and commission him to help, putting him in charge of the reconstruction of Tokyo. He accepts the job, on condition that no salary be paid him. He wants to stay free.

During the reconstruction of Tokyo, Kagawa sees the way to attack the big-city slums. He has not forgotten Shinkawa. For years he keeps dinning it into the ears of the regime that the

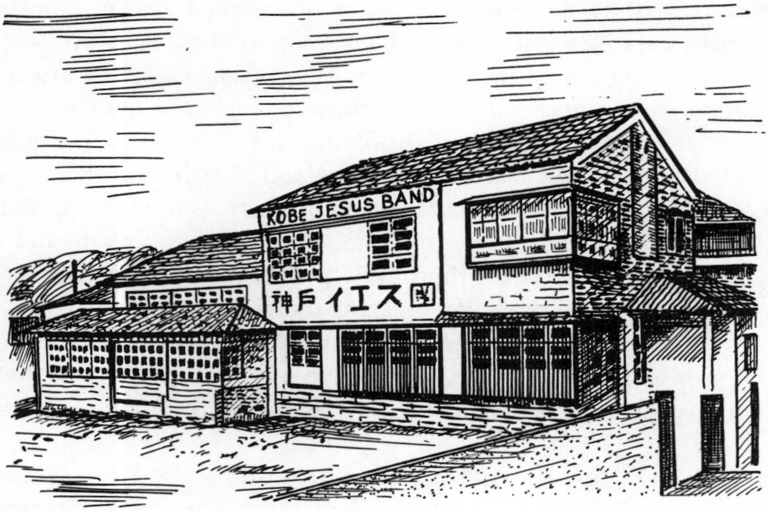

The mission to the poor is still going on in Kobe, Japan, where Toyohiko Kagawa began his work.

slums should be torn down and replaced by bright, modern workers' settlements, something like the new Tokyo. In 1926 the government yields; in six large cities, including Kobe, Kagawa is able to carry out his plans. The slums come down, modern housing developments go up. Even Shinkawa, which was built on alluvial deposits (from which it derives its name), is transformed. A Christian mission station, a hospital, and a dispensary replace the "haunted" hut.

But the service that this consumptive renders his people and mankind is not finished. Kagawa agrees with Tolstoy and Gandhi on the question of violence. And when overpopulated Japan deems it necessary to seize by armed force the land on the continent nearby, the apostle of peace sadly leaves his own camp and sides with those who are threatened. He visits Chinese cities and with tears in his eyes he begs forgiveness for the sins of his own people; he stands in the dock for them, as it were. Nowhere can we see more clearly how serious this Japanese is about living the Christian faith. Kagawa is also on hand during the greatest catastrophe ever to befall his nation. The dreadful bloodletting perpetrated during World War II by the Japanese Army, whose victims in the areas they seized included countless numbers of Christians, is paid for by the dreadful atomic bombs dropped by the United States on Hiroshima and Nagasaki. Kagawa is not a young man anymore; but he is on hand when he is needed. Once more, he doesn't ask about money or thanks; instead, he appeals for a spirit of brotherhood and cooperative relief.

When representatives of America's Christian churches come to Japan to do their part in helping to atone for the great common guilt, Kagawa approaches them at the airport in silence. He and the incoming passengers know that when men sin against each other, there is only one way they can give and receive pardon. They know that pardon cannot be bought with eloquence, but that it is offered men in Jesus Christ. And so in that hour the Christians of Japan and the United States go together to the Lord's Table and receive Communion. Then together they set about the task of redressing wrong and alleviating need.

The Jungle Hospital

Redressing wrong and alleviating need is also the work of the third great humanitarian who must be mentioned here: Albert Schweitzer. Schweitzer is a European, but his field is Africa, that part of the world so greatly sinned against by the West. Since the days when David Livingstone followed the secret slave trails of the Arabs and—in his journals, published by Stanley—focused world attention upon these atrocities, the slave traffic has been largely eliminated; but the life of the African national is still a grim one. Decades after slavery is officially abolished, the Africans are still in effect slaves on the farms and the plantations and in the factories. Slaves with few rights, second-class human beings, helpless against the forces of nature and the ravages of disease.

At the time Albert Schweitzer decides to go to these oppressed people, he has already established himself as a pastor, a theology professor, and an organist of world renown. By European standards he has everything he could wish for, and a brilliant future in prospect. But he realizes that his course is wrong. He returns to the university and gets his degree in medicine. In 1913 he goes to

Lambaréné as sketched by an African boy.

West Africa with his wife under the auspices of the Paris Missionary Society. The mission has a construction site available for him at its Lambaréné station on the shores of the Ogowe River. With medical supplies and equipment purchased with the proceeds from his organ recitals, he starts setting up his jungle hospital. The building is made of wood, with a corrugated roof. An office, an operating room, and a dispensary—that is all. The sick are accommodated in large bamboo huts situated around the hospital compound.

Schweitzer runs the hospital until 1917 when he and his wife, being Alsatians and hence German subjects, are interned by the French. He is not able to resume his work in Lambaréné until February of 1924. However he now has a large group of supporters, including a sizable number of Swedes enlisted by the Swedish archbishop, Nathan Söderblom.

Picking up the work after several years' absence is not much easier than starting it had been originally. The barrack-hospital is still standing, but the huts have to be rebuilt. Undismayed, Schweitzer starts in. One day reserves arrive from Alsace, among them another doctor. Soon their quarters are too cramped for them. At first there are forty patients, then sixty, then the number rapidly grows to eighty and a hundred. When both a severe famine and an epidemic of dysentery break out in 1925, Schweitzer is faced with an insoluble problem. How can he isolate the sixty dysentery patients? He also faces the problem of feeding the native families who usually come with the patients and camp near the hospital.

There is only one answer: the hospital must be moved to a larger site. Schweitzer finds a suitable one some two miles upstream and is able to work out the necessary arrangements with the government. By the end of 1925 he is clearing the site, and for the next two years he leaves his medical work to the other doctors while he himself becomes construction engineer, bricklayer, and carpenter. By January, 1927, there are enough houses built to make the move practicable. Now, mothers-to-be, lung patients, and mental cases can be accommodated in separate quarters. By 1948 the number of buildings has grown to forty-five.

Schweitzer is able to carry on his work during World War II, though often under the most difficult conditions; and after the war he begins treating leprosy patients, now that promising new remedies have been developed. In 1953 he is awarded the Nobel Peace Prize. He is now internationally known and honored. Money and medicine are sent to him from every part of the world.

Schweitzer set an example for all mankind, but unfortunately mankind has not yet come very far along the paths of goodness and peace. Gandhi, Kagawa, and Schweitzer, who protest with all their strength against armed force and war, live to witness two global conflagrations. Their service in the cause of mankind is rendered in a century of almost incredible inhumanity.

"Lay Down Your Arms"

The most glaring example of twentieth-century inhumanity is provided by the first and second world wars. The ruthlessness of modern strategists and tacticians, and the dreadful power of modern weapons of destruction, turned these wars into genocide on an unprecedented scale. A single invention gave them their nightmarish dimensions: dynamite, the explosive discovered by Alfred Nobel of Sweden.

Why—one might ask—does this book include a man whose name would seem to belong in a history of inhumanity? We have mentioned the Nobel Peace Prize several times—a prize endowed by none other than Alfred Nobel for the promotion of world peace. Between these two poles, the invention of one of the most deadly tools of war and the endowment of the peace prize, is bracketed the life of a man who wanted good and who created an instrument of evil. It is a life we might justly call tragic.

The Nobels have an explosives factory in Sweden. They build no bombs and sell no war matériel; their products are used for blasting rock and grading roads. One day the factory blows up and the owners are killed, all except one of them who happens to be out of the country at the time. This lone survivor, Alfred Nobel, soon afterward discovers the most powerful explosive of his time: nitroglycerin in kieselguhr, a porus substance. He calls the new product "dynamite," and soon begins producing it in new factories. It makes him fabulously rich. Nobel has his own ideas about the possible uses of dynamite. His is the age of railroads, and everywhere there are routes to be graded, boulders to be blasted, and tunnels to be built. With the new explosive these jobs will take months instead of years. Nobel is thinking big: soon, all Europe will be crisscrossed with railroads, bringing its nations closer together. Dynamite will literally clear all the obstacles from the path.

Nobel is not unaware that he has a deadly weapon on his hands. Monopolized by one nation, it could threaten all Europe. But—he thinks—in the hands of all nations it will be a universal deterrent to future war; the fear of self-annihilation will guarantee peace. (Who would blame him for such reasoning? It is, after all, the same reasoning applied to atomic weapons today.) Nobel follows his blueprint precisely, selling dynamite to any country that wants it.

They all want it. In fact, there is a virtual stampede to get it. Everyone wants to be first and have the most. Nobel's company extends itself over half the world; new factories spring up everywhere, and their owner's fortune reaches staggering proportions. Now, he thinks, the day can't be far off when two opposing armies will be able to blow each other up almost instantly. In such circumstances, who would risk starting a war? Peace on earth is surely in sight.

But Nobel is mistaken. Nations are not only stockpiling large reserves of dynamite; they are also manufacturing bombs and shells and loading them with the new explosive, and they are developing more and more ways to deliver these deadly charges swiftly and surely to their target. The very thing that Nobel dreamed would contribute toward peace on earth and the well-being of all mankind turns out to be an instrument of monstrous peril. Many inventions have shared a similar fate. From the useful invention of the automobile comes the tank; from man's dream of flying, a dream as ancient as Icarus, comes the modern air force, which brings death and devastation not only to the front lines but also to peaceful towns and villages far beyond; from the submarine comes that silent courier of death, the torpedo. By the time Nobel sees his dreadful mistake, it is too late. His conscience drives him to take his whole immense fortune and use it to endow a prestigious prize. Part of the money is to be used to pay tribute to achievements of enduring human value in the fields of medicine, science, and literature. Part of it is set aside for men and women who have made outstanding contributions to the cause of peace. Thus his wealth, which he owes to a truly demonic invention, is invested to promote a better and more peaceful life on earth.

Nobel has come to see that playing with fire in order to control fire is a dangerous game; it can even become a deadly game. He has also seen that there are other, better ways to safeguard peace. Not the least important contribution to his enlightenment is made by a woman, Countess Bertha Kinski, who is better known by her married name, Bertha von Suttner.

In 1876 Nobel hires Countess Kinski as a secretary. After barely a fortnight, she leaves to marry Artur Gundaccar, Baron von Suttner, against the wishes of his family, and she goes with him to Russia. After a rather carefree start to their new life, they settle down to some writing. Meanwhile, the Russo-Turkish War has broken out, and its shadow reaches even the inhabitants of the quiet valley in the Caucasus. Hearing repeatedly of the carnage on the battlefields, Bertha thinks of the Swedish dynamite king. She was unconvinced by his visions of the abolition of war when she was working for him, and now his theory is being controverted by what is going on around her. She stops writing idyllic novels and begins to write for peace.

After a reconciliation with Artur's parents, the couple leave Russia and settle at Harmannsdorf, the von Suttner castle in lower Austria. Here Bertha learns of the founding of the International Peace and Arbitration Association in London. The association wants to establish a world tribunal for the peaceful settlement of all international disputes. She sees that she is not alone in her views, and, inspired by the idea of a kind of international freemasonry of peace on earth, she writes her greatest work, *Lay Down Your Arms*. The book, which prospective publishers at first consider too controversial because of its politics, arouses the world to a degree hardly matched by best sellers today. Everywhere it appears, the reaction is tremendous, for it is indeed loaded with political, if not actual, dynamite. It warns, exhorts, accuses, and expresses a burning, prophetic concern for humanity. Soon it is published in a dozen or more languages. Nobel himself writes to Bertha:

> I have just finished reading your masterpiece. There are said to be two thousand languages (it would be 1,999 too many), and surely your wonderful book ought to be published, read, and pondered in every one of them.

The impact of the book is felt everywhere. More peace societies are founded in many countries. There are manifestos and appeals. Response pours in from people who want to do their part to achieve the goal of world peace. Bertha von Suttner continues to carry the banner. She is elected president of the Austrian Peace Society and gives her first major speech at the Peace Congress in Rome. This petite and elegant lady speaks to an audience of several thousand, and holds them spellbound.

She meets Nobel again in 1892 in Zurich, and he tells her of his plans for a peace prize. In 1905 she herself is the recipient of the prize, *pro pace et fraternitate gentium*—for peace and the brotherhood of peoples. In her acceptance speech she stresses that only a beginning has been made, that not only the peoples but the governments of all nations must make peace and brotherhood their aim. She is looking far ahead toward a united Europe.

But something else is in store for Europe and for the world. People are not ready for the ideas of Bertha von Suttner. Or is it only the mighty of the earth who, yielding to their overweening ambition, incite their peoples against other peoples and make death and terror into a satanic game? Loading Nobel's dynamite into their cannon, they plunge the whole world from America to Asia, from the North Sea to the Cape of Good Hope, into a world holocaust. It is ignited by the guns of August 1914. Bertha von Suttner is mercifully spared the sight; she dies a few weeks before, on June 21. In her unfulfilled desire for peace on earth she still speaks for all men of goodwill.

For four years the war rages on: in Europe, in the African bush and the Far East, on the sea and in the air. Whole divisions of troops are cut down by bullets or overrun by tanks; cities and villages go up in flames. Airplanes drop bombs on residential communities. Entire regions are depopulated or evacuated. The people flee to escape the advancing enemy, or to get out of the way of their own soldiers—or else the war, suddenly erupting in their communities, drives them before it into faraway places and extreme hardship. The Red Cross is undergoing its big test. Now it will be seen whether Dunant's ideas are right. Now humanity must prove itself in the midst of inhumanity. Now the solidarity of mercy must act as an international force, superseding international enmity and armed confrontation. Now it will also be seen whether the ideas of Bertha von Suttner and all peace crusaders have gained acceptance or whether they have been lost in the heady atmosphere of battle and victory, in the roar of nations cheering on their heroes. Where are the men who will lay down their arms while the rest of the world continues to mobilize? Where are the volunteers who will sacrifice personal safety for the sake of the brother who might by lying out there in the rubble at the far edge of some distant battlefield?

Without question, much is being done. There are quiet and vocal protests, and there are volunteers—unknown, nameless volunteers. World history has nothing to say about them. The generals who wipe out enemy armies loom larger in the history books than the simple people who rescue the casualties.

There are the Mennonites, who stick to their pacifist principles and accept the consequences: imprisonment and exile. Many Quakers do likewise, becoming conscientious objectors or attacking the problem of hunger, which grows progressively more acute as the war drags on. The Red Cross is on hand too, its volunteers busy in the service of mercy on battlefields that are bloodier than ever before.

In 1919 the Treaty of Versailles and other international treaties put a formal end to the war, but unrest is still widespread. There follows a round of civil wars, revolutions, riots, strikes, border skirmishes, and assassination plots. With the outbreak of the Second World War in 1939, Armageddon seems to be near. And yet in this cowering huddle of humanity, care is still alive; the commandment of love from heart to heart unfailingly proves to be the one bridge across the battlefields and the graveyards.

This caring becomes a beacon. Its beam is inextinguishable during the persecution of the Armenians and Jews, famine in Russia, slavery in Hitler's Germany, and in the labyrinthine ways pursued by children in a century in which men and women have lost their vision. In these and a thousand personal griefs and tragedies care survives. The century of world war becomes a century of world relief programs, programs which cross national borders and geographical boundaries. Under the sponsorship of public and private organizations, including Christian charities, they prove effective aid for entire nations. Here again, as in every age, in the forefront are individuals, men and women who dedicate their lives to serving their neighbors: the imprisoned, the hungry, the refugees.

The Angel of Siberia

The impact of war is felt far beyond the battlefields. The hunger, expulsion, and imprisonment that go with it are often more terrible than death and the wounds it inflicts. A single place-name epitomizes the anguish suffered by many: Siberia. Here, in an almost endless waste of snow, whipped by the icy winds of the steppes, the Russian czars set up penal colonies for felons and political prisoners. Anyone deported to Siberia rarely returns. The hunger, the cold, the grueling labor, and—not least importantly—the unrelieved isolation soon take their toll. And who cares?

There is a Finnish woman named Mathilda Wrede who does what she can for these exiles. She visits the prisons. She is on the railroad platforms when the loaded transport trains leave for Siberia. She distributes food and tries to bolster morale. She visits the loved ones left behind and does what she can to help. Often she is not able to do very much: pitted against the overwhelming need, her strength and resources are not enough to have any long-range effect. But she proves that something, at least, can be done. She proves that wherever someone really wants to help, ways can be found.

When world war breaks out, huge prisoner of war camps are built near the penal colonies; and the life of the POWs is, if possible, even harder than that of the Russian exiles. They are exposed to the Siberian winter without the barest essentials of clothing, and to infection and disease without medicine or treatment. Totally vulnerable, they die by the thousands. Siberia becomes a mass grave for enemy prisoners.

In 1915 the first shocking reports from the Russian prison camps reach Germany. The response is an outpouring of aid from the whole people: in a short time, the enormous sum of twenty million marks is raised for the prisoners. The money is to be sent via the Swedish envoy in St. Petersburg (Petrograd), General Edvard Brändström. The general is well aware that the success of the relief action depends completely on the proper transmission of the money, and he is also aware of the corruptibility of the czarist officers and officials. But there is nothing he can do; his place is in St. Petersburg. Then one day his daughter Elsa asks him to let her go to Siberia as a delegate of the Red Cross. Coming from a twenty-seven-year-old socialite, the request is almost preposterous. But the general consents. His answer to the remonstrances of his friends is merely, "Why should I worry? She is going the way of the Lord."

It is around Christmastime 1915 when Elsa and her friend, Ethel von Heidenstam, arrive at the Sretensk camp in eastern Siberia with large amounts of money and clothing. She shudders at what she sees. Typhus is raging throughout the camp; the prisoners are lying uncovered on the bare floor; a scanty mugful of water per prisoner must do for washing, drinking, and soup-making. The Russian commandant has never seen the inside of the prisoners' compound, and he does his best to keep the Swedish visitor out as well. But Miss Brändström persists, and eventually she talks him into visiting the camp with her. When he sees the unspeakable conditions, he recoils in shock.

This visit transforms his attitude. He gives the Swedish Red Cross nurse a completely free hand and helps her in setting up a 550-bed hospital. Miss Brändström procures medical supplies and equipment, covers and clothing, and sees to it that the patients are adequately fed.

To the prisoners she is an angel; later she will in fact be called the "angel of Siberia." Not long after her arrival in Sretensk, she comes down with typhus herself, and the whole camp fears for her life. Barely recovered, she gets up and leaves Sretensk to carry on the work in other camps, thus saving the lives of thousands of German soldiers.

Miss Brändström knows that physical and material relief is not enough. She writes: "The prisoners must feel that the one who brings them the gifts from the homeland is a warmhearted human being, for whom every prisoner is a real person. The distributing itself takes little skill; the thing is to use it as a means of thawing out frozen, unfeeling hearts." And so she is always on the go, visiting camp after camp, standing beside sickbeds, comforting the dying and bringing hope to the living. She travels on an open sled through the icy Siberian plains and spends days on the rattling cars of the Trans-Siberian Railroad. Failing other means of transportation, she goes by horse or on foot, helping where the need is greatest. In the early part of 1916, when prisoners of war in Siberia are shipped off to work in the western part of Russia, she plants herself at the little station in Pensa where for weeks she hands out food and clothing and takes down the names of the prisoners' relatives in her notebook in order that they can be notified. The prisoners leave Pensa knowing that this young woman has made their concern her own.

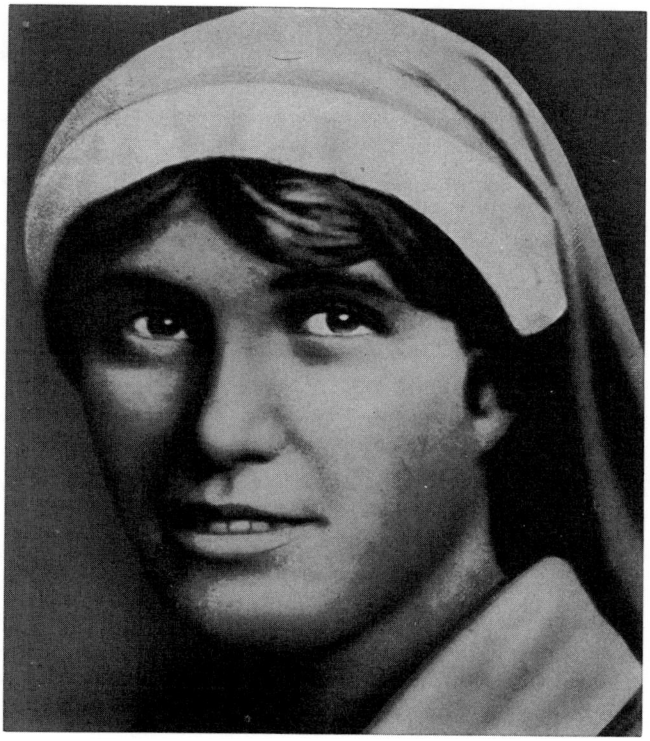

Elsa Brändström, the "angel of Siberia," ministers to prisoners of war in World War I.

Historisches Bildarchiv Handke, Bad Berneck

After the Treaty of Brest-Litovsk in 1918, all ties between the prisoners of war and their homeland are severed. The Red and White armies face each other across the barricades, and no one has any precise information about the political and military situation. All traffic and all communication lines to Siberia are blocked. Miss Brändström is in western Russia at the time, but when the German government appeals to her for help she sets off with a small Red Cross delegation, hoping to go to Siberia to investigate the state of the prisoners and to rescue them if possible. The delegates take plenty of funds with them, as before, but they soon fall into the hands of the Czechs, who detain them for weeks and put them through a round of interrogations. It would be easy to buy their way out, but Miss Brändström and her companions have no intentions of doing that. The money belongs to the prisoners.

The delegation is finally set free, and soon thereafter Miss Brändström reaches her first destination: Omsk in Siberia. She spends Christmas at the internment camp in Tomsk, then travels to Krasnoyarsk where she finds that the whole camp is being put through a drumhead court-martial, the purpose of which is to divert attention from the mutiny of a nearby Russian regiment. In a makeshift barrack-courtroom, death sentences are being handed out day after day. Miss Brändström demands to be admitted to the proceedings. In response to an attempt to scare her off, she says merely, "You can shoot me, but you won't silence the voice of the Swedish people that way." Finally allowed to enter, she stays for two days, observing the "judges" until the blood purge is stopped.

In the fall of 1919 the Red forces take over Siberia. Shortly thereafter the Red Cross is forbidden to carry on its work and Elsa Brändström is arrested. But her presence is so forceful and her achievements so conspicuous that no one dares lay a hand on her. Leon Trotsky himself, at that time in command of the Red Army, signs a pass permitting her to resume her tour of the POW camps. Not until the summer of 1920 does she decide to return to Sweden, where her father, critically ill, is awaiting her.

But her work is not done. In 1923 she goes to the United States on a lecture tour and returns with $100,000 which she uses to found a home for war orphans. She takes on other jobs as well: numbers of returnees from Siberia, for example, have her to thank for taking care of their resettlement problems. In 1929 she marries a German university professor. He is forced to leave Nazi Germany in 1935, and she accompanies him to the United States, from where she continues to aid German refugees and, after the war, the impoverished German people as well. She is preparing to revisit Germany—the German Protestant Relief Agency has asked her for help during the postwar crisis—when on March 3, 1948, she dies.

Nansen and the "Nansen Passes"

Elsa Brändström did much to help the prisoners of war while they were interned, but she was not able to win their release.

Their ordeal continues for years after the end of the war, and the issue is finally taken up by the fledgling League of Nations in Geneva. The new Soviet government in Moscow has agreed in principle to the repatriation of prisoners of war, but the logistics problems have not been worked out. At this point another Scandinavian is enlisted in the cause: Fridtjof Nansen, the Norwegian polar explorer and university professor. Initially Nansen is reluctant to leave his academic work. As he sees it, the job the League of Nations has in mind for him would be better handled by a politician or a diplomat than a professor. So Philip Noel Baker of the League's secretariat goes to Oslo and calls on Nansen at his home, situated high above the Oslo Fjord. Baker is persistent. He quotes figures: prisoners of twenty-six nationalities are waiting to return to their homes; almost half a million people are languishing in Siberian camps under conditions of cold, hunger, isolation, and the constant threat of death. They must be helped. Nansen reads the reports that Baker gives him, including some compiled by Elsa Brändström. Deeply shaken, he agrees to take the job.

At the behest of the League of Nations Nansen goes to Moscow to negotiate with Georgi Chicherin, People's Commissar for Foreign Affairs in the Bolshevist regime. Money is being raised in Europe, and Nansen organizes large shipments of food and medical supplies. At the same time, he makes arrangements with European relief organizations, ship lines, and railway companies. Then his coordinated repatriation plan is launched. Carloads of food and medical supplies head eastward, and carloads of internees head westward. Within five months 100,000 soldiers are home again; within a year the number is 400,000. In 1922, when Nansen is able to report that he has carried out his assignment, the number of those who owe their lives and liberty to him is almost 430,000.

Nansen is not merely the master organizer who directs the action from the conference room. This grand old Scandinavian is in the middle of the action—right in the Siberian camps distributing food rations to half-starved prisoners. If any part of his organizational machinery threatens to jam, he is on the spot himself to make the necessary repairs and adjustments, and generally to act as troubleshooter. If necessary he runs the entire operation. All told, he is said to have spent an average of $8.60 per prisoner—$8.60 per life saved. He sees not only the plight of the prisoners but also the tribulation of the Russian people, who have been through war, civil war, and revolution. In 1921, when drought and crop failures deplete the granaries of Russia and threaten thirty million people with starvation, Nansen appeals to other governments for assistance. "In the name of humanity," he says, "in the name of everything noble and sacred, I beg you—you who have wives and children of your own—to consider what it means to see women and children starving to death. . . . I call upon you, upon the whole world, to help."

The governments are silent. But their people hear the call. The first response comes from the United States. Large and small private donations pour in; and once more ships and trains carrying food and medicine are dispatched to Russia. Nansen goes along, personally delivering the food to the Russian peasantry, and the medical supplies to the overcrowded hospitals.

In addition to being the League of Nations High Commissioner for repatriation and the Red Cross representative in charge of the Russian relief program, Nansen agrees to serve as the League's High Commissioner for refugee aid. Refugees are trekking endlessly through Europe in headlong flight from civil war in Russia and the Greek-Turkish confrontation in Asia Minor. They make their way through the Baltic provinces, through Poland and Czechoslovakia, and pour into the Balkan states. Homeless, hungry, welcomed nowhere, frequently driven onward or expelled, they drift about: the flotsam and jetsam of the war, men and women in despair.

Nansen's territory is now Moscow, Constantinople, Athens, and the areas between. He soon sees that the number of refugees is far larger than was ever supposed. Two million Russians, an equal number of Bulgarians and Greeks, and no one knows how many Armenians, Ruthenians, Galicians, and Jews are waiting for help. Nansen tackles the food problem first. More carloads of provisions roll through Europe, destined mainly for the Balkans.

Nansen does one more thing. He gives back to the refugees once again their names. For all practical purposes, these people had lost their identity as well as their homes; they had become unpersons. Who believes their stories? Who opens his arms to anonymous foreigners? They have no official papers and no passports. Being stateless, they are no one's worry. Nansen's intervention at this point is perhaps the most important thing he does. He issues the refugees a small piece of paper, a refugee pass which is internationally recognized and which means a new lease on life for its bearer. These identification papers are soon known as Nansen Passes. Unfortunately, the fifty-two states recognizing them as passports decline to help their bearers to resettle. This comes as a jolt to Nansen; but the Red Cross and a number of welfare organizations and private individuals step into the breach with large donations, and Nansen is gradually able to cope with the refugee crisis. In December 1922 he is awarded the Nobel Peace Prize. Nansen uses all of it, more than ten thousand dollars, to help Greek refugees and to buy food for famine-stricken Russia. The League of Nations pays tribute to him in these words: "We express our gratitude to him as a benefactor of mankind."

The Ordeal of the Armenians

Among the refugees aided by Nansen, the Armenians probably suffer the most. Since 1895 they have been repeatedly exposed to persecution, hunger, and disease. Clara Barton, founder of the American Red Cross and Good Samaritan on many battlefields, is the first to organize a relief program for them. In the First World War, the Turks diligently pursue a plan for the "systematic solution of the Armenian question," which is actually a program to liquidate an entire people. The Armenians are marched to the arid wastes of southwest Turkey, hastened along by the bayonets of the Turkish soldiers. For the majority, it is a death march. Looting, rape, murder, and slavery in Turkish households are commonplace. When Kemal Pasha (later Ataturk) drives the Greeks out in 1922, thousands of the surviving Armenians are driven out as well. To save these refugees Nansen needs 900,000 pounds sterling, which he estimates is equal to the amount spent to operate a battleship for two years. He doesn't get the money.

While a concerted world relief effort fails to materialize, individual volunteers are quietly working among the Armenians. Notable among these are Dr. Johannes Lepsius, founder of the "Deutsche Orient-Mission" and a consistent advocate of the Armenian cause, and Jakob Künzler, a Swiss lay missionary. Even before World War I, Künzler is active in Turkey as an assistant to a physician named Dr. Christ in the Urfa mission hospital. Urfa becomes the end of the road for the Armenians marching into the desert. Dr. Christ, who has gone home on leave, has been prevented by the war situation from returning, which leaves the work up to "Brother Jakob," as Künzler is generally known. He fills in for the doctor as best he can, daily passing out food to the columns of refugees filing by. Some of the Armenian women call out to him to give them poison instead of food—that would cut short their ordeal. Brother Jakob knows that bread alone is never enough, that what he must provide is balm for grief, even when he himself is near despair. Refugees who are unable to continue the march are permitted to remain in Urfa, and Brother Jakob takes those who have collapsed to the hospital. The quarters are desperately cramped, all the rooms having been filled beyond normal capacity long ago, but there is no other way to save at least some.

On the heels of the Armenian crisis follows a deliberate campaign of persecution against the Kurds; and once more long lines of refugees file past Urfa. The same scenes are reenacted, but the roles are reversed. The Kurds were among the most savage persecutors of the Armenians. Now they are in flight, and it is up to Brother Jakob to help them. He does so without hesitation. What matters to him is the human need, nothing else.

At the end of the war, orders are issued in Turkey to release all Armenians still being held under duress as menials. But where are they to go? Their land is ravaged, their houses burned, their fields devastated. The children particularly face a future bereft of hope. Brother Jakob intercedes once more. Besides running the Urfa hospital, he must now take care of Armenian orphans. Before long he has seven hundred orphan dependents, and he remains their protector until he is able to find an American relief organization to take them. But as the Turkish authorities make things increasingly difficult for the Americans, it is decided to get the children out of Turkey. Künzler arranges their transportation: first they are taken to Jerablus, a border station; from there, some are put on trains bound for Beirut, but space is limited and time is running out, so several groups of children are carried across the Taurus Mountains by mule trains that Brother Jakob manages to get together. Crates are strapped to the mules, one on each side, and the children are put in the crates. It is a rather pathetic-looking procession, and the way is long and arduous, but the children come to no harm. As they pass through the Kurdish regions, the people, grateful for the aid they received, reciprocate by providing what food and lodging they can. Eight thousand Armenian children and over twelve hundred Greek children are evacuated in this way.

In 1922 Künzler takes charge of an American orphanage in the Lebanon mountains; and when the home is closed in 1931, Künzler, now over sixty years of age, finds new tasks awaiting him. Using funds from Switzerland and England, he builds a number of small houses, including a forty-house settlement for Armenians who had been driven out of a partly Turkish area over which the French had relinquished control. Finally, he builds the large Armenian sanatorium in the Lebanon mountains. It is made possible by the gifts of Armenians scattered all over the world, who are grateful for their rescue from dreadful persecution. When Brother Jakob dies in 1949, he is mourned by an entire people.

Tribute should be paid here to one more man, the Quaker Herbert Hoover. Later to become president of the United States, Hoover is one of those who act to alleviate the acute food shortage visited upon the innocent in the aftermath of World War I. The rapid German advance through Belgium to France turned the two small states of Belgium and Holland (both densely populated, both economically dependent on imports) into a disaster area. Hoover organizes the extensive American relief program to which thousands of Belgian and Dutch people owe their lives. Hoover is also the first to respond to Nansen's appeal for aid to Russia, after all other governments have refused to help. In later years as well, Hoover is frequently called upon to handle relief programs.

12. The Annals of Inhumanity

The Final Solution

It takes years for the nations of the world to recover from the havoc wrought by World War I and return to a measure of calm—and the surcease is short-lived. Economic crises and repressive governments bring on new catastrophes. Before, during, and after World War II, the sufferings of individuals and peoples mount to proportions that the mind can scarcely conceive. "Total war" is no respecter of the aged, or of women or children, however far from the front they may be. Mass extermination campaigns are not limited to one nationality; the fate of the Armenians is now visited in a variety of ways upon other peoples. But none suffers as horribly as do the Jews in Germany and in those parts of Europe occupied by Germany. In the Nazi holocaust, anti-Semitism is carried to such lengths that what is officially called the *Endlösung*, the "Final Solution" to the "Jewish question," turns out to be a program aiming at the utter extermination of an entire people.

The operation proceeds like clockwork; the annihilation of six million Jews in the gas chambers and crematoriums of the concentration camps is planned to the last detail. A bureaucratic officialdom takes pains to see that the nightmare is invested with order and system. The lists of those slated for destruction are kept in perfect order. The transport trains leave on schedule; and the Jews herded together in them are worse off than cattle. The march to the gas chambers proceeds with military precision. E. F.

L. Russell, Baron of Liverpool, quotes a Polish government report describing one such march:

> After unloading at the siding, all the victims were assembled in one place . . . where they had to take off their clothes and shoes. The men did this in the courtyard, the women and children in a hut nearby. The women then had all their hair cut off and the whole convoy, men, women and children, now naked and shorn, were driven along the road to the gas chambers. . . .
>
> When they reached the lethal chambers they were driven in with their hands above their heads so that as many might be squeezed in as possible. The children were piled on top. Sometimes the infants were first killed. . . . The actual gassing in the chamber lasted about fifteen minutes.

Behind this stark description is a tragedy no words can frame. Who will help? Indeed, who is able to help, when people are being fed by the millions into the highly sophisticated apparatus of mass destruction? Who would dare to involve himself, when the risk of getting caught in the refined governmental machinery himself is so great? Given the thorough organization of the Final Solution, who would dare put his hand into the fire?

Yet there are some who do. At enormous risk, friendly families hide Jewish children, or give them false names and pass them off as their own. Identification papers are forged, so that their Jewish bearers can emigrate safely and without being discovered. Jewish men and women are spirited across the border into Switzerland or other neighboring countries.

And what is the church doing? Rescue operations are planned wherever possible. In the Freiburg headquarters of Caritas, Dr. Gertrud Luckner works for years in close cooperation with Caritas International, helping numbers of Jews to escape. In Berlin it is notably the regular Protestant groups that befriend the fugitives. Other Christian fellowships, including the free churches, also help out. Much assistance comes from ordinary citizens, often as an act of neighborly solidarity. Foreign relief committees are also active. Father Benoit helps in Marseilles. Abbé Pierre handles smuggling operations in the Alps. Raoul Wallenberg, a young Swede, goes to Budapest, where he forges identification papers that enable Hungarian Jews to escape to freedom. Wallenberg is later caught and

Since A.D. *70 the Jews have lived in dispersion. They have also been the victims of repeated persecutions, those during the Hitler regime being carried out with incredible savagery. This 1642 copper engraving shows the looting of Frankfurt's "Judengasse" or ghetto in 1624.*

Württemberg Landesbibliothek, Stuttgart

executed. In Warsaw Janusz Korczak keeps a brave vigil over the children of his orphanage; when the Nazis come and all avenues of escape are cut off, Korczak chooses to be executed with his charges. Holland has an active underground that assists the Jews. A number of its agents land in German concentration camps.

Some people undertake rescue ventures virtually under the noses of the chief architects of the Final Solution. Dr. Felix Kersten, a native of Sweden and personal physician to SS Chief Heinrich Himmler, uses every available means to get people out of the concentration camps. Near the end of the war, the Swedish Count Folke Bernadotte gets permission to remove Scandinavian internees in a convoy of Red Cross buses. He packs in as many people as will fit, without asking them a lot of questions; and in this way he saves many non-Scandinavians as well, including Jews.

Euthanasia at the Gates of Bethel

The demonic Final Solution has its counterpart in the murder of the mentally ill and the disabled. Both operations are carried out in a deafening silence. The murderers arrive and do their work in stealth, so that the public will not know what is going on. For a long time, the people suspect nothing. Anyone who does know something had better keep quiet; otherwise his own life will be in danger. This means that all assistance to the potential victims must be unpublicized as well. "Pastor Fritz" Bodelschwingh (son of the founder of the Bethel Community) battles for the life of the patients in his charge. But his defiance of those who would exterminate the people "unfit to live" necessarily takes place offstage. There is too much at stake to do it any other way.

How does this extermination program come about? The idea of killing off the "unfit" is old. It was practiced in ancient Greece, for example. Even today, who objects to putting an old horse or dog out of its unrelievable misery? Doctors often speak of euthanasia, but euthanasia goes beyond the Christian ethic of love and is still in dispute today. The real question is: Is there such a thing as a "life without value"? The people at Bethel have long recognized that even "the least of these" has value in God's sight. And even supposing for the moment that upon the request of a patient with a terminal illness his doctor has the right to give him an injection to shorten his pain and ease him gently and imperceptibly across the threshold—even so, where is the evidence that the extermination program unleashed by Hitler has as its purpose delivery of the sick from unbearable pain at their own request?

Using private stationery, Hitler wrote the following directive, which never gained legal status:

> *Reichsleiter* [Philipp] Bouhler and Dr. [Karl] Brandt are to be given the responsibility of enlarging the authority of certain doctors, to be designated by name, who should perform the operation of euthanasia on persons whose condition, according to human judgment, is held to be incurable after most careful diagnosis of their state of health.

The health authorities of the Third Reich go by this directive. So does Dr. Brandt, Hitler's personal physician. Brandt is not a Christian, and he is convinced that euthanasia is justified. He does not want to kill people arbitrarily, but the program for which he is responsible—and after the war he pays with his life for that responsibility—soon begins to move according to laws that are largely beyond his control. All invalid homes and institutions of healing begin receiving registration forms on which the names of all patients, along with their complaints and medical history, are to be entered in precise detail. Doctors, nurses, and institution directors innocently fill them out, not suspecting that in most cases their entries amount to a death sentence. Nor do they suspect anything when the sick are picked up and taken off to the main state institutions by the buses of a "Public Service Invalid Transportation Company"—organized especially for the purpose. These buses travel all through Germany, and their invalid passengers never return.

The German people are engaged in a life and death struggle—so runs one argument for the mass liquidation program—and this struggle demands the harnessing of all of its strength; hence it is no longer reasonable to continue to sustain the incurably ill, who represent an intolerable burden on the population. But the notices sent to the next of kin speak only of the "sad and painful duty to inform you that your son has died of pneumonia," "your daughter has died of a circulatory disorder," "your wife has died of sepsis caused by a severe angina infection"—adding that "all the efforts of our doctors to save the life of the patient were unavailing." The authorities are cynical enough to convey the news by printed forms on which the name of the deceased is written in but everything else is already set in type, including the cause of death!

The registration forms arrive at Bethel too, but meanwhile people are beginning to sit up and take notice. Precise details are still not known, but the suspicion is that what has seemed an innocent undertaking is really an enormity. One day Pastor Fritz gets the facts from an associate in Berlin. When the registration forms arrive, they are ignored, and Pastor Fritz goes to Berlin himself.

He calls on the heads of ministries, tries to find who is in charge of the program, and draws a blank everywhere. No one knows anything about the business, and nobody wants to know. Finally Bodelschwingh turns to Hermann Göring, "Marshal of the Reich." Although he remains evasive himself, Göring does clear the path to Dr. Brandt. Now that Pastor Fritz has found the man in charge, he hangs on to him. Saving his main ammunition for later, Bodelschwingh urges Dr. Brandt to come to Bethel. Brandt agrees to do so, meanwhile assuring Bodelschwingh that until his visit Bethel would be left alone.

But Bethel is not left alone. One day a commission of doctors and nurses appears at the Community to fill out the medical forms themselves. Pastor Fritz guesses that they might be acting without Brandt's knowledge, but there is nothing he can do. At this point Dr. Brandt is suddenly announced, and it turns out that he knows nothing of the commission's intervention. Alternating arguments with pleas, Pastor Fritz now begins a last-ditch fight for his patients. He knows there is no such thing as "life without value." (His father had once called the sick "teachers of love.") He also knows that faith can work wonders, even in the weak, even in the bodies of the moribund. He knows it better than all the doctors and nurses in the ideological labyrinths of the Third Reich.

Bodelschwingh next begins talking to Dr. Brandt as believer to unbeliever. The conversation turns into a contest. At the end, Dr. Brandt, who had come to Bethel so sure of himself and his mission, leaves with his head bowed in silence. He has experienced something of the power of faith. Shortly thereafter the whole operation aimed at the institutions of mercy is called off. No patient is ever bussed out of Bethel.

Pastor Fritz fights this battle single-handedly. Other men fight similar one-man battles in their places of service. In Württemberg, Bishop Theophil Wurm's diocese, the murderers have wrested the Grafeneck nursing home away from the Inner Mission and are going methodically about their work. Bishop Wurm sends a scorching protest to the government. The unshakable count Clemens August von Galen, Catholic bishop of Münster, uses his pulpit to oppose the tactics of mass murder. And in the city of

Brandenburg, a nameless district judge with jurisdiction over "wards of the court" protects those in his custody from being transferred to the extermination camps.

On May 8, 1945, Germany capitulates. Hitler has already taken his own life. A few weeks later the first atomic bombs are dropped on Hiroshima and Nagasaki, ending the war in the Far East and leaving chaos and misery behind. The victors of yesterday are now the persecuted and oppressed, while the losers of the earlier skirmishes become the avengers and oppressors. The ordeal of war prisoners in Siberia begins all over again; women and girls become the quarry of a soldiery gone wild. Children all over the world go hungry again. Refugees trudging through snow and ice . . . overcrowded camps and the attendant moral dangers . . . divided families—the range of suffering seems almost infinite. It is not only cities that are a mass of rubble; mankind itself resembles a ruined cathedral.

The Postwar SOS and the Response

Once again, out of the ruins there emerges a spirit of brotherhood. We have noted how Kagawa receives the American Christians in Japan. We know of Count Bernadotte, who is commissioned by the United Nations to mediate between the Israelis and the Arabs in Palestine, and who later pays with his life. The International Red Cross is on the scene, and Caritas gets its relief operation going. The newly founded Protestant Relief Agency in Germany joins forces with the Inner Mission. Quakers and Mennonites consider it their unquestioned duty to care for those in need. Smaller nations such as Sweden and Switzerland, who have been spared the ravages of war, do not stand aloof; and the larger nations are likewise conscious of a common responsibility. Organizations in the United States and Canada send whole shiploads of food to famine-stricken areas in Europe and Asia. Victor Gollancz, an English publisher, founds the "Save Europe Now" movement, encouraging aid to the nation responsible for the death of so many of his fellow Jews. The United Nations founds relief organizations that act to alleviate hunger and hardship. Young people, formerly enemies by virtue of nationality, build settlements together. Governments allocate large amounts of aid for other nations going through economic crises.

Some of the aid may have been politically motivated, but the manifest spirit of international cooperation shows that humanity has not completely succumbed to inhumanity. This is demonstrated not only in postwar aid but in the relief action undertaken in the wake of natural disasters: earthquakes in Japan, Greece, Morocco, and Chile, floods in Holland, Pacific tidal waves, tornados, hurricanes, droughts, and in such man-made disasters as air and highway collisions and mining tragedies the world over.

The postwar crisis is especially conspicuous in three areas: the forgotten generation of young people, the acute housing shortage, and the disastrous famines particularly in the developing countries. But volunteers are active in all three areas. As always, it is the lifelines thrown out by individuals that spell survival. We cannot pay tribute to all those of our contemporaries who have dedicated their lives to the ministry of Samaritan love; the contribution of a few of them may serve once more to represent the deeds of many others.

It was once thought that we live in the "century of the child." At the beginning of the 1900s there is Maria Montessori, who works with the waifs and strays of San Lorenzo, a slum district in Rome. There is the German Youth Hostel Movement, founded in 1909. In the same year that the United States enters the First World War, the Irish-born Father Flanagan founds his Boys Town in Nebraska; it becomes the prototype for other Boys Towns all over the world, and thus a blueprint for an international movement in which Father Flanagan is active until his death in 1948. In London following World War I, an Englishwoman named Eglantyne Jebb founds the international "Save the Children" fund; and some years later Franz Bakule starts a program for crippled children living in underprivileged communities on the outskirts of Prague. In 1931 Don Zeno Saltini builds his Italian youth village of "Nomadelfia" in San Giacomo Roncolo; and in 1934 in Ben Schemen, Palestine, Dr. Siegfried Lehmann supervises the building of a village for Jewish refugee children from Germany. But what happens to this "century of the child"?

In both world wars, children in uniform meet on the battlefield, fight like savages, and die. Following World War II, the youth workers must begin all over again.

The initiative is taken by Walter R. Corti of Switzerland. Corti looks beyond the security and comfort of his own situation and sees nations at war. He is especially concerned for children who have lost home and parents. The letters he sends out and the appeals he makes start a chain reaction of aid. In 1946 he is able to realize his objective: ground is broken for a children's village in the Swiss community of Trogen. Children of all nationalities—French, Finnish, Yugoslavian, Polish, German—are accommodated and cared for in one-family houses. The number of houses grows to ten, fifteen, and more—young people from many nations helping to build them. Thus the village becomes an international colony in which political controversy or nationalistic animus cannot take root. Bridges are built here from nationality to nationality; isn't it the young people who best know how to build them? The village in Trogen is named after Pestalozzi, and all the colonies modeled after it in other lands are also called Pestalozzi villages.

In Austria a similar movement is launched by Hermann Gmeiner. Originally having planned to study medicine, Gmeiner is aroused by the SOS of the youth of the world, and from that point on he does not rest until he is able to found the first "SOS Children's Village" in the Tirolese community of Imst. It too becomes the model for similar havens for homeless children in other countries. Colonies which include vocational training are also founded.

There is no doubt that much is done—by Christians and non-Christians—for young people. Nor is there any doubt that the primary motivation is the desire to help. On the other hand, many extensive youth programs are deliberately designed to lead young people astray and seduce them politically. He who wins the youth holds the future: this age-old maxim has given rise to grave error and to flagrant wrongs committed against youth. Aiding and educating youth can have only one purpose: to help the child and the adolescent to grow into mature adulthood. That was Pestalozzi's view, and it is still valid today.

The youth colonies provide care for homeless boys and girls, but what is being done for adults? The aftermath of World War

II brings a desperate housing shortage, vestiges of which are still evident in some places. In postwar Germany conditions are worse than during the economic hangover of the early 1870s. Millions of people are crammed together in barracks, bomb-cratered houses, hovels, and shacks. There is a growing army of beggars vagrants, and slum-dwellers. Even the surprisingly rapid pace of West German reconstruction is not able to cope with the shortage. Though cities appear as if by magic, though new developments are established, new houses built, communities planned, and though federal and regional authorities grant subsidies and loans, it is still not enough. In this struggle, too, individual action counts for much. No nation can do without the initiative of the open heart.

In 1946, a Frankfurt pastor named Otto Fricke begins working on plans for the first Protestant "Construction Community," the purpose of which is to provide a Christian community for refugees and people who have been bombed out of their homes. A Swedish pastor, Birger Forell, in cooperation with the Protestant Relief Agency, starts a refugee settlement in a former munitions complex in Espelkamp, Westphalia, which grows to a flourishing town of over ten thousand. These are only two of many examples. We cannot give a complete survey of the huge international postwar aid programs. But there are two men whose relief projects merit a close look, for they show that individual initiative can mean help for untold numbers of people. One of the men is Abbé Pierre, a Frenchman who founds the "Emmaus" movement. The other is a Belgian named Father Dominique Pire, who launches the "European Village" project.

Abbé Pierre

After seven years in a Capuchin monastery, Abbé Pierre (H. A. Groués) becomes active in hospital work during World War II. Following the French surrender of 1940, he serves as a curé and works in the French underground, sheltering political fugitives, especially Jews, and helping them across the border. Of this period his biographer writes:

> He was faced with the terrifying privilege of saving hunted souls at the risk of his own life.

Following the war Abbe Pierre is elected to the French Chamber of Deputies. One day he rents a moldering house in a suburb of Paris. The property includes a yard and garden, both overgrown. Here he plans to set up a kind of meeting place. He works hard to get the house in shape, and soon young people of many nationalities are meeting here in order to overcome with brotherhood the hatred fomented in bygone years. The youth center, which Abbé Pierre dubs "Emmaus" is soon widely known, and its founder is invited to a number of congresses. He becomes a traveling spokesman for international reconciliation.

Then the abbé is challenged to do something about the needy close by. The "clochards"—homeless vagrants of Paris—begin to come to Emmaus, a few at a time at first, and then more and more. Abbe Pierre turns none of them away. One of his principles is to serve without thought of reward. And so he serves the people who come to him for asylum, giving them a place to sleep. In return they help him around the house and in the garden. He never asks anyone where he comes from or why he has come to Emmaus. Each one's need is reason enough. Ragpickers, homeless beggars, ex-prisoners, washouts—they all are made welcome.

While the abbé does not inquire of his guests where they come from, he does make inquiries about the scope and urgency of the vagrancy problem. And he finds out. He discovers a large number of families who have no home, who must sleep in the open air, and whose children die of exposure and are buried in mass graves. He also finds—in the government—a splendidly humming bureaucracy which has no advice or assistance to offer the needy individual, and whose functionaries send him from department to department, from office to office, until he gives up in frustration or despair. He finds rooms renting at black market rates no laborer can afford, and he finds landlords who summarily evict their tenants with impunity. Behind the glittering facade of fashionable, cosmopolitan Paris, he discovers abysmal squalor.

Abbé Pierre assembles his *clochards* and begins to build. The authorities take a dim view of his primitive cabins—for which he has no building permit—but for the vagrants they mean a place to live. The abbé uses every opportunity to promote the work. He goes from door to door handing out leaflets, and he wins the big prize on a circus quiz show. Every sou is important to him; his people collect rags, go through garbage dumps, and rummage about in attics. A dilapidated old truck serves as transportation. Everything in his homes-for-the-homeless is makeshift. Faced with urgent need, he cannot wait for legislation and official permits.

The results prove him right. Paris begins to take notice: What is going on out there is accomplishing something; the abbé hasn't built a model settlement, but he has saved people from starving and freezing to death. The awareness of his work spreads, first around Paris and then all over France. The makeshift beginnings turn into a national relief movement. The old "Emmaus House" becomes the "Emmaus Movement" for the homeless and spreads to other countries. Abbé Pierre has started an avalanche. Personal animosities and political recriminations do not stop him from carrying out his plan, which is so simple: to help where the need is, and to help quickly—without asking a lot of questions.

Father Pire

Father Pire also starts an avalanche. He too is concerned about the homeless and about the many refugees; and in 1950 he and some friends found an old people's home in Belgium. Father Pire is aware of the obligations that church and society have toward the aged. Many people are talking about the younger generation, and the younger generation is also lobbying in its own cause; but who will take care of the old people? In bygone centuries, didn't the young take care of their parents out of filial respect for the prerogatives of old age? Now everything is changed. In an apartment there is no room for grandma and grandpa. Old folks' homes come to be a necessity, even for people with roots in their communities—and still more so for aged refugees.

Since the problems of the aging are a consequence of the problems of the family, Father Pire does not deal only with the one task. After the war, countless families have to live in camps. Many people have become inured to this cheerless atmosphere, with all its dangers to health and morality, but the grim housing conditions in the camps are the undoing of many a family and many a child. Man is forced to live in conditions incompatible with human dignity. Man's dignity must be restored to him.

So Father Pire and his friends resolve to provide housing: full-fledged settlements with an adequate number of one-family houses and job opportunities for the men. They envision a regular village. A site is found near Aachen, one that seems particularly appropriate; for in Aachen, Charlemagne's city, you *have* to think "European." That is what Father Pire thinks, at any rate, for he intends to build a European village in which all national barriers will be dissolved. Later, bitterly disappointed, he is forced to see that a united Europe is still a long way off. But the name "European Village" sticks. From the planning stage to the actual laying of the cornerstone for the first house is a long and arduous way: the authorities are obstinate, the construction plans get bogged down, the financing is a headache. Father Pire gives lectures to promote his ideas; he enlists the help of the news media, and slowly, very slowly, the public is won over. On May 6, 1956 the work begins. There are plans for twenty houses; initially, six are built. At the end of the first day, Father Pire and his friends are already planning their second European Village.

After the second village, they build the third and then the fourth. The one in Luxembourg is named after Albert Schweitzer, the one in Belgium after Fridtjof Nansen, and the one in Norway after the brave Jewish girl, Anne Frank. Soon there are plans for villages in Bregenz in Austria and Augsburg in Germany, each to have more than twenty houses, all of them to be compact little communities for homeless foreigners.

The European Villages help many people. But there are still the slums of Johannesburg, Arab refugee camps, and Hong Kong.

Hong Kong, the British Crown Colony on Chinese territory, used to be a city of six hundred thousand; today there are three million people there: mostly Chinese in flight from communism. Of course, new buildings are going up in Hong Kong, too; but the new construction is a drop in the ocean. The number of refugee shanties all over the city stays constant, except when an occasional fire destroys some of them, and with them the last possessions of the poorest people. In the city proper, the doorsteps of the stores are still rented out as overnight lodgings, and refugees are charged exorbitant prices for a square yard or two of roof space on top of the modern buildings. Anyone who can pay the price can secure accommodations of sorts for a couple of nights.

Just outside the borders of the new state of Israel are the wretched camps of the Arab evacuees. Thousands of them, with no prospects of a home or a job, have been living here for years in pathetic-looking barracks and hovels, partitioned into rooms by lathing and blankets. Every room is occupied, often by several families, and every cranny is put to use.

And in Johannesburg there are still the teeming warrens of Sophiatown. Its corrugated huts and rubbish-filled streets are the breeding grounds for disease and crime.

These three examples could be multiplied; but who would want to catalogue all the slums and ghettos of the world? Who would want to total up all the need and suffering in every country on earth? Many more European Villages must be built in every land; many more people must follow in the footsteps of the French abbé and the Belgian priest.

Finally, there is the problem of hunger. Wherever men live in squalor—in slums, camps, emergency quarters—hunger is sure to be their constant companion. Wherever jobs are short, food will be scarce. This applies not only to the developing countries but to large areas in the developed countries as well. And it is symptomatic of our age that stark need is concealed behind a facade of affluence and well-being and happiness. It is far easier to cover it up than to do something about it.

Danilo Dolci

Thus mankind cannot pay sufficient tribute to the Italian, Danilo Dolci, for consistently exposing the squalor behind the glittering facades in his country. Dolci is from Trieste. He plans to become an architect, but he has also tried his hand at verse. His first poems appear in an anthology of Christian lyric poetry. "Words are stones," he says, "if they remain merely words." He takes his own words seriously, interrupting his studies and laying aside his first architectural monographs to work in Nomadelfia, Don Zeno Saltini's youth village. But Nomadelfia is only a way station. The spirit of the first Christians, which Don Zeno is trying to instill in his community, seems too narrow for Dolci. He withdraws into solitude, searching for his own course. At this point he doesn't know where it will lead him, but he has the courage to wait. And one day he finds his bearings. They point him to Trappeto, on the Gulf of Castellammare.

Trappeto is one of the most idyllic spots on the island of Sicily, renowned for its magnificent view of the sea and for the unexplored grottoes along its coast. Of course, Dolci does not settle at Trappeto for the sake of its beauty; he is drawn by the Sicilian fishermen, who live there in abject poverty. He resolves to share their life with them, a poor man living among poor men, a brother among brothers. Dolci has found his Lambaréné in his own homeland.

For a long time the people are suspicious of him, for he asks a lot of questions. Maybe he's a police informer, or a Communist, or some other kind of revolutionary.

A revolutionary—Dolci is that, all right. He is a special kind of rebel, as the fishermen would soon find out. With the precision of a John Howard, Dolci begins examining the social conditions of this degraded class. He asks about school attendance and the level of education, about job opportunities and wages, about prison terms and about God's commandments. He wants to know how many people sleep in a room and whether they have their own running water. He wants to know how much they make a year. Finally, he wants to know about the bandits.

It is the bandits who actually run things in the vicious triangle formed by Trappeto, Partinico, and Montelepre. Their activities include robbery, smuggling, and blackmail, and they still adhere to the immemorial Sicilian custom of the vendetta. But where do these people get their power? Dolci soon finds out. If you go to work for the bandits, you can earn a thousand lire a day and more. If you cross over to Montelepre to work in a run-down factory, you can't expect to get more than three hundred lire, barely enough to buy a couple of loaves of bread. And—Dolci figures—if you live in Trappeto and commute to Camporeale to work, after you deduct the cost of bread and beans you will be out five lire a day.

And so these people stick with the bandits. Not because they don't want to work but because they don't want to starve. All the government does is jail the robbers and smugglers it catches; no one asks why they rob and smuggle. So Dolci goes to them, too, and asks them his questions. He is appalled to learn that of 147 "bandits," 108 have served a total of more than 1,000 years in prison but have had only about 350 years of schooling among them.

The first thing Dolci does is to open a home for children whose parents are either in prison or have been the victims of a vendetta. He wants them to learn to love and trust each other. In this way Dolci hopes to check the wave of vendettas. Then he calls on the government for thirty million lire to deal with the worst of the evils. He is laughed at. His visits to the various authorities and agencies come to nothing. And so in 1952 he applies Gandhi's nonviolent methods: he begins a fast.

The winter before, Dolci saw a baby die of hunger and cold. He now lies down himself on the same straw mat on which it died and says he will fast until the government comes up with the money. The fast arouses the concern of people all over Italy, and in other countries as well. Faced with a national scandal of potentially disastrous consequences, the Italian government backs down and authorizes the money.

Dolci is a national figure overnight. People from all over the world volunteer their services. Sicily's poor call him *il santo,* the saint. A year following the fast he marries a widow with five children whose husband was killed by bandits. Under his direction the children's home he had started grows into a "Hamlet of God," and he succeeds in setting up a program of adult education beginning with reading and writing classes for the area's numerous illiterates. Things are looking up in Trappeto. The city will need relief assistance for a long time, but the worst of the evils have been checked.

That means it is time for Dolci to leave. The main work behind him, he turns to a place where he is needed more. Giving his house to an unemployed man he moves with his sizable family into a three-room flat in the Partinico slums, which are known as the "holy crown of thorns." A number of his friends object to what they see as an exaggerated romanticism, but he answers, "One must be involved in order to really understand." That is the basis of his whole thought and action: he wants to identify with the needy in order to help them.

In Partinico he begins, as before, with a fact-finding survey. Precise, documented facts would be his ammunition in the war against need. He publishes the results of his investigations, and they do not make pleasant reading. *Act Quickly (And Well) For People Are Dying* is the title of one of his books. *Outlaws* is another. He probes relentlessly into the pathology of the human condition: prostitution and procuring, robbery and blackmail, bloodlettings and gangsterism. In particular he exposes crimes against children, who are often trained in a special pickpocketing technique while very young.

Dolci goes on two more fasts. He campaigns for men who can get no jobs; and he protests against the motorized trawler-fleets of the large fisheries, by which a syndicate with connections to the ubiquitous Mafia—Dolci's natural enemy—raids the gulf waters and robs the poverty-stricken inshore fishermen of their take, which is meager enough as it is. He stages a "strike-in-reverse" with about one hundred fifty unemployed men, clearing and repairing a nearly impassable road—without pay. He is going to show that "do-nothings" have a right to work. When the police arrive and tell them they are breaking the law, Dolci says:

> By the Constitution work isn't only a right—it's a duty of us all. . . . Whoever prevents us from working is a murderer.

As the police take him away he calls to the others, "Go on working, go on digging!" But he does not resist arrest. Here, too, he may be compared to Gandhi or Kagawa, who also interceded for fishermen, peasants, and laborers, without resorting to violence.

Dolci is tried twice and sentenced to prison, but both sentences are eventually rescinded, indicating that even the jurists are unsure of themselves. Has he spoken to their consciences too?

Dolci also goes to the slums of Palermo, situated directly behind the glamorous sections that the guides show the tourists.

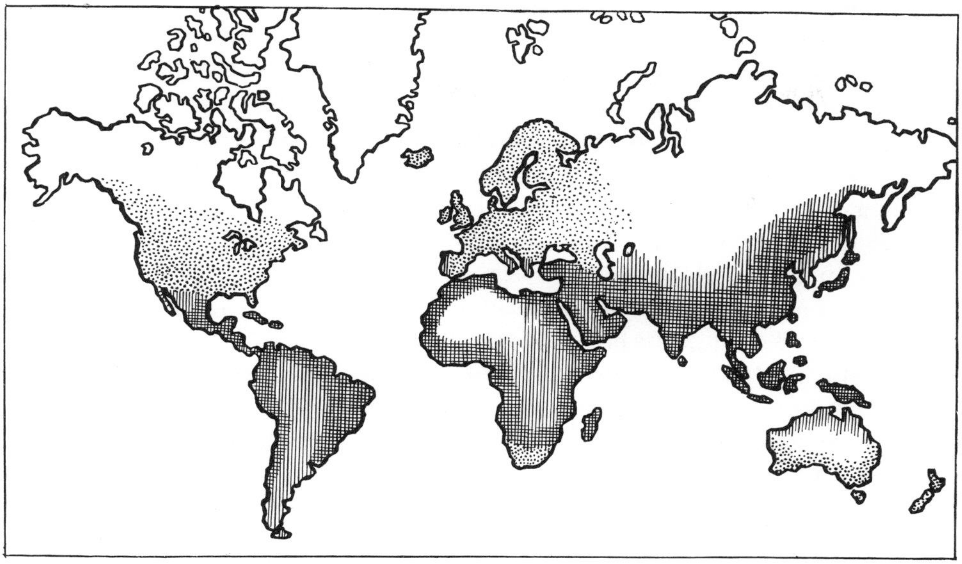

▒ *rich countries*

▥ *poor countries*

▦ *countries undergoing severe economic crises owing to rapid population increases*

Herder Verlag, Freiburg

No visitor is ever taken into these dark streets; to venture down them is to risk one's life. In 1956, when Dolci arrives, the Palermo slums are populated by over a hundred thousand people living in grottoes, bombed-out hulks of buildings, and crumbling shacks. The inhabitants are pickpockets, smugglers, pimps, prostitutes, thieves, fences, gangsters, and murderers. But Dolci and his friends have safe-conduct because of their involvement with the poor. Nothing happens to them, because the slum-dwellers know why they have come: in order to help, to live here with us, to fight for us.

The conditions described in Dolci's famous *Report from Palermo* are so shocking that some passages read like the product of a diseased mind. But the statements are true. Dolci wrote them down, word for word, as they came from the lips of the bandits and the unemployed. His book might have been banned as obscene were not its revelations of moral decay, degeneracy, and depravity so dreadfully and bitterly true.

When the Dolci-inspired Congress for Full Employment meets in Palermo, Dolci submits a report of over a hundred pages dealing with the "Possibilities of full agricultural employment in the Sicilian agrarian economy." After the congress he goes on another fast to stir the public conscience.

Though an idealist, Danilo Dolci is not a visionary. He is a realistic thinker and can hold his own in debates with the experts. He is also sophisticated enough to realize that social evils cannot be got rid of without applying the insights of modern sociology. But above all Dolci is a man who is totally committed to his mission, prepared if necessary to give his life for it. He is Italy's gadfly, the conscience of the nation; and he comes to be a spokesman for the conscience of mankind. As in Italy, so in the world: millions upon millions of the earth's population go hungry because they have no work. Words alone are not enough. Action is needed.

The Mosaic of Human Kindness

We have reached the middle of the twentieth century in our survey. Much has perforce been left unsaid, but the little we have presented here of our own times shows how multicolored is the mosaic of man's humanity to man. The great army of those who are committed to the ministry of mercy, either by full-time or volunteer service, continues to grow. The number of centers and institutions dedicated to helping people is increasing yearly. Hospitals, nursing homes, and other institutions are being built at great expense and with the most modern equipment—even in the remotest jungles. Lambaréné is no longer an isolated phenomenon. Increasingly, social legislation is providing and regulating care for the needy and enabling people of all social levels to enjoy adequate living conditions. Nations are learning from each other. International relief agencies are constantly helping to overcome barriers of prejudice and boundaries of race, religion, and nationality.

Even so, it is still true that organized care and state-regulated welfare will not be enough in themselves. Human kindness cannot be legislated into existence. And the modern welfare state's potential for good does not eliminate the need for individual initiative. As always, the individual must make room in his heart for goodwill and good works. Only in this way can the "chain reaction of goodwill," of which Hermann Gmeiner speaks, become reality.

The world will always need the individual who gets involved, the courageous visionary who stirs up the complacent. There will always be a need for the man who acts as the conscience of the community, the rebel whose cause is humanity. Only in the spirit in which God himself walked on earth as a man two thousand years ago to show us how to love one another, in the spirit in which the apostle Paul told the Galatians to "bear one another's burdens"—only in this spirit is true humanness possible.

It is to the ministry of mercy, of neighbor loving neighbor, that we owe our very existence. Without the good works of good men, the world would have foundered on its own inhumanity long ago. Surrounded as we are by all these servants of mankind, by those who have set about loving their neighbor and fulfilling the law of Christ, it would be irresponsible of us not to follow in their steps.

There are so many possibilities! Not everyone can be a jungle doctor or serve on an Alpine rescue squad, or build a whole village of mercy institutions or go on a hunger strike. But we all have some task we can do, often very close to home, and to do it is not only our right but our duty. It is up to each of us, in the place where we are, to do our own works of love and mercy.

Thus it is necessary here at the end that our focus be redirected from far horizons and remote continents to our own immediate situation. Whatever is to happen in the great wide world out there will have its beginnings in the small and limited world of our own home territory. In the many tiny sectors in which we move, our lives are to be so lived that they can bear the scrutiny of him who became one with us because he wanted us to become truly men, the human beings God intended us to be.

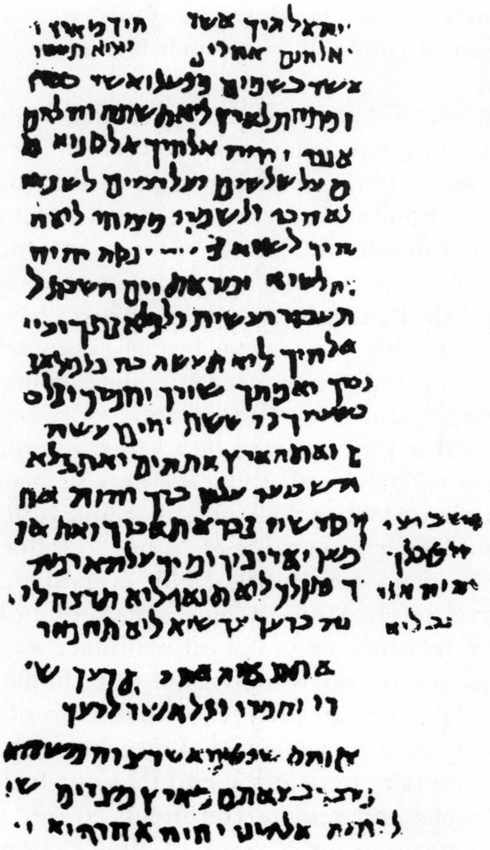

The Nash papyrus, one of the most ancient of Old Testament documents, includes the Ten Commandments, God's basic guide to true humanness.

Sources of Quotations

Index

Sources of Quotations

Page

15–16 Luke 10:25–37.

17 John 13:1–17.

32–33 Sulpicius Severus, *St. Martin of Tours* (London: Sands, 1928), pp. 98–99.

113 Martin Luther, "Preface to the Epistle of St. Paul to the Romans," *Luther's Works*, ed. Helmut T. Lehmann (Philadelphia: Fortress, 1960), volume 35, p. 370.

130 Marion Dexter Learned, *The Life of Francis Daniel Pastorius, the Founder of Germantown* (Philadelphia: William J. Campbell, 1908), pp. 261–262. According to Learned, the Protest is in both the style and the handwriting of Pastorius.

132 John Woolman, "A Plea for the Poor," *The Journal and Essays of John Woolman*, ed. Amelia Mott Gummere (New York: Macmillan, 1922), p. 427.

133 Wilbur H. Siebert, *The Underground Railroad from Slavery to Freedom* (New York: Arno Press, 1968), p. 110.

168 Patrick Pringle, *The Prisoners' Friend: The Story of Elizabeth Fry* (New York: Roy, 1954), p. 75.

171 Thomas Timpson, *Memoirs of Mrs. Elizabeth Fry* (New York: Stanford & Swords, 1847), p. 261.

188 Anthony Ashley-Cooper, Lord Shaftesbury, "Mines and Collieries," quoted in J. Wesley Bready, *Lord Shaftesbury and Social-Industrial Progress* (London: Allen & Unwin, 1926), p. 286.

193–94 Edwin Hodder, *The Life and Work of the Seventh Earl of Shaftesbury, K.G.* (London: Cassell & Company, 1887), pp. 146, 157.

195 Antony Ashley-Cooper, *Speeches of the Earl of Shaftesbury, K.G.* (London: Chapman & Hall, 1868), p. 32.

206 Anna Sticker, *Theodor und Friederike Fliedner* (Neukirchen: Neukirchener Verlag des Erziehungsvereins, 1965), p. 66. Sticker gives the quotation in English.

229–30 J. F. Maguire, *Father Mathew, A Biography* (London: Longman, Green, Longman, Roberts, & Green, 1863), p. 397.

240–41 Leo Tolstoy, *A Confession, The Gospel in Brief, and What I Believe* (London: Oxford, 1940), pp. 64–65.

256 Hertha Pauli, *Cry of the Heart* (New York: Washburn, 1957), p. 129.

269 E. F. L. Russell, *The Scourge of the Swastika* (New York: Philosophical Library, 1954), p. 243.

271 J. S. Conway, *The Nazi Persecution of the Churches, 1933–1945* (New York: Basic Books, 1968), p. 267.

277 Boris Simon, *Abbé Pierre and the Ragpickers of Emmaus* (New York: P. J. Kenedy & Sons, 1955), p. 98.

284 James McNeish, *Fire Under the Ashes* (Boston: Beacon, 1966), pp. 122–123.

Index

Type, 11 on 13 and 10 on 11 Baskerville
Display, Baskerville